CONTENTS

5 Standards-Based Assessment 104

6 Assessing Listening 116

9   Assessing Writing   **218**

PREFACE

The field of second language acquisition and pedagogy has enjoyed a half century of academic prosperity, with exponentially increasing numbers of books, journals, articles, and dissertations now constituting our stockpile of knowledge. Surveys of even a subdiscipline within this growing field now require hundreds of bibliographic entries to document the state of the art. In this mélange of topics and issues, assessment remains an area of intense fascination. What is the best way to assess learners' ability? What are the most practical assessment instruments available? Are current standardized tests of language proficiency accurate and reliable? In an era of communicative language teaching, do our classroom tests measure up to standards of authenticity and meaningfulness? How can a teacher design tests that serve as motivating learning experiences rather than anxiety-provoking threats?

All these and many more questions now being addressed by teachers, researchers, and specialists can be overwhelming to the novice language teacher, who is already baffled by linguistic and psychological paradigms and by a multitude of methodological options. This book provides the teacher trainee with a clear, reader-friendly presentation of the essential foundation stones of language assessment, with ample practical examples to illustrate their application in language classrooms. It is a book that simplifies the issues without oversimplifying. It doesn't dodge complex questions, and it treats them in ways that classroom teachers can comprehend. Readers do not have to become testing experts to understand and apply the concepts in this book, nor do they have to become statisticians adept in manipulating mathematical equations and advanced calculus.

PURPOSE AND AUDIENCE

This book is designed to offer a comprehensive survey of essential principles and tools for second language assessment. It has been used in pilot forms for teacher-training courses in teacher certification and in Master of Arts in TESOL programs. As the third in a trilogy of teacher education textbooks, it is designed to follow my other two books, *Principles of Language Learning and Teaching* (Fourth Edition,

Pearson Education, 2000) and *Teaching by Principles* (Second Edition, Pearson Education, 2001). References to those two books are sprinkled throughout the current book. In keeping with the tone set in the previous two books, this one features uncomplicated prose and a systematic, spiraling organization. Concepts are introduced with a maximum of practical exemplification and a minimum of weighty definition. Supportive research is acknowledged and succinctly explained without burdening the reader with ponderous debate over minutiae.

The testing discipline sometimes possesses an aura of sanctity that can cause teachers to feel inadequate as they approach the task of mastering principles and designing effective instruments. Some testing manuals, with their heavy emphasis on jargon and mathematical equations, don't help to dissipate that mystique. By the end of *Language Assessment: Principles and Classroom Practices,* readers will have gained access to this not-so-frightening field. They will have a working knowledge of a number of useful fundamental principles of assessment and will have applied those principles to practical classroom contexts. They will have acquired a storehouse of useful, comprehensible tools for evaluating and designing practical, effective assessment techniques for their classrooms.

PRINCIPAL FEATURES

Notable features of this book include the following:

- clearly framed <u>fundamental principles</u> for evaluating and designing assessment procedures of all kinds
- focus on the most common pedagogical challenge: <u>classroom-based assessment</u>
- many <u>practical examples</u> to illustrate principles and guidelines
- concise but comprehensive treatment of assessing all <u>four skills</u> (listening, speaking, reading, writing)
- in each skill, classification of assessment techniques that range from <u>controlled to open-ended item types</u> on a specified continuum of micro- and macroskills of language
- thorough discussion of large-scale <u>standardized tests:</u> their purpose, design, validity, and utility
- a look at testing <u>language proficiency</u>, or "ability"
- explanation of what <u>standards-based assessment</u> is, why it is so popular, and what its pros and cons are
- consideration of the <u>ethics of testing</u> in an educational and commercial world driven by tests
- a comprehensive presentation of <u>alternatives in assessment</u>, namely, portfolios, journals, conferences, observations, interviews, and self- and peer-assessment

- systematic discussion of <u>letter grading</u> and overall evaluation of student performance in a course
- <u>end-of-chapter exercises</u> that suggest whole-class discussion and individual, pair, and group work for the teacher education classroom
- a few suggested <u>additional readings</u> at the end of each chapter

WORDS OF THANKS

Language Assessment: Principles and Classroom Practices is the product of many years of teaching language testing and assessment in my own classrooms. My students have collectively taught me more than I have taught them, which prompts me to thank them all, everywhere, for these gifts of knowledge. I am further indebted to teachers in many countries around the world where I have offered occasional workshops and seminars on language assessment. I have memorable impressions of such sessions in Brazil, the Dominican Republic, Egypt, Japan, Peru, Thailand, Turkey, and Yugoslavia, where cross-cultural issues in assessment have been especially stimulating.

I am also grateful to my graduate assistant, Amy Shipley, for tracking down research studies and practical examples of tests, and for preparing artwork for some of the figures in this book. I offer an appreciative thank you to my friend Maryruth Farnsworth, who read the manuscript with an editor's eye and artfully pointed out some idiosyncrasies in my writing. My gratitude extends to my staff at the American Language Institute at San Francisco State University, especially Kathy Sherak, Nicole Frantz, and Nadya McCann, who carried the ball administratively while I completed the bulk of writing on this project. And thanks to my colleague Pat Porter for reading and commenting on an earlier draft of this book. As always, the embracing support of faculty and graduate students at San Francisco State University is a constant source of stimulation and affirmation.

H. Douglas Brown
San Francisco, California
September 2003

TEXT CREDITS

Grateful acknowledgment is made to the following publishers and authors for permission to reprint copyrighted material.

American Council on Teaching Foreign Languages (ACTFL), for material from *ACTFL Proficiency Guidelines: Speaking* (1986); *Oral Proficiency Inventory (OPI): Summary Highlights*.

Blackwell Publishers, for material from Brown, James Dean & Bailey, Kathleen M. (1984). A categorical instrument for scoring second language writing skills. *Language Learning, 34,* 21–42.

California Department of Education, for material from *California English Language Development (ELD) Standards: Listening and Speaking*.

Chauncey Group International (a subsidiary of ETS), for material from *Test of English for International Communication (TOEIC®)*.

Educational Testing Service (ETS), for material from *Test of English as a Foreign Language (TOEFL®); Test of Spoken English (TSE®); Test of Written English (TWE®)*.

English Language Institute, University of Michigan, for material from *Michigan English Language Assessment Battery (MELAB)*.

Ordinate Corporation, for material from *PhonePass®*.

Pearson/Longman ESL, and Deborah Phillips, for material from Phillips, Deborah. (2001). *Longman Introductory Course for the TOEFL® Test.* White Plains, NY: Pearson Education.

Second Language Testing, Inc. (SLTI), for material from *Modern Language Aptitude Test*.

University of Cambridge Local Examinations Syndicate (UCLES), for material from *International English Language Testing System*.

Yasuhiro Imao, Roshan Khan, Eric Phillips, and Sheila Viotti, for unpublished material.

CHAPTER 1

TESTING, ASSESSING,

AND TEACHING

If you hear the word *test* in any classroom setting, your thoughts are not likely to be positive, pleasant, or affirming. The anticipation of a test is almost always accompanied by feelings of anxiety and self-doubt—along with a fervent hope that you will come out of it alive. Tests seem as unavoidable as tomorrow's sunrise in virtually every kind of educational setting. Courses of study in every discipline are marked by periodic tests—milestones of progress (or inadequacy)—and you intensely wish for a miraculous exemption from these ordeals. We live by tests and sometimes (metaphorically) die by them.

For a quick revisiting of how tests affect many learners, take the following vocabulary quiz. All the words are found in standard English dictionaries, so you should be able to answer all six items correctly, right? Okay, take the quiz and circle the correct definition for each word.

Circle the correct answer. You have 3 minutes to complete this examination!

1. polygene
  a. the first stratum of lower-order protozoa containing multiple genes
  b. a combination of two or more plastics to produce a highly durable material
  c. one of a set of cooperating genes, each producing a small quantitative effect
  d. any of a number of multicellular chromosomes

2. cynosure
  a. an object that serves as a focal point of attention and admiration; a center of interest or attention
  b. a narrow opening caused by a break or fault in limestone caves
  c. the cleavage in rock caused by glacial activity
  d. one of a group of electrical impulses capable of passing through metals

---

3. gudgeon

   a. a jail for commoners during the Middle Ages, located in the villages of Germany and France

   b. a strip of metal used to reinforce beams and girders in building construction

   c. a tool used by Alaskan Indians to carve totem poles

   d. a small Eurasian freshwater fish

4. hippogriff

   a. a term used in children's literature to denote colorful and descriptive phraseology

   b. a mythological monster having the wings, claws, and head of a griffin and the body of a horse

   c. ancient Egyptian cuneiform writing commonly found on the walls of tombs

   d. a skin transplant from the leg or foot to the hip

5. reglet

   a. a narrow, flat molding

   b. a musical composition of regular beat and harmonic intonation

   c. an Australian bird of the eagle family

   d. a short sleeve found on women's dresses in Victorian England

6. fictile

   a. a short, oblong-shaped projectile used in early eighteenth-century cannons

   b. an Old English word for the leading character of a fictional novel

   c. moldable plastic; formed of a moldable substance such as clay or earth

   d. pertaining to the tendency of certain lower mammals to lose visual depth perception with increasing age

Now, how did that make you feel? Probably just the same as many learners feel when they take many multiple-choice (or shall we say multiple-guess?), timed, "tricky"tests. To add to the torment, if this were a commercially administered standardized test, you might have to wait weeks before learning your results. You can check *your* answers on this quiz now by turning to page 16. If you correctly identified three or more items, congratulations! You just exceeded the average.

Of course, this little pop quiz on obscure vocabulary is not an appropriate example of classroom-based achievement testing, nor is it intended to be. It's simply an illustration of how tests make us *feel* much of the time. Can tests be positive experiences? Can they build a person's confidence and become learning experiences? Can they bring out the best in students? The answer is a resounding *yes!* Tests need not be degrading, artificial, anxiety-provoking experiences. And that's partly what this book is all about: helping you to create more authentic, intrinsically motivating assessment procedures that are appropriate for their context and designed to offer constructive feedback to your students.

Before we look at tests and test design in second language education, we need to understand three basic interrelated concepts: testing, assessment, and teaching. Notice that the title of this book is *Language Assessment,* not *Language Testing.* There are important differences between these two constructs, and an even more important relationship among testing, assessing, and teaching.

WHAT IS A TEST?

A test, in simple terms, is a *method of measuring a person's ability, knowledge, or performance in a given domain.* Let's look at the components of this definition. A test is first a <u>method</u>. It is an instrument—a set of techniques, procedures, or items—that requires performance on the part of the test-taker. To qualify as a test, the method must be explicit and structured: multiple-choice questions with prescribed correct answers; a writing prompt with a scoring rubric; an oral interview based on a question script and a checklist of expected responses to be filled in by the administrator.

Second, a test must <u>measure</u>. Some tests measure general ability, while others focus on very specific competencies or objectives. A multi-skill proficiency test determines a general ability level; a quiz on recognizing correct use of definite articles measures specific knowledge. The way the results or measurements are communicated may vary. Some tests, such as a classroom-based short-answer essay test, may earn the test-taker a letter grade accompanied by the instructor's marginal comments. Others, particularly large-scale standardized tests, provide a total numerical score, a percentile rank, and perhaps some subscores. If an instrument does not specify a form of reporting measurement—a means for offering the test-taker some kind of result—then that technique cannot appropriately be defined as a test.

Next, a test measures an <u>individual's</u> ability, knowledge, or performance. Testers need to understand who the test-takers are. What is their previous experience and background? Is the test appropriately matched to their abilities? How should test-takers interpret their scores?

A test measures *performance,* but the results imply the test-taker's ability, or, to use a concept common in the field of linguistics, <u>competence</u>. Most language tests measure one's ability to perform language, that is, to speak, write, read, or listen to a subset of language. On the other hand, it is not uncommon to find tests designed to tap into a test-taker's knowledge <u>about</u> language: defining a vocabulary item, reciting a grammatical rule, or identifying a rhetorical feature in written discourse. Performance-based tests sample the test-taker's actual use of language, but from those samples the test administrator infers general competence. A test of reading comprehension, for example, may consist of several short reading passages each followed by a limited number of comprehension questions—a small sample of a second language learner's total reading behavior. But from the results of that test, the examiner may infer a certain level of general reading ability.

Finally, a test measures a given <u>domain</u>. In the case of a proficiency test, even though the actual performance on the test involves only a sampling of skills, that domain is overall proficiency in a language—general competence in all skills of a language. Other tests may have more specific criteria. A test of pronunciation might well be a test of only a limited set of phonemic minimal pairs. A vocabulary test may focus on only the set of words covered in a particular lesson or unit. One of the biggest obstacles to overcome in constructing adequate tests is to measure the desired criterion and not include other factors inadvertently, an issue that is addressed in Chapters 2 and 3.

A well-constructed test is an instrument that provides an accurate measure of the test-taker's ability within a particular domain. The definition sounds fairly simple, but in fact, constructing a good test is a complex task involving both science and art.

ASSESSMENT AND TEACHING

Assessment is a popular and sometimes misunderstood term in current educational practice. You might be tempted to think of testing and assessing as synonymous terms, but they are not. Tests are prepared administrative procedures that occur at identifiable times in a curriculum when learners muster all their faculties to offer peak performance, knowing that their responses are being measured and evaluated.

Assessment, on the other hand, is an ongoing process that encompasses a much wider domain. Whenever a student responds to a question, offers a comment, or tries out a new word or structure, the teacher subconsciously makes an assessment of the student's performance. Written work—from a jotted-down phrase to a formal essay—is performance that ultimately is assessed by self, teacher, and possibly other students. Reading and listening activities usually require some sort of productive performance that the teacher implicitly judges, however peripheral that judgment may be. A good teacher never ceases to assess students, whether those assessments are incidental or intended.

Tests, then, are a subset of assessment; they are certainly not the only form of assessment that a teacher can make. Tests can be useful devices, but they are only one among many procedures and tasks that teachers can ultimately use to assess students.

But now, you might be thinking, if you make assessments every time you teach something in the classroom, does all teaching involve assessment? Are teachers constantly assessing students with no interaction that is assessment-free?

The answer depends on your perspective. For optimal learning to take place, students in the classroom must have the freedom to experiment, to try out their own hypotheses about language without feeling that their overall competence is being judged in terms of those trials and errors. In the same way that tournament tennis players must, before a tournament, have the freedom to practice their skills with no implications for their final placement on that day of days, so also must learners have ample opportunities to "play" with language in a classroom without being formally graded. Teaching sets up the practice games of language learning: the opportunities for learners to listen, think, take risks, set goals, and process feedback from the "coach" and then recycle through the skills that they are trying to master. (A diagram of the relationship among testing, teaching, and assessment is found in Figure 1.1.)

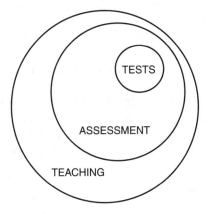

Figure 1.1. Tests, assessment, and teaching

At the same time, during these practice activities, teachers (and tennis coaches) are indeed observing students' performance and making various evaluations of each learner: How did the performance compare to previous performance? Which aspects of the performance were better than others? Is the learner performing up to an expected potential? How does the performance compare to that of others in the same learning community? In the ideal classroom, all these observations feed into the way the teacher provides instruction to each student.

Informal and Formal Assessment

One way to begin untangling the lexical conundrum created by distinguishing among tests, assessment, and teaching is to distinguish between informal and formal assessment. **Informal assessment** can take a number of forms, starting with incidental, unplanned comments and responses, along with coaching and other impromptu feedback to the student. Examples include saying "Nice job!" "Good work!" "Did you say *can* or *can't?*" "I think you meant to say you *broke* the glass, not you *break* the glass," or putting a ☺ on some homework.

Informal assessment does not stop there. A good deal of a teacher's informal assessment is embedded in classroom tasks designed to elicit performance without recording results and making fixed judgments about a student's competence. Examples at this end of the continuum are marginal comments on papers, responding to a draft of an essay, advice about how to better pronounce a word, a suggestion for a strategy for compensating for a reading difficulty, and showing how to modify a student's note-taking to better remember the content of a lecture.

On the other hand, **formal assessments** are exercises or procedures specifically designed to tap into a storehouse of skills and knowledge. They are systematic, planned sampling techniques constructed to give teacher and student an appraisal of student achievement. To extend the tennis analogy, formal assessments are the tournament games that occur periodically in the course of a regimen of practice.

Is formal assessment the same as a test? We can say that all tests are formal assessments, but not all formal assessment is testing. For example, you might use a student's journal or portfolio of materials as a formal assessment of the attainment of certain course objectives, but it is problematic to call those two procedures "tests." A systematic set of observations of a student's frequency of oral participation in class is certainly a formal assessment, but it too is hardly what anyone would call a test. Tests are usually relatively time-constrained (usually spanning a class period or at most several hours) and draw on a limited sample of behavior.

Formative and Summative Assessment

Another useful distinction to bear in mind is the function of an assessment: How is the procedure to be used? Two functions are commonly identified in the literature: formative and summative assessment. Most of our classroom assessment is **formative assessment:** evaluating students in the process of "forming" their competencies and skills with the goal of helping them to continue that growth process. The key to such formation is the delivery (by the teacher) and internalization (by the student) of appropriate feedback on performance, with an eye toward the future continuation (or formation) of learning.

For all practical purposes, virtually all kinds of informal assessment are (or should be) formative. They have as their primary focus the ongoing development of the learner's language. So when you give a student a comment or a suggestion, or call attention to an error, that feedback is offered in order to improve the learner's language ability.

Summative assessment aims to measure, or summarize, what a student has grasped, and typically occurs at the end of a course or unit of instruction. A summation of what a student has learned implies looking back and taking stock of how well that student has accomplished objectives, but does not necessarily point the way to future progress. Final exams in a course and general proficiency exams are examples of summative assessment.

One of the problems with prevailing attitudes toward testing is the view that *all* tests (quizzes, periodic review tests, midterm exams, etc.) are summative. At various points in your past educational experiences, no doubt you've considered such tests as summative. You may have thought, "Whew! I'm glad that's over. Now I don't have to remember that stuff anymore!" A challenge to you as a teacher is to change that attitude among your students: Can you instill a more formative quality to what your students might otherwise view as a summative test? Can you offer your students an opportunity to convert tests into "learning experiences"? We will take up that challenge in subsequent chapters in this book.

Norm-Referenced and Criterion-Referenced Tests

Another dichotomy that is important to clarify here and that aids in sorting out common terminology in assessment is the distinction between norm-referenced and criterion-referenced testing. In **norm-referenced tests,** each test-taker's score is interpreted in relation to a mean (average score), median (middle score), standard deviation (extent of variance in scores), and/or percentile rank. The purpose in such tests is to place test-takers along a mathematical continuum in rank order. Scores are usually reported back to the test-taker in the form of a numerical score (for example, 230 out of 300) and a percentile rank (such as 84 percent, which means that the test-taker's score was higher than 84 percent of the total number of test-takers, but lower than 16 percent in that administration). Typical of norm-referenced tests are standardized tests like the Scholastic Aptitude Test (SAT®) or the Test of English as a Foreign Language (TOEFL®), intended to be administered to large audiences, with results efficiently disseminated to test-takers. Such tests must have fixed, predetermined responses in a format that can be scored quickly at minimum expense. Money and efficiency are primary concerns in these tests.

Criterion-referenced tests, on the other hand, are designed to give test-takers feedback, usually in the form of grades, on specific course or lesson objectives. Classroom tests involving the students in only one class, and connected to a curriculum, are typical of criterion-referenced testing. Here, much time and effort on the part of the teacher (test administrator) are sometimes required in order to deliver useful, appropriate feedback to students, or what Oller (1979, p. 52) called "instructional value." In a criterion-referenced test, the distribution of students' scores across a continuum may be of little concern as long as the instrument assesses appropriate objectives. In *Language Assessment,* with an audience of classroom language teachers and teachers in training, and with its emphasis on classroom-based assessment (as opposed to standardized, large-scale testing), criterion-referenced testing is of more prominent interest than norm-referenced testing.

APPROACHES TO LANGUAGE TESTING: A BRIEF HISTORY

Now that you have a reasonably clear grasp of some common assessment terms, we now turn to one of the primary concerns of this book: the creation and use of tests, particularly classroom tests. A brief history of language testing over the past half-century will serve as a backdrop to an understanding of classroom-based testing.

Historically, language-testing trends and practices have followed the shifting sands of teaching methodology (for a description of these trends, see Brown,

Teaching by Principles [hereinafter *TBP*], Chapter 2).[1] For example, in the 1950s, an era of behaviorism and special attention to contrastive analysis, testing focused on specific language elements such as the phonological, grammatical, and lexical contrasts between two languages. In the 1970s and 1980s, communicative theories of language brought with them a more integrative view of testing in which specialists claimed that "the whole of the communicative event was considerably greater than the sum of its linguistic elements" (Clark, 1983, p. 432). Today, test designers are still challenged in their quest for more authentic, valid instruments that simulate real-world interaction.

Discrete-Point and Integrative Testing

This historical perspective underscores two major approaches to language testing that were debated in the 1970s and early 1980s. These approaches still prevail today, even if in mutated form: the choice between discrete-point and integrative testing methods (Oller, 1979). **Discrete-point tests** are constructed on the assumption that language can be broken down into its component parts and that those parts can be tested successfully. These components are the skills of listening, speaking, reading, and writing, and various units of language (discrete points) of phonology/graphology, morphology, lexicon, syntax, and discourse. It was claimed that an overall language proficiency test, then, should sample all four skills and as many linguistic discrete points as possible.

Such an approach demanded a decontextualization that often confused the test-taker. So, as the profession emerged into an era of emphasizing communication, authenticity, and context, new approaches were sought. Oller (1979) argued that language competence is a unified set of interacting abilities that cannot be tested separately. His claim was that communicative competence is so global and requires such integration (hence the term "integrative" testing) that it cannot be captured in additive tests of grammar, reading, vocabulary, and other discrete points of language. Others (among them Cziko, 1982, and Savignon, 1982) soon followed in their support for integrative testing.

What does an **integrative test** look like? Two types of tests have historically been claimed to be examples of integrative tests: cloze tests and dictations. A **cloze test** is a reading passage (perhaps 150 to 300 words) in which roughly every sixth or seventh word has been deleted; the test-taker is required to supply words that fit into those blanks. (See Chapter 8 for a full discussion of cloze testing.) Oller (1979)

---

[1] Frequent references are made in this book to companion volumes by the author. *Principles of Language Learning and Teaching (PLLT)* (Fourth Edition, 2000) is a basic teacher reference book on essential foundations of second language acquisition on which pedagogical practices are based. *Teaching by Principles (TBP)* (Second Edition, 2001) spells out that pedagogy in practical terms for the language teacher.

claimed that cloze test results are good measures of overall proficiency. According to theoretical constructs underlying this claim, the ability to supply appropriate words in blanks requires a number of abilities that lie at the heart of competence in a language: knowledge of vocabulary, grammatical structure, discourse structure, reading skills and strategies, and an internalized "expectancy" grammar (enabling one to predict an item that will come next in a sequence). It was argued that successful completion of cloze items taps into all of those abilities, which were said to be the essence of global language proficiency.

Dictation is a familiar language-teaching technique that evolved into a testing technique. Essentially, learners listen to a passage of 100 to 150 words read aloud by an administrator (or audiotape) and write what they hear, using correct spelling. The listening portion usually has three stages: an oral reading without pauses; an oral reading with long pauses between every phrase (to give the learner time to write down what is heard); and a third reading at normal speed to give test-takers a chance to check what they wrote. (See Chapter 6 for more discussion of dictation as an assessment device.)

Supporters argue that dictation is an integrative test because it taps into grammatical and discourse competencies required for other modes of performance in a language. Success on a dictation requires careful listening, reproduction in writing of what is heard, efficient short-term memory, and, to an extent, some expectancy rules to aid the short-term memory. Further, dictation test results tend to correlate strongly with other tests of proficiency. Dictation testing is usually classroom-centered since large-scale administration of dictations is quite impractical from a scoring standpoint. Reliability of scoring criteria for dictation tests can be improved by designing multiple-choice or exact-word cloze test scoring.

Proponents of integrative test methods soon centered their arguments on what became known as the **unitary trait hypothesis,** which suggested an "indivisible" view of language proficiency: that vocabulary, grammar, phonology, the "four skills," and other discrete points of language could not be disentangled from each other in language performance. The unitary trait hypothesis contended that there is a general factor of language proficiency such that all the discrete points do *not* add up to that whole.

Others argued strongly against the unitary trait position. In a study of students in Brazil and the Philippines, Farhady (1982) found significant and widely varying differences in performance on an ESL proficiency test, depending on subjects' native country, major field of study, and graduate versus undergraduate status. For example, Brazilians scored very low in listening comprehension and relatively high in reading comprehension. Filipinos, whose scores on five of the six components of the test were considerably higher than Brazilians' scores, were actually lower than Brazilians in reading comprehension scores. Farhady's contentions were supported in other research that seriously questioned the unitary trait hypothesis. Finally, in the face of the evidence, Oller retreated from his earlier stand and admitted that "the unitary trait hypothesis was wrong" (1983, p. 352).

Communicative Language Testing

By the mid-1980s, the language-testing field had abandoned arguments about the unitary trait hypothesis and had begun to focus on designing communicative language-testing tasks. Bachman and Palmer (1996, p. 9) include among "fundamental" principles of language testing the need for a correspondence between language test performance and language use: "In order for a particular language test to be useful for its intended purposes, test performance must correspond in demonstrable ways to language use in non-test situations." The problem that language assessment experts faced was that tasks tended to be artificial, contrived, and unlikely to mirror language use in real life. As Weir (1990, p. 6) noted, "Integrative tests such as cloze only tell us about a candidate's linguistic competence. They do not tell us anything directly about a student's performance ability."

And so a quest for authenticity was launched, as test designers centered on communicative performance. Following Canale and Swain's (1980) model of communicative competence, Bachman (1990) proposed a model of language competence consisting of organizational and pragmatic competence, respectively subdivided into grammatical and textual components, and into illocutionary and sociolinguistic components. (Further discussion of both Canale and Swain's and Bachman's models can be found in *PLLT,* Chapter 9.) Bachman and Palmer (1996, pp. 70f) also emphasized the importance of **strategic competence** (the ability to employ communicative strategies to compensate for breakdowns as well as to enhance the rhetorical effect of utterances) in the process of communication. All elements of the model, especially pragmatic and strategic abilities, needed to be included in the constructs of language testing and in the actual performance required of test-takers.

Communicative testing presented challenges to test designers, as we will see in subsequent chapters of this book. Test constructors began to identify the kinds of real-world tasks that language learners were called upon to perform. It was clear that the contexts for those tasks were extraordinarily widely varied and that the sampling of tasks for any one assessment procedure needed to be validated by what language users actually do with language. Weir (1990, p. 11) reminded his readers that "to measure language proficiency . . . account must now be taken of: where, when, how, with whom, and why language is to be used, and on what topics, and with what effect." And the assessment field became more and more concerned with the authenticity of tasks and the genuineness of texts. (See Skehan, 1988, 1989, for a survey of communicative testing research.)

Performance-Based Assessment

In language courses and programs around the world, test designers are now tackling this new and more student-centered agenda (Alderson, 2001, 2002). Instead of just offering paper-and-pencil selective response tests of a plethora of separate items, performance-based assessment of language typically involves oral production, written production, open-ended responses, integrated performance (across skill areas), group performance, and other interactive tasks. To be sure, such assessment is time-consuming and therefore expensive, but those extra efforts are paying off in the form of more direct testing because students are assessed as they perform actual or simulated real-world tasks. In technical terms, higher content validity (see Chapter 2 for an explanation) is achieved because learners are measured in the process of performing the targeted linguistic acts.

In an English language-teaching context, performance-based assessment means that you may have a difficult time distinguishing between formal and informal assessment. If you rely a little less on formally structured tests and a little more on evaluation while students are performing various tasks, you will be taking some steps toward meeting the goals of performance-based testing. (See Chapter 10 for a further discussion of performance-based assessment.)

A characteristic of many (but not all) performance-based language assessments is the presence of interactive tasks. In such cases, the assessments involve learners in actually performing the behavior that we want to measure. In interactive tasks, test-takers are measured in the act of speaking, requesting, responding, or in combining listening and speaking, and in integrating reading and writing. Paper-and-pencil tests certainly do not elicit such communicative performance.

A prime example of an interactive language assessment procedure is an oral interview. The test-taker is required to listen accurately to someone else and to respond appropriately. If care is taken in the test design process, language elicited and volunteered by the student can be personalized and meaningful, and tasks can approach the authenticity of real-life language use (see Chapter 7).

CURRENT ISSUES IN CLASSROOM TESTING

The design of communicative, performance-based assessment rubrics continues to challenge both assessment experts and classroom teachers. Such efforts to improve various facets of classroom testing are accompanied by some stimulating issues, all of which are helping to shape our current understanding of effective assessment. Let's look at three such issues: the effect of new theories of intelligence on the testing industry; the advent of what has come to be called "alternative" assessment; and the increasing popularity of computer-based testing.

New Views on Intelligence

Intelligence was once viewed strictly as the ability to perform (a) linguistic and (b) logical-mathematical problem solving. This "IQ" (intelligence quotient) concept of intelligence has permeated the Western world and its way of testing for almost a century. Since "smartness" in general is measured by timed, discrete-point tests consisting of a hierarchy of separate items, why shouldn't every field of study be so measured? For many years, we have lived in a world of standardized, norm-referenced tests that are timed in a multiple-choice format consisting of a multiplicity of logic-constrained items, many of which are inauthentic.

However, research on intelligence by psychologists like Howard Gardner, Robert Sternberg, and Daniel Goleman has begun to turn the psychometric world upside down. Gardner (1983, 1999), for example, extended the traditional view of intelligence to seven different components.[2] He accepted the traditional conceptualizations of linguistic intelligence and logical-mathematical intelligence on which standardized IQ tests are based, but he included five other "frames of mind" in his theory of multiple intelligences:

- spatial intelligence (the ability to find your way around an environment, to form mental images of reality)
- musical intelligence (the ability to perceive and create pitch and rhythmic patterns)
- bodily-kinesthetic intelligence (fine motor movement, athletic prowess)
- interpersonal intelligence (the ability to understand others and how they feel, and to interact effectively with them)
- intrapersonal intelligence (the ability to understand oneself and to develop a sense of self-identity)

Robert Sternberg (1988, 1997) also charted new territory in intelligence research in recognizing creative thinking and manipulative strategies as part of intelligence. All "smart" people aren't necessarily adept at fast, reactive thinking. They may be very innovative in being able to think beyond the normal limits imposed by existing tests, but they may need a good deal of processing time to enact this creativity. Other forms of smartness are found in those who know how to manipulate their environment, namely, other people. Debaters, politicians, successful salespersons, smooth talkers, and con artists are all smart in their manipulative ability to persuade others to think their way, vote for them, make a purchase, or do something they might not otherwise do.

More recently, Daniel Goleman's (1995) concept of "EQ" (emotional quotient) has spurred us to underscore the importance of the emotions in our cognitive processing. Those who manage their emotions—especially emotions that can be detrimental—tend to be more capable of fully intelligent processing. Anger, grief, resentment, self-doubt, and other feelings can easily impair peak performance in everyday tasks as well as higher-order problem solving.

These new conceptualizations of intelligence have not been universally accepted by the academic community (see White, 1998, for example). Nevertheless, their intuitive appeal infused the decade of the 1990s with a sense of both freedom and responsibility in our testing agenda. Coupled with parallel educational reforms at the time (Armstrong, 1994), they helped to free us from relying exclusively on

---

[2] For a summary of Gardner's theory of intelligence, see Brown (2000, pp. 100–102).

timed, discrete-point, analytical tests in measuring language. We were prodded to cautiously combat the potential tyranny of "objectivity" and its accompanying impersonal approach. But we also assumed the responsibility for tapping into whole language skills, learning processes, and the ability to negotiate meaning. Our challenge was to test interpersonal, creative, communicative, interactive skills, and in doing so to place some trust in our subjectivity and intuition.

Traditional and "Alternative" Assessment

Implied in some of the earlier description of performance-based classroom assessment is a trend to supplement traditional test designs with alternatives that are more authentic in their elicitation of meaningful communication. Table 1.1 highlights differences between the two approaches (adapted from Armstrong, 1994, and Bailey, 1998, p. 207).

Two caveats need to be stated here. First, the concepts in Table 1.1 represent some overgeneralizations and should therefore be considered with caution. It is difficult, in fact, to draw a clear line of distinction between what Armstrong (1994) and Bailey (1998) have called traditional and alternative assessment. Many forms of assessment fall in between the two, and some combine the best of both.

Second, it is obvious that the table shows a bias toward alternative assessment, and one should not be misled into thinking that everything on the left-hand side is tainted while the list on the right-hand side offers salvation to the field of language assessment! As Brown and Hudson (1998) aptly pointed out, the assessment traditions available to us should be valued and utilized for the functions that they provide. At the same time, we might all be stimulated to look at the right-hand list and ask ourselves if, among those concepts, there are alternatives to assessment that we can constructively use in our classrooms.

It should be noted here that considerably more time and higher institutional budgets are required to administer and score assessments that presuppose more

Table 1.1. Traditional and alternative assessment

Traditional Assessment	Alternative Assessment
One-shot, standardized exams	Continuous long-term assessment
Timed, multiple-choice format	Untimed, free-response format
Decontextualized test items	Contextualized communicative tasks
Scores suffice for feedback	Individualized feedback and washback
Norm-referenced scores	Criterion-referenced scores
Focus on the "right" answer	Open-ended, creative answers
Summative	Formative
Oriented to product	Oriented to process
Non-interactive performance	Interactive performance
Fosters extrinsic motivation	Fosters intrinsic motivation

subjective evaluation, more individualization, and more interaction in the process of offering feedback. The payoff for the latter, however, comes with more useful feedback to students, the potential for intrinsic motivation, and ultimately a more complete description of a student's ability. (See Chapter 10 for a complete treatment of alternatives in assessment.) More and more educators and advocates for educational reform are arguing for a de-emphasis on large-scale standardized tests in favor of building budgets that will offer the kind of contextualized, communicative performance-based assessment that will better facilitate learning in our schools. (In Chapter 4, issues surrounding standardized testing are addressed at length.)

Computer-Based Testing

Recent years have seen a burgeoning of assessment in which the test-taker performs responses on a computer. Some computer-based tests (also known as "computer-assisted" or "web-based" tests) are small-scale "home-grown" tests available on websites. Others are standardized, large-scale tests in which thousands or even tens of thousands of test-takers are involved. Students receive prompts (or probes, as they are sometimes referred to) in the form of spoken or written stimuli from the computerized test and are required to type (or in some cases, speak) their responses. Almost all computer-based test items have fixed, closed-ended responses; however, tests like the Test of English as a Foreign Language (TOEFL®) offer a written essay section that must be scored by humans (as opposed to automatic, electronic, or machine scoring). As this book goes to press, the designers of the TOEFL are on the verge of offering a spoken English section.

A specific type of computer-based test, a **computer-adaptive test,** has been available for many years but has recently gained momentum. In a computer-adaptive test (CAT), each test-taker receives a set of questions that meet the test specifications and that are generally appropriate for his or her performance level. The CAT starts with questions of moderate difficulty. As test-takers answer each question, the computer scores the question and uses that information, as well as the responses to previous questions, to determine which question will be presented next. As long as examinees respond correctly, the computer typically selects questions of greater or equal difficulty. Incorrect answers, however, typically bring questions of lesser or equal difficulty. The computer is programmed to fulfill the test design as it continuously adjusts to find questions of appropriate difficulty for test-takers at all performance levels. In CATs, the test-taker sees only one question at a time, and the computer scores each question before selecting the next one. As a result, test-takers cannot skip questions, and once they have entered and confirmed their answers, they cannot return to questions or to any earlier part of the test.

Computer-based testing, with or without CAT technology, offers these advantages:

- classroom-based testing
- self-directed testing on various aspects of a language (vocabulary, grammar, discourse, one or all of the four skills, etc.)

- practice for upcoming high-stakes standardized tests
- some individualization, in the case of CATs
- large-scale standardized tests that can be administered easily to thousands of test-takers at many different stations, then scored electronically for rapid reporting of results

Of course, some disadvantages are present in our current predilection for computerizing testing. Among them:

- Lack of security and the possibility of cheating are inherent in classroom-based, unsupervised computerized tests.
- Occasional "home-grown" quizzes that appear on unofficial websites may be mistaken for validated assessments.
- The multiple-choice format preferred for most computer-based tests contains the usual potential for flawed item design (see Chapter 3).
- Open-ended responses are less likely to appear because of the need for human scorers, with all the attendant issues of cost, reliability, and turn-around time.
- The human interactive element (especially in oral production) is absent.

More is said about computer-based testing in subsequent chapters, especially Chapter 4, in a discussion of large-scale standardized testing. In addition, the following websites provide further information and examples of computer-based tests:

Educational Testing Service	**www.ets.org**
Test of English as a Foreign Language	**www.toefl.org**
Test of English for International Communication	**www.toeic.com**
International English Language Testing System	**www.ielts.org**
Dave's ESL Café (computerized quizzes)	**www.eslcafe.com**

Some argue that computer-based testing, pushed to its ultimate level, might mitigate against recent efforts to return testing to its artful form of being tailored by teachers for their classrooms, of being designed to be performance-based, and of allowing a teacher–student dialogue to form the basis of assessment. This need not be the case. Computer technology can be a boon to communicative language testing. Teachers and test-makers of the future will have access to an ever-increasing range of tools to safeguard against impersonal, stamped-out formulas for assessment. By using technological innovations creatively, testers will be able to enhance authenticity, to increase interactive exchange, and to promote autonomy.

§   §   §   §   §

As you read this book, I hope you will do so with an appreciation for the place of testing in assessment, and with a sense of the interconnection of assessment and teaching. Assessment is an integral part of the teaching–learning cycle. In an interactive, communicative curriculum, assessment is almost constant. Tests, which are a subset of assessment, can provide authenticity, motivation, and feedback to the learner. Tests are essential components of a successful curriculum and one of several partners in the learning process. Keep in mind these basic principles:

1. Periodic assessments, both formal and informal, can increase motivation by serving as milestones of student progress.
2. Appropriate assessments aid in the reinforcement and retention of information.
3. Assessments can confirm areas of strength and pinpoint areas needing further work.
4. Assessments can provide a sense of periodic closure to modules within a curriculum.
5. Assessments can promote student autonomy by encouraging students' self-evaluation of their progress.
6. Assessments can spur learners to set goals for themselves.
7. Assessments can aid in evaluating teaching effectiveness.

> Answers to the vocabulary quiz on pages 1 and 2: 1c, 2a, 3d, 4b, 5a, 6c.

EXERCISES

[Note: (**I**) Individual work; (**G**) Group or pair work; (**C**) Whole-class discussion.]

1. (**G**) In a small group, look at Figure 1.1 on page 5 that shows tests as a subset of assessment and the latter as a subset of teaching. Do you agree with this diagrammatic depiction of the three terms? Consider the following classroom teaching techniques: choral drill, pair pronunciation practice, reading aloud, information gap task, singing songs in English, writing a description of the weekend's activities. What proportion of each has an assessment facet to it? Share your conclusions with the rest of the class.
2. (**G**) The chart below shows a hypothetical line of distinction between formative and summative assessment, and between informal and formal assessment. As a group, place the following techniques/procedures into one of the four cells and justify your decision. Share your results with other groups and discuss any differences of opinion.

   Placement tests
   Diagnostic tests
   Periodic achievement tests
   Short pop quizzes

Standardized proficiency tests
Final exams
Portfolios
Journals
Speeches (prepared and rehearsed)
Oral presentations (prepared, but not rehearsed)
Impromptu student responses to teacher's questions
Student-written response (one paragraph) to a reading assignment
Drafting and revising writing
Final essays (after several drafts)
Student oral responses to teacher questions after a videotaped lecture
Whole class open-ended discussion of a topic

	Formative	**Summative**
Informal		
Formal		

3. **(I/C)** Review the distinction between norm-referenced and criterion-referenced testing. If norm-referenced tests typically yield a distribution of scores that resemble a bell-shaped curve, what kinds of distributions are typical of classroom achievement tests in your experience?

4. **(I/C)** Restate in your own words the argument between unitary trait proponents and discrete-point testing advocates. Why did Oller back down from the unitary trait hypothesis?

5. **(I/C)** Why are cloze and dictation considered to be integrative tests?

6. **(G)** Look at the list of Gardner's seven intelligences. Take one or two intelligences, as assigned to your group, and brainstorm some teaching activities that foster that type of intelligence. Then, brainstorm some assessment tasks

that may presuppose the same intelligence in order to perform well. Share your results with other groups.

7. **(C)** As a whole-class discussion, brainstorm a variety of test tasks that class members have experienced in learning a foreign language. Then decide which of those tasks are performance-based, which are not, and which ones fall in between.

8. **(G)** Table 1.1 lists traditional and alternative assessment tasks and characteristics. In pairs, quickly review the advantages and disadvantages of each, on both sides of the chart. Share your conclusions with the rest of the class.

9. **(C)** Ask class members to share any experiences with computer-based testing and evaluate the advantages and disadvantages of those experiences.

FOR YOUR FURTHER READING

McNamara, Tim. (2000). *Language testing.* Oxford: Oxford University Press.

One of a number of Oxford University Press's brief introductions to various areas of language study, this 140-page primer on testing offers definitions of basic terms in language testing with brief explanations of fundamental concepts. It is a useful little reference book to check your understanding of testing jargon and issues in the field.

Mousavi, Seyyed Abbas. (2002). *An encyclopedic dictionary of language testing.* Third Edition. Taipei: Tung Hua Book Company.

This publication may be difficult to find in local bookstores, but it is a highly useful compilation of virtually every term in the field of language testing, with definitions, background history, and research references. It provides comprehensive explanations of theories, principles, issues, tools, and tasks. Its exhaustive 88-page bibliography is also downloadable at **http://www.abbas-mousavi.com**. A shorter version of this 942-page tome may be found in the previous version, Mousavi's (1999) *Dictionary of language testing* (Tehran: Rahnama Publications).

CHAPTER 2

PRINCIPLES OF

LANGUAGE ASSESSMENT

This chapter explores how principles of language assessment can and should be applied to formal tests, but with the ultimate recognition that these principles also apply to assessments of all kinds. In this chapter, these principles will be used to evaluate an existing, previously published, or created test. Chapter 3 will center on how to use those principles to design a good test.

How do you know if a test is effective? For the most part, that question can be answered by responding to such questions as: Can it be given within appropriate administrative constraints? Is it dependable? Does it accurately measure what you want it to measure? These and other questions help to identify five cardinal criteria for "testing a test": practicality, reliability, validity, authenticity, and washback. We will look at each one, but with no priority order implied in the order of presentation.

PRACTICALITY

An effective test is **practical**. This means that it

- is not excessively expensive,
- stays within appropriate time constraints,
- is relatively easy to administer, and
- has a scoring/evaluation procedure that is specific and time-efficient.

A test that is prohibitively expensive is impractical. A test of language proficiency that takes a student five hours to complete is impractical—it consumes more time (and money) than necessary to accomplish its objective. A test that requires individual one-on-one proctoring is impractical for a group of several hundred test-takers and only a handful of examiners. A test that takes a few minutes for a student to take and several hours for an examiner to evaluate is impractical for most classroom situations. A test that can be scored only by computer is impractical if the test takes place a thousand miles away from the nearest computer. The value and quality of a test sometimes hinge on such nitty-gritty, practical considerations.

Here's a little horror story about practicality gone awry. An administrator of a six-week summertime short course needed to place the 50 or so students who had enrolled in the program. A quick search yielded a copy of an old English Placement Test from the University of Michigan. It had 20 listening items based on an audiotape and 80 items on grammar, vocabulary, and reading comprehension, all multiple-choice format. A scoring grid accompanied the test. On the day of the test, the required number of test booklets had been secured, a proctor had been assigned to monitor the process, and the administrator and proctor had planned to have the scoring completed by later that afternoon so students could begin classes the next day. Sounds simple, right? Wrong.

The students arrived, test booklets were distributed, and directions were given. The proctor started the tape. Soon students began to look puzzled. By the time the tenth item played, everyone looked bewildered. Finally, the proctor checked a test booklet and was horrified to discover that the wrong tape was playing; it was a tape for another form of the same test! Now what? She decided to randomly select a short passage from a textbook that was in the room and give the students a dictation. The students responded reasonably well. The next 80 non-tape-based items proceeded without incident, and the students handed in their score sheets and dictation papers.

When the red-faced administrator and the proctor got together later to score the tests, they faced the problem of how to score the dictation—a more subjective process than some other forms of assessment (see Chapter 6). After a lengthy exchange, the two established a point system, but after the first few papers had been scored, it was clear that the point system needed revision. That meant going back to the first papers to make sure the new system was followed.

The two faculty members had barely begun to score the 80 multiple-choice items when students began returning to the office to receive their placements. Students were told to come back the next morning for their results. Later that evening, having combined dictation scores and the 80-item multiple-choice scores, the two frustrated examiners finally arrived at placements for all students.

It's easy to see what went wrong here. While the listening comprehension section of the test was apparently highly practical, the administrator had failed to check the materials ahead of time (which, as you will see below, is a factor that touches on unreliability as well). Then, they established a scoring procedure that did not fit into the time constraints. In classroom-based testing, time is almost always a crucial practicality factor for busy teachers with too few hours in the day!

RELIABILITY

A **reliable** test is consistent and dependable. If you give the same test to the same student or matched students on two different occasions, the test should yield similar results. The issue of reliability of a test may best be addressed by considering a number of factors that may contribute to the unreliability of a test. Consider the following possibilities (adapted from Mousavi, 2002, p. 804): fluctuations in the student, in scoring, in test administration, and in the test itself.

Student-Related Reliability

The most common learner-related issue in reliability is caused by temporary illness, fatigue, a "bad day," anxiety, and other physical or psychological factors, which may make an "observed" score deviate from one's "true" score. Also included in this category are such factors as a test-taker's "test-wiseness" or strategies for efficient test taking (Mousavi, 2002, p. 804).

Rater Reliability

Human error, subjectivity, and bias may enter into the scoring process. **Inter-rater reliability** occurs when two or more scorers yield inconsistent scores of the same test, possibly for lack of attention to scoring criteria, inexperience, inattention, or even preconceived biases. In the story above about the placement test, the initial scoring plan for the dictations was found to be unreliable—that is, the two scorers were not applying the same standards.

Rater-reliability issues are not limited to contexts where two or more scorers are involved. **Intra-rater reliability** is a common occurrence for classroom teachers because of unclear scoring criteria, fatigue, bias toward particular "good" and "bad" students, or simple carelessness. When I am faced with up to 40 tests to grade in only a week, I know that the standards I apply—however subliminally—to the first few tests will be different from those I apply to the last few. I may be "easier" or "harder" on those first few papers or I may get tired, and the result may be an inconsistent evaluation across all tests. One solution to such intra-rater unreliability is to read through about half of the tests before rendering any final scores or grades, then to recycle back through the whole set of tests to ensure an even-handed judgment. In tests of writing skills, rater reliability is particularly hard to achieve since writing proficiency involves numerous traits that are difficult to define. The careful specification of an analytical scoring instrument, however, can increase rater reliability (J. D. Brown, 1991).

Test Administration Reliability

Unreliability may also result from the conditions in which the test is administered. I once witnessed the administration of a test of aural comprehension in which a tape recorder played items for comprehension, but because of street noise outside the building, students sitting next to windows could not hear the tape accurately. This was a clear case of unreliability caused by the conditions of the test administration. Other sources of unreliability are found in photocopying variations, the amount of light in different parts of the room, variations in temperature, and even the condition of desks and chairs.

Test Reliability

Sometimes the nature of the test itself can cause measurement errors. If a test is too long, test-takers may become fatigued by the time they reach the later items and hastily respond incorrectly. Timed tests may discriminate against students who do not perform well on a test with a time limit. We all know people (and you may be included in this category!) who "know" the course material perfectly but who are adversely affected by the presence of a clock ticking away. Poorly written test items (that are ambiguous or that have more than one correct answer) may be a further source of test unreliability.

VALIDITY

By far the most complex criterion of an effective test—and arguably the most important principle—is **validity,** "the extent to which inferences made from assessment results are appropriate, meaningful, and useful in terms of the purpose of the assessment" (Gronlund, 1998, p. 226). A valid test of reading ability actually measures reading ability—not 20/20 vision, nor previous knowledge in a subject, nor some other variable of questionable relevance. To measure writing ability, one might ask students to write as many words as they can in 15 minutes, then simply count the words for the final score. Such a test would be easy to administer (practical), and the scoring quite dependable (reliable). But it would not constitute a valid test of writing ability without some consideration of comprehensibility, rhetorical discourse elements, and the organization of ideas, among other factors.

How is the validity of a test established? There is no final, absolute measure of validity, but several different kinds of evidence may be invoked in support. In some cases, it may be appropriate to examine the extent to which a test calls for performance that matches that of the course or unit of study being tested. In other cases, we may be concerned with how well a test determines whether or not students have reached an established set of goals or level of competence. Statistical correlation with other related but independent measures is another widely accepted form of evidence. Other concerns about a test's validity may focus on the consequences—beyond measuring the criteria themselves—of a test, or even on the test-taker's perception of validity. We will look at these five types of evidence below.

Content-Related Evidence

If a test actually samples the subject matter about which conclusions are to be drawn, and if it requires the test-taker to perform the behavior that is being measured, it can claim content-related evidence of validity, often popularly referred to as **content validity** (e.g., Mousavi, 2002; Hughes, 2003). You can usually identify content-related evidence observationally if you can clearly define the achievement that you are measuring. A test of tennis competency that asks someone to run a 100-yard dash obviously lacks content validity. If you are trying to assess a person's ability to speak a second language in a conversational setting, asking the learner to answer paper-and-pencil multiple-choice questions requiring grammatical judgments does not achieve content validity. A test that requires the learner actually to speak within some sort of authentic context does. And if a course has perhaps ten objectives but only two are covered in a test, then content validity suffers.

Consider the following quiz on English articles for a high-beginner level of a conversation class (listening and speaking) for English learners.

English articles quiz

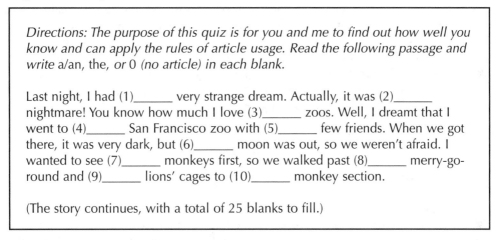

Directions: The purpose of this quiz is for you and me to find out how well you know and can apply the rules of article usage. Read the following passage and write a/an, the, *or* 0 *(no article) in each blank.*

Last night, I had (1)_____ very strange dream. Actually, it was (2)_____ nightmare! You know how much I love (3)_____ zoos. Well, I dreamt that I went to (4)_____ San Francisco zoo with (5)_____ few friends. When we got there, it was very dark, but (6)_____ moon was out, so we weren't afraid. I wanted to see (7)_____ monkeys first, so we walked past (8)_____ merry-go-round and (9)_____ lions' cages to (10)_____ monkey section.

(The story continues, with a total of 25 blanks to fill.)

The students had had a unit on zoo animals and had engaged in some open discussions and group work in which they had practiced articles, all in listening and speaking modes of performance. In that this quiz uses a familiar setting and focuses on previously practiced language forms, it is somewhat content valid. The fact that it was administered in written form, however, and required students to read the passage and write their responses makes it quite low in content validity for a listening/speaking class.

There are a few cases of highly specialized and sophisticated testing instruments that may have questionable content-related evidence of validity. It is possible to contend, for example, that standard language proficiency tests, with their context-reduced, academically oriented language and limited stretches of discourse, lack content validity since they do not require the full spectrum of communicative performance on the part of the learner (see Bachman, 1990, for a full discussion). There is good reasoning behind such criticism; nevertheless, what such proficiency tests lack in content-related evidence they may gain in other forms of evidence, not to mention practicality and reliability.

Another way of understanding content validity is to consider the difference between **direct** and **indirect** testing. Direct testing involves the test-taker in actually performing the target task. In an indirect test, learners are not performing the task itself but rather a task that is related in some way. For example, if you intend to test learners' oral production of syllable stress and your test task is to have learners mark (with written accent marks) stressed syllables in a list of written words, you could, with a stretch of logic, argue that you are indirectly testing their oral production. A direct test of syllable production would have to require that students actually produce target words orally.

The most feasible rule of thumb for achieving content validity in classroom assessment is to test performance directly. Consider, for example, a listening/speaking class that is doing a unit on greetings and exchanges that includes discourse for asking for personal information (name, address, hobbies, etc.) with some form-focus on the verb *to be,* personal pronouns, and question formation. The test on that unit should include all of the above discourse and grammatical elements and involve students in the actual performance of listening and speaking.

What all the above examples suggest is that content is not the *only* type of evidence to support the validity of a test, but classroom teachers have neither the time nor the budget to subject quizzes, midterms, and final exams to the extensive scrutiny of a full construct validation (see below). Therefore, it is critical that teachers hold content-related evidence in high esteem in the process of defending the validity of classroom tests.

Criterion-Related Evidence

A second form of evidence of the validity of a test may be found in what is called criterion-related evidence, also referred to as **criterion-related validity,** or the extent to which the "criterion" of the test has actually been reached. You will recall that in Chapter 1 it was noted that most classroom-based assessment with teacher-designed tests fits the concept of criterion-referenced assessment. In such tests, specified classroom objectives are measured, and implied predetermined levels of performance are expected to be reached (80 percent is considered a minimal passing grade).

In the case of teacher-made classroom assessments, criterion-related evidence is best demonstrated through a comparison of results of an assessment with results of some other measure of the same criterion. For example, in a course unit whose objective is for students to be able to orally produce voiced and voiceless stops in all possible phonetic environments, the results of one teacher's unit test might be compared with an independent assessment—possibly a commercially produced test in a textbook—of the same phonemic proficiency. A classroom test designed to assess mastery of a point of grammar in communicative use will have criterion validity if test scores are corroborated either by observed subsequent behavior or by other communicative measures of the grammar point in question.

Criterion-related evidence usually falls into one of two categories: concurrent and predictive validity. A test has **concurrent validity** if its results are supported by other concurrent performance beyond the assessment itself. For example, the validity of a high score on the final exam of a foreign language course will be substantiated by actual proficiency in the language. The **predictive validity** of an assessment becomes important in the case of placement tests, admissions assessment batteries, language aptitude tests, and the like. The assessment criterion in such cases is not to measure concurrent ability but to assess (and predict) a test-taker's likelihood of future success.

Construct-Related Evidence

A third kind of evidence that can support validity, but one that does not play as large a role for classroom teachers, is construct-related validity, commonly referred to as **construct validity**. A construct is any theory, hypothesis, or model that attempts to explain observed phenomena in our universe of perceptions. Constructs may or may not be directly or empirically measured—their verification often requires inferential data. "Proficiency" and "communicative competence" are linguistic constructs; "self-esteem" and "motivation" are psychological constructs. Virtually every issue in language learning and teaching involves theoretical constructs. In the field of assessment, construct validity asks, "Does this test actually tap into the theoretical construct as it has been defined?" Tests are, in a manner of speaking, operational definitions of constructs in that they operationalize the entity that is being measured (see Davidson, Hudson, & Lynch, 1985).

For most of the tests that you administer as a classroom teacher, a formal construct validation procedure may seem a daunting prospect. You will be tempted, perhaps, to run a quick content check and be satisfied with the test's validity. But don't let the concept of construct validity scare you. An informal construct validation of the use of virtually every classroom test is both essential and feasible.

Imagine, for example, that you have been given a procedure for conducting an oral interview. The scoring analysis for the interview includes several factors in the final score: pronunciation, fluency, grammatical accuracy, vocabulary use, and sociolinguistic appropriateness. The justification for these five factors lies in a theoretical construct that claims those factors to be major components of oral proficiency. So if you were asked to conduct an oral proficiency interview that evaluated only pronunciation and grammar, you could be justifiably suspicious about the construct validity of that test. Likewise, let's suppose you have created a simple written vocabulary quiz, covering the content of a recent unit, that asks students to correctly define a set of words. Your chosen items may be a perfectly adequate sample of what was covered in the unit, but if the lexical objective of the unit was the communicative use of vocabulary, then the writing of definitions certainly fails to match a construct of communicative language use.

Construct validity is a major issue in validating large-scale standardized tests of proficiency. Because such tests must, for economic reasons, adhere to the principle of practicality, and because they must sample a limited number of domains of language, they may not be able to contain all the content of a particular field or skill. The TOEFL®, for example, has until recently not attempted to sample oral production, yet oral production is obviously an important part of academic success in a university course of study. The TOEFL's omission of oral production content, however, is ostensibly justified by research that has shown positive correlations between oral production and the behaviors (listening, reading, grammaticality detection, and writing) actually sampled on the TOEFL (see Duran et al., 1985). Because of the crucial need to offer a financially affordable proficiency test and the high cost of administering and scoring oral production tests, the omission of oral content from the TOEFL has been justified as an economic necessity. (Note: As this book goes to press, oral production tasks are being included in the TOEFL, largely stemming from the demands of the professional community for authenticity and content validity.)

Consequential Validity

As well as the above three widely accepted forms of evidence that may be introduced to support the validity of an assessment, two other categories may be of some interest and utility in your own quest for validating classroom tests. Messick (1989), Gronlund (1998), McNamara (2000), and Brindley (2001), among others, underscore the potential importance of the consequences of using an assessment. Consequential validity encompasses all the consequences of a test, including such considerations as its accuracy in measuring intended criteria, its impact on the preparation of test-takers, its effect on the learner, and the (intended and unintended) social consequences of a test's interpretation and use.

As high-stakes assessment has gained ground in the last two decades, one aspect of consequential validity has drawn special attention: the effect of test preparation courses and manuals on performance. McNamara (2000, p. 54) cautions against test results that may reflect socioeconomic conditions such as opportunities for coaching that are "differentially available to the students being assessed (for example, because only some families can afford coaching, or because children with more highly educated parents get help from their parents)." The social consequences of large-scale, high-stakes assessment are discussed in Chapter 6.

Another important consequence of a test falls into the category of *washback*, to be more fully discussed below. Gronlund (1998, pp. 209–210) encourages teachers to consider the effect of assessments on students' motivation, subsequent performance in a course, independent learning, study habits, and attitude toward school work.

Face Validity

An important facet of consequential validity is the extent to which "students view the assessment as fair, relevant, and useful for improving learning" (Gronlund, 1998, p. 210), or what is popularly known as **face validity**. "Face validity refers to the degree to which a test *looks* right, and *appears* to measure the knowledge or abilities it claims to measure, based on the subjective judgment of the examinees who take it, the administrative personnel who decide on its use, and other psychometrically unsophisticated observers" (Mousavi, 2002, p. 244).

Sometimes students don't know what is being tested when they tackle a test. They may feel, for a variety of reasons, that a test isn't testing what it is "supposed" to test. Face validity means that the students perceive the test to be valid. Face validity asks the question "Does the test, on the 'face' of it, appear from the learner's perspective to test what it is designed to test?" Face validity will likely be high if learners encounter

- a well-constructed, expected format with familiar tasks,
- a test that is clearly doable within the allotted time limit,
- items that are clear and uncomplicated,
- directions that are crystal clear,
- tasks that relate to their course work (content validity), and
- a difficulty level that presents a reasonable challenge.

Remember, face validity is *not* something that can be empirically tested by a teacher or even by a testing expert. It is purely a factor of the "eye of the beholder"—how the test-taker, or possibly the test giver, intuitively perceives the instrument. For this reason, some assessment experts (see Stevenson, 1985) view face validity as a superficial factor that is dependent on the whim of the perceiver.

The other side of this issue reminds us that the psychological state of the learner (confidence, anxiety, etc.) is an important ingredient in peak performance by a learner. Students can be distracted and their anxiety increased if you "throw a curve" at them on a test. They need to have rehearsed test tasks before the fact and feel comfortable with them. A classroom test is not the time to introduce new tasks because you won't know if student difficulty is a factor of the task itself or of the objectives you are testing.

I once administered a dictation test and a cloze test (see Chapter 8 for a discussion of cloze tests) as a placement test for a group of learners of English as a second language. Some learners were upset because such tests, on the face of it, did not appear to them to test their true abilities in English. They felt that a multiple-choice grammar test would have been the appropriate format to use. A few claimed they didn't perform well on the cloze and dictation because they were not accustomed to these formats. As it turned out, the tests served as superior instruments for placement, but the students would not have thought so. Face validity was low, content validity was moderate, and construct validity was very high.

As already noted above, content validity is a very important ingredient in achieving face validity. If a test samples the actual content of what the learner has achieved or expects to achieve, then face validity will be more likely to be perceived.

Validity is a complex concept, yet it is indispensable to the teacher's understanding of what makes a good test. If in your language teaching you can attend to the practicality, reliability, and validity of tests of language, whether those tests are classroom tests related to a part of a lesson, final exams, or proficiency tests, then you are well on the way to making accurate judgments about the competence of the learners with whom you are working.

AUTHENTICITY

A fourth major principle of language testing is **authenticity,** a concept that is a little slippery to define, especially within the art and science of evaluating and designing tests. Bachman and Palmer (1996, p. 23) define authenticity as "the degree of correspondence of the characteristics of a given language test task to the features of a target language task," and then suggest an agenda for identifying those target language tasks and for transforming them into valid test items.

Essentially, when you make a claim for authenticity in a test task, you are saying that this task is likely to be enacted in the "real world." Many test item types fail to simulate real-world tasks. They may be contrived or artificial in their attempt to target a grammatical form or a lexical item. The sequencing of items that bear no relationship to one another lacks authenticity. One does not have to look very long to find reading comprehension passages in proficiency tests that do not reflect a real-world passage.

In a test, authenticity may be present in the following ways:

- The language in the test is as natural as possible.
- Items are contextualized rather than isolated.
- Topics are meaningful (relevant, interesting) for the learner.
- Some thematic organization to items is provided, such as through a story line or episode.
- Tasks represent, or closely approximate, real-world tasks.

The authenticity of test tasks in recent years has increased noticeably. Two or three decades ago, unconnected, boring, contrived items were accepted as a necessary component of testing. Things have changed. It was once assumed that large-scale testing could not include performance of the productive skills and stay within budgetary constraints, but now many such tests offer speaking and writing components. Reading passages are selected from real-world sources that test-takers are likely to have encountered or will encounter. Listening comprehension sections feature natural language with hesitations, white noise, and interruptions. More and more tests offer items that are "episodic" in that they are sequenced to form meaningful units, paragraphs, or stories.

You are invited to take up the challenge of authenticity in your classroom tests. As we explore many different types of task in this book, especially in Chapters 6 through 9, the principle of authenticity will be very much in the forefront.

WASHBACK

A facet of consequential validity, discussed above, is "the effect of testing on teaching and learning" (Hughes, 2003, p. 1), otherwise known among language-testing specialists as **washback**. In large-scale assessment, washback generally refers to the effects the tests have on instruction in terms of how students prepare for the test.

"Cram" courses and "teaching to the test" are examples of such washback. Another form of washback that occurs more in classroom assessment is the information that "washes back" to students in the form of useful diagnoses of strengths and weaknesses. Washback also includes the effects of an assessment on teaching and learning prior to the assessment itself, that is, on preparation for the assessment. Informal performance assessment is by nature more likely to have built-in washback effects because the teacher is usually providing interactive feedback. Formal tests can also have positive washback, but they provide no washback if the students receive a simple letter grade or a single overall numerical score.

The challenge to teachers is to create classroom tests that serve as learning devices through which washback is achieved. Students' incorrect responses can become windows of insight into further work. Their correct responses need to be praised, especially when they represent accomplishments in a student's interlanguage. Teachers can suggest strategies for success as part of their "coaching" role. Washback enhances a number of basic principles of language acquisition: intrinsic motivation, autonomy, self-confidence, language ego, interlanguage, and strategic investment, among others. (See *PLLT* and *TBP* for an explanation of these principles.)

One way to enhance washback is to comment generously and specifically on test performance. Many overworked (and underpaid!) teachers return tests to students with a single letter grade or numerical score and consider their job done. In reality, letter grades and numerical scores give absolutely no information of intrinsic interest to the student. Grades and scores reduce a mountain of linguistic and cognitive performance data to an absurd molehill. At best, they give a relative indication of a formulaic judgment of performance as compared to others in the class—which fosters competitive, not cooperative, learning.

With this in mind, when you return a written test or a data sheet from an oral production test, consider giving more than a number, grade, or phrase as your feedback. Even if your evaluation is not a neat little paragraph appended to the test, you can respond to as many details throughout the test as time will permit. Give praise for strengths—the "good stuff"—as well as constructive criticism of weaknesses. Give strategic hints on how a student might improve certain elements of performance. In other words, take some time to make the test performance an intrinsically motivating experience from which a student will gain a sense of accomplishment and challenge.

A little bit of washback may also help students through a specification of the numerical scores on the various subsections of the test. A subsection on verb tenses, for example, that yields a relatively low score may serve the diagnostic purpose of showing the student an area of challenge.

Another viewpoint on washback is achieved by a quick consideration of differences between **formative** and **summative** tests, mentioned in Chapter 1. Formative tests, by definition, provide washback in the form of information to the learner on progress toward goals. But teachers might be tempted to feel that summative tests, which provide assessment at the end of a course or program, do not need to offer much in the way of washback. Such an attitude is unfortunate because the end of every language course or program is always the beginning of further pursuits, more learning, more goals, and more challenges to face. Even a final examination in a course should carry with it some means for giving washback to students.

In my courses I never give a final examination as the last scheduled classroom session. I always administer a final exam during the penultimate session, then complete the evaluation of the exams in order to return them to students during the last class. At this time, the students receive scores, grades, and comments on their work, and I spend some of the class session addressing material on which the students were not completely clear. My summative assessment is thereby enhanced by some beneficial washback that is usually not expected of final examinations.

Finally, washback also implies that students have ready access to you to discuss the feedback and evaluation you have given. While you almost certainly have known teachers with whom you wouldn't dare argue about a grade, an interactive, cooperative, collaborative classroom nevertheless can promote an atmosphere of dialogue between students and teachers regarding evaluative judgments. For learning to continue, students need to have a chance to feed back on your feedback, to seek clarification of any issues that are fuzzy, and to set new and appropriate goals for themselves for the days and weeks ahead.

APPLYING PRINCIPLES TO THE EVALUATION OF CLASSROOM TESTS

The five principles of practicality, reliability, validity, authenticity, and washback go a long way toward providing useful guidelines for both evaluating an existing assessment procedure and designing one on your own. Quizzes, tests, final exams, and standardized proficiency tests can all be scrutinized through these five lenses.

Are there other principles that should be invoked in evaluating and designing assessments? The answer, of course, is yes. Language assessment is an extraordinarily broad discipline with many branches, interest areas, and issues. The process of designing effective assessment instruments is far too complex to be reduced to five principles. Good test construction, for example, is governed by research-based rules of test preparation, sampling of tasks, item design and construction, scoring responses, ethical standards, and so on. But the five principles cited here serve as an excellent foundation on which to evaluate existing instruments and to build your own.

We will look at how to design tests in Chapter 3 and at standardized tests in Chapter 4. The questions that follow here, indexed by the five principles, will help you evaluate existing tests for your own classroom. It is important for you to remember, however, that the sequence of these questions does not imply a priority order. Validity, for example, is certainly the most significant cardinal principle of assessment evaluation. Practicality may be a secondary issue in classroom testing. Or, for a particular test, you may need to place authenticity as your primary consideration. When all is said and done, however, if *validity* is not substantiated, all other considerations may be rendered useless.

1. Are the test procedures practical?

Practicality is determined by the teacher's (and the students') time constraints, costs, and administrative details, and to some extent by what occurs before and after the test. To determine whether a test is practical for your needs, you may want to use the checklist below.

Practicality checklist

> ☐ **1.** Are administrative details clearly established before the test?
> ☐ **2.** Can students complete the test reasonably within the set time frame?
> ☐ **3.** Can the test be administered smoothly, without procedural "glitches"?
> ☐ **4.** Are all materials and equipment ready?
> ☐ **5.** Is the cost of the test within budgeted limits?
> ☐ **6.** Is the scoring/evaluation system feasible in the teacher's time frame?
> ☐ **7.** Are methods for reporting results determined in advance?

As this checklist suggests, after you account for the administrative details of *giving* a test, you need to think about the practicality of your plans for *scoring* the test. In teachers' busy lives, time often emerges as the most important factor, one that overrides other considerations in evaluating an assessment. If you need to tailor a test to fit your own time frame, as teachers frequently do, you need to accomplish this without damaging the test's validity and washback. Teachers should, for example, avoid the temptation to offer only quickly scored multiple-choice selection items that may be neither appropriate nor well-designed. Everyone knows teachers secretly hate to grade tests (almost as much as students hate to take them!) and will do almost anything to get through that task as quickly and effortlessly as possible. Yet good teaching almost always implies an investment of the teacher's time in giving feedback—comments and suggestions—to students on their tests.

2. Is the test reliable?

Reliability applies to both the test and the teacher, and at least four sources of unreliability must be guarded against, as noted in the second section of this chapter. Test and test administration reliability can be achieved by making sure that all students receive the same quality of input, whether written or auditory. Part of achieving test reliability depends on the physical context—making sure, for example, that

- every student has a cleanly photocopied test sheet,
- sound amplification is clearly audible to everyone in the room,
- video input is equally visible to all,
- lighting, temperature, extraneous noise, and other classroom conditions are equal (and optimal) for all students, and
- objective scoring procedures leave little debate about correctness of an answer.

Rater reliability, another common issue in assessments, may be more difficult, perhaps because we too often overlook this as an issue. Since classroom tests rarely involve two scorers, inter-rater reliability is seldom an issue. Instead, *intra*-rater reliability is of constant concern to teachers: What happens to our fallible concentration and stamina over the period of time during which we are evaluating a test? Teachers need to find ways to maintain their concentration and stamina over the time it takes to score assessments. In open-ended response tests, this issue is of paramount importance. It is easy to let mentally established standards erode over the hours you require to evaluate the test.

Intra-rater reliability for open-ended responses may be enhanced by the following guidelines:

- Use consistent sets of criteria for a correct response.
- Give uniform attention to those sets throughout the evaluation time.
- Read through tests at least twice to check for your consistency.
- If you have made "mid-stream" modifications of what you consider as a correct response, go back and apply the same standards to all.
- Avoid fatigue by reading the tests in several sittings, especially if the time requirement is a matter of several hours.

3. Does the procedure demonstrate content validity?

The major source of validity in a classroom test is content validity: the extent to which the assessment requires students to perform tasks that were included in the previous classroom lessons and that directly represent the objectives of the unit on which the assessment is based. If you have been teaching an English language class to fifth graders who have been reading, summarizing, and responding to short passages, and if your assessment is based on this work, then to be content valid, the test needs to include performance in those skills.

There are two steps to evaluating the content validity of a classroom test.

1. Are classroom objectives identified and appropriately framed? Underlying every good classroom test are the objectives of the lesson, module, or unit of the course in question. So the first measure of an effective classroom test is the identification of objectives. Sometimes this is easier said than done. Too often teachers work through lessons day after day with little or no cognizance of the objectives they seek to fulfill. Or perhaps those objectives are so poorly framed that determining whether or not they were accomplished is impossible. Consider the following objectives for lessons, all of which appeared on lesson plans designed by students in teacher preparation programs:

- **a.** Students should be able to demonstrate some reading comprehension.
- **b.** To practice vocabulary in context.
- **c.** Students will have fun through a relaxed activity and thus enjoy their learning.

    d. To give students a drill on the /i/ – /I/ contrast.
    e. Students will produce yes/no questions with final rising intonation.

Only the last objective is framed in a form that lends itself to assessment. In (a), the modal *should* is ambiguous and the expected performance is not stated. In (b), everyone can fulfill the act of "practicing"; no standards are stated or implied. For obvious reasons, (c) cannot be assessed. And (d) is really just a teacher's note on the type of activity to be used.

    Objective (e), on the other hand, includes a *performance* verb and a specific *linguistic target.* By specifying acceptable and unacceptable levels of performance, the goal can be tested. An appropriate test would elicit an adequate number of samples of student performance, have a clearly framed set of standards for evaluating the performance (say, on a scale of 1 to 5), and provide some sort of feedback to the student.

    2. Are lesson objectives represented in the form of test specifications? The next content-validity issue that can be applied to a classroom test centers on the concept of test **specifications.** Don't let this word scare you. It simply means that a test should have a structure that follows logically from the lesson or unit you are testing. Many tests have a design that

- divides them into a number of sections (corresponding, perhaps, to the objectives that are being assessed),
- offers students a *variety* of item types, and
- gives an appropriate relative **weight** to each section.

Some tests, of course, do not lend themselves to this kind of structure. A test in a course in academic writing at the university level might justifiably consist of an in-class written essay on a given topic—only one "item" and one response, in a manner of speaking. But in this case the specs (specifications) would be embedded in the prompt itself and in the scoring or evaluation rubric used to grade it and give feedback. We will return to the concept of test specs in the next chapter.

    The content validity of an existing classroom test should be apparent in how the objectives of the unit being tested are represented in the form of the content of items, clusters of items, and item types. Do you clearly perceive the performance of test-takers as reflective of the classroom objectives? If so, and you can argue this, content validity has probably been achieved.

4. Is the procedure face valid and "biased for best"?

This question integrates the concept of face validity with the importance of structuring an assessment procedure to elicit the optimal performance of the student. Students will generally judge a test to be face valid if

- directions are clear,
- the structure of the test is organized logically,

- its difficulty level is appropriately pitched,
- the test has no "surprises," and
- timing is appropriate.

A phrase that has come to be associated with face validity is "biased for best," a term that goes a little beyond how the student views the test to a degree of strategic involvement on the part of student and teacher in preparing for, setting up, and following up on the test itself. According to Swain (1984), to give an assessment procedure that is "biased for best," a teacher

- offers students appropriate review and preparation for the test,
- suggests strategies that will be beneficial, and
- structures the test so that the best students will be modestly challenged and the weaker students will not be overwhelmed.

It's easy for teachers to forget how challenging some tests can be, and so a well-planned testing experience will include some strategic suggestions on how students might optimize their performance. In evaluating a classroom test, consider the extent to which before-, during-, and after-test options are fulfilled.

Test-taking strategies

Before the Test

1. Give students all the information you can about the test: Exactly what will the test cover? Which topics will be the most important? What kind of items will be on it? How long will it be?
2. Encourage students to do a systematic review of material. For example, they should skim the textbook and other material, outline major points, write down examples.
3. Give them practice tests or exercises, if available.
4. Facilitate formation of a study group, if possible.
5. Caution students to get a good night's rest before the test.
6. Remind students to get to the classroom early.

During the Test

1. After the test is distributed, tell students to look over the whole test quickly in order to get a good grasp of its different parts.
2. Remind them to mentally figure out how much time they will need for each part.
3. Advise them to concentrate as carefully as possible.
4. Warn students a few minutes before the end of the class period so that they can finish on time, proofread their answers, and catch careless errors.

After the Test

1. When you return the test, include feedback on specific things the student did well, what he or she did not do well, and, if possible, the reasons for your comments.
2. Advise students to pay careful attention in class to whatever you say about the test results.
3. Encourage questions from students.
4. Advise students to pay special attention in the future to points on which they are weak.

Keep in mind that what comes before and after the test also contributes to its face validity. Good class preparation will give students a comfort level with the test, and good feedback—washback—will allow them to learn from it.

5. Are the test tasks as authentic as possible?

Evaluate the extent to which a test is authentic by asking the following questions:

- Is the language in the test as natural as possible?
- Are items as contextualized as possible rather than isolated?
- Are topics and situations interesting, enjoyable, and/or humorous?
- Is some thematic organization provided, such as through a story line or episode?
- Do tasks represent, or closely approximate, real-world tasks?

Consider the following two excerpts from tests, and the concept of authenticity may become a little clearer.

Multiple-choice tasks—contextualized

"Going To"

1. **What _____ this weekend?**
   a. you are going to do
   b. are you going to do
   c. your gonna do
2. **I'm not sure. _____ anything special?**
   a. Are you going to do
   b. You are going to do
   c. Is going to do

3. **My friend Melissa and I _____ a party. Would you like to come?**
   a. am going to
   b. are going to go to
   c. go to
4. **I'd love to! _____**
   a. What's it going to be?
   b. Who's going to be?
   c. Where's it going to be?
5. **It is _____ to be at Ruth's house.**
   a. go
   b. going
   c. gonna

—Sheila Viotti, from *Dave's ESL Café*

Multiple-choice tasks—decontextualized

1. **There are three countries I would like to visit. One is Italy.**
   a. The other is New Zealand and other is Nepal.
   b. The others are New Zealand and Nepal.
   c. Others are New Zealand and Nepal.
2. **When I was twelve years old, I used _____ every day.**
   a. swimming
   b. to swimming
   c. to swim
3. **When Mr. Brown designs a website, he always creates it _____ .**
   a. artistically
   b. artistic
   c. artist
4. **Since the beginning of the year, I _____ at Millennium Industries.**
   a. am working
   b. had been working
   c. have been working
5. **When Mona broke her leg, she asked her husband _____ her to work.**
   a. to drive
   b. driving
   c. drive

—Brown (2000), *New Vistas,* Book 4

The sequence of items in the contextualized tasks achieves a modicum of authenticity by contextualizing all the items in a story line. The conversation is one that might occur in the real world, even if with a little less formality. The sequence of items in the decontextualized tasks takes the test-taker into five different topic areas with no context for any. Each sentence is likely to be written or spoken in the real world, but not in that sequence. Given the constraints of a multiple-choice format, on a measure of authenticity I would say the first excerpt is "good" and the second excerpt is only "fair."

6. Does the test offer beneficial washback to the learner?

The design of an effective test should point the way to beneficial washback. A test that achieves content validity demonstrates relevance to the curriculum in question and thereby sets the stage for washback. When test items represent the various objectives of a unit, and/or when sections of a test clearly focus on major topics of the unit, classroom tests can serve in a diagnostic capacity even if they aren't specifically labeled as such.

Other evidence of washback may be less visible from an examination of the test itself. Here again, what happens before and after the test is critical. Preparation time before the test can contribute to washback since the learner is reviewing and focusing in a potentially broader way on the objectives in question. By spending classroom time after the test reviewing the content, students discover their areas of strength and weakness. Teachers can raise the washback potential by asking students to use test results as a guide to setting goals for their future effort. The key is to play down the "Whew, I'm glad that's over" feeling that students are likely to have, and play up the learning that can now take place from their knowledge of the results.

Some of the "alternatives" in assessment referred to in Chapter 1 may also enhance washback from tests. (See also Chapter 10.) Self-assessment may sometimes be an appropriate way to challenge students to discover their own mistakes. This can be particularly effective for writing performance: once the pressure of assessment has come and gone, students may be able to look back on their written work with a fresh eye. Peer discussion of the test results may also be an alternative to simply listening to the teacher tell everyone what they got right and wrong and why. Journal writing may offer students a specific place to record their feelings, what they learned, and their resolutions for future effort.

§   §   §   §   §

The five basic principles of language assessment were expanded here into six essential questions you might ask yourself about an assessment. As you use the principles and the guidelines to evaluate various forms of tests and procedures, be sure to allow each one of the five to take on greater or lesser importance, depending on the context. In large-scale standardized testing, for example, practicality is usually more important than washback, but the reverse may be true of a number of class-room tests. Validity is of course always the final arbiter. And remember, too, that these principles, important as they are, are not the only considerations in evaluating or making an effective test. Leave some space for other factors to enter in.

In the next chapter, the focus is on how to design a test. These same five principles underlie test construction as well as test evaluation, along with some new facets that will expand your ability to apply principles to the practicalities of language assessment in your own classroom.

EXERCISES

[Note: **(I)** Individual work; **(G)** Group or pair work; **(C)** Whole-class discussion.]

1. **(I/C)** Review the five basic principles of language assessment that are defined and explained in this chapter. Be sure to differentiate among several types of evidence that support the validity of a test, as well as four kinds of reliability.
2. **(G)** A checklist for gauging *practicality* is provided on page 31. In your group, construct a similar checklist for either face validity, authenticity, or washback, as assigned to your group. Present your lists to the class and, in the case of multiple groups, synthesize findings into one checklist for each principle.
3. **(I/C)** Do you think that consequential and face validity are appropriate considerations in classroom-based assessment? Explain.
4. **(G)** In the section on washback, it is stated that "Washback enhances a number of basic principles of language acquisition: intrinsic motivation, autonomy, self-confidence, language ego, interlanguage, and strategic investment, among others" (page 29). In a group, discuss the connection between washback and the above-named general principles of language learning and teaching. Come up with some specific examples for each. Report your examples to the rest of the class.
5. **(I/C)** Washback is described here as a positive effect. Can tests provide negative washback? Explain.
6. **(G)** In a small group, decide how you would evaluate each of the 12 assessment scenarios described in the chart on pages 39–40, according to the six factors listed there. Fill in the chart with 5-4-3-2-1 scores, with 5 indicating that the principle is highly fulfilled and 1 indicating very low or no fulfillment. Use your best intuition to supply these evaluations, even though you don't have complete information on each context. Report your group's findings to the rest of the class and compare.

	Practicality	Rater Reliability	Test Reliability	Content Validity	Face Validity	Authenticity
Scenario 1: Standardized multiple-choice proficiency test, no oral or written production. S receives a report form listing a total score and part scores for listening, grammar, proofreading, and reading comprehension.						
Scenario 2: Timed impromptu test of written English (TWE). S receives a report form listing one holistic score ranging between 0 and 6.						
Scenario 3: One-on-one oral interview to assess overall oral production ability. S receives one holistic score ranging between 0 and 5.						
Scenario 4: Multiple-choice listening quiz provided by a textbook with taped prompts, covering the content of a three-week module of a course. S receives a total score from T with no indication of which items were correct/incorrect.						
Scenario 5: S is given a sheet with 10 vocabulary items and directed to write 10 sentences using each word. T marks each item as acceptable/ unacceptable, and S receives the test sheet back with items marked and a total score ranging from 0 to 10.						
Scenario 6: S reads a passage of three paragraphs and responds to six multiple-choice general comprehension items. S receives a score report showing which items were correct and incorrect.						
Scenario 7: S gives a 5-minute prepared oral presentation in class. T evaluates by filling in a rating sheet indicating S's success in delivery, rapport, pronunciation, grammar, and content.						
Scenario 8: S listens to a 15-minute video lecture and takes notes. T makes individual comments on each S's notes.						
Scenario 9: S writes a take-home (overnight) one-page essay on an assigned topic. T reads paper and comments on organization and content only, and returns essay to S for a subsequent draft.						

(continued)

	Practicality	Rater Reliability	Test Reliability	Content Validity	Face Validity	Authenticity
Scenario 10: S creates multiple drafts of a three-page essay, peer- and T-reviewed, and turns in a final version. T comments on grammatical/rhetorical errors only, and returns it to S.						
Scenario 11: S assembles a portfolio of materials over a semester-long course. T conferences with S on the portfolio at the end of the semester.						
Scenario 12: S writes a dialogue journal over the course of a semester. T comments on entries every two weeks.						

7. **(G)** Page 33 stresses the importance of stating objectives in terms of performance verbs that can be observed and assessed. In pairs, write two or three other potential lesson objectives (addressing a proficiency level and skill area as assigned to your pair) that you think are effective. Present them to the rest of the class for analysis and evaluation.

8. **(I/G)** In an accessible language class, ask the teacher to allow you to observe an assessment procedure that is about to take place (a test, an in-class periodic assessment, a quiz, etc.). Conduct (a) a brief interview with the teacher before the test, (b) an observation (if possible) of the actual administration of the assessment, and (c) a short interview with the teacher after the fact to form your data. Evaluate the effectiveness of the assessment in terms of (a) the five basic principles of assessment and/or (b) the six steps for test evaluation described in this chapter. Present your findings either as a written report to your instructor and/or orally to the class.

FOR YOUR FURTHER READING

Alderson, J. Charles. (2001). Language testing and assessment (Part 1). *Language Teaching, 34,* 213–236.

Alderson, J. Charles. (2002). Language testing and assessment (Part 2). *Language Teaching, 35,* 79–113.

These two highly informative state-of-the-art articles summarize current issues and controversies in the field of language testing. A comprehensive bibliography is provided at the end of each part. Part 1 covers such issues as ethics and politics in language testing, standards-based assessment, computer-based testing, self-assessment, and other alternatives in testing. Part 2 focuses on assessment of the skills of reading, listening, speaking, and writing, along with grammar and vocabulary.

Hughes, Arthur. (2003). *Testing for language teachers.* Second Edition. Cambridge: Cambridge University Press.

A widely used training manual for teachers, Hughes's book contains useful information on basic principles and techniques for testing language across the four skills. The chapters on validity, reliability, and washback ("backwash") provide quick alternatives to the definitions of the same terms used in this book.

CHAPTER 3

DESIGNING CLASSROOM

LANGUAGE TESTS

The previous chapters introduced a number of building blocks for designing language tests. You now have a sense of where tests belong in the larger domain of assessment. You have sorted through differences between formal and informal tests, formative and summative tests, and norm- and criterion-referenced tests. You have traced some of the historical lines of thought in the field of language assessment. You have a sense of major current trends in language assessment, especially the present focus on communicative and process-oriented testing that seeks to transform tests from anguishing ordeals into challenging and intrinsically motivating learning experiences. By now, certain foundational principles have entered your vocabulary: practicality, reliability, validity, authenticity, and washback. And you should now possess a few tools with which you can evaluate the effectiveness of a classroom test.

In this chapter, you will draw on those foundations and tools to begin the process of designing tests or revising existing tests. To start that process, you need to ask some critical questions:

1. What is the purpose of the test? Why am I creating this test or why was it created by someone else? For an evaluation of overall proficiency? To place students into a course? To measure achievement within a course? Once you have established the major purpose of a test, you can determine its objectives.

2. What are the objectives of the test? What specifically am I trying to find out? Establishing appropriate objectives involves a number of issues, ranging from relatively simple ones about forms and functions covered in a course unit to much more complex ones about constructs to be operationalized in the test. Included here are decisions about what language abilities are to be assessed.

3. How will the test specifications reflect both the purpose and the objectives? To evaluate or design a test, you must make sure that the objectives are incorporated into a structure that appropriately weights the various competencies being assessed. (These first three questions all center, in one way or another, on the principle of validity.)

4. How will the test tasks be selected and the separate items arranged? The tasks that the test-takers must perform need to be practical in the ways defined in the previous chapter. They should also achieve content validity by presenting tasks that mirror those of the course (or segment thereof) being assessed. Further, they should be able to be evaluated reliably by the teacher or scorer. The tasks themselves should strive for authenticity, and the progression of tasks ought to be biased for best performance.

5. *What kind of scoring, grading, and/or feedback is expected?* Tests vary in the form and function of feedback, depending on their purpose. For every test, the way results are reported is an important consideration. Under some circumstances a letter grade or a holistic score may be appropriate; other circumstances may require that a teacher offer substantive washback to the learner.

These five questions should form the basis of your approach to designing tests for your classroom.

TEST TYPES

The first task you will face in designing a test for your students is to determine the purpose for the test. Defining your purpose will help you choose the right kind of test, and it will also help you to focus on the specific objectives of the test. We will look first at two test types that you will probably not have many opportunities to create as a classroom teacher—language aptitude tests and language proficiency tests—and three types that you will almost certainly need to create—placement tests, diagnostic tests, and achievement tests.

Language Aptitude Tests

One type of test—although admittedly not a very common one—predicts a person's success prior to exposure to the second language. A **language aptitude test** is designed to measure capacity or general ability to learn a foreign language and ultimate success in that undertaking. Language aptitude tests are ostensibly designed to apply to the classroom learning of any language.

Two standardized aptitude tests have been used in the United States: the *Modern Language Aptitude Test* (MLAT) (Carroll & Sapon, 1958) and the *Pimsleur Language Aptitude Battery* (PLAB) (Pimsleur, 1966). Both are English language tests and require students to perform a number of language-related tasks. The MLAT, for example, consists of five different tasks.

Tasks in the Modern Language Aptitude Test

1. <u>Number learning</u>: Examinees must learn a set of numbers through aural input and then discriminate different combinations of those numbers.
2. <u>Phonetic script</u>: Examinees must learn a set of correspondences between speech sounds and phonetic symbols.

3. <u>Spelling clues</u>: Examinees must read words that are spelled somewhat phonetically, and then select from a list the one word whose meaning is closest to the "disguised" word.
4. <u>Words in sentences</u>: Examinees are given a key word in a sentence and are then asked to select a word in a second sentence that performs the same grammatical function as the key word.
5. <u>Paired associates</u>: Examinees must quickly learn a set of vocabulary words from another language and memorize their English meanings.

More information on the MLAT may be obtained from the following website: **http://www.2lti.com/mlat.htm#2**.

The MLAT and PLAB show some significant correlations with ultimate performance of students in language courses (Carroll, 1981). Those correlations, however, presuppose a foreign language course in which success is measured by similar processes of mimicry, memorization, and puzzle-solving. There is no research to show unequivocally that those kinds of tasks predict communicative success in a language, especially untutored acquisition of the language.

Because of this limitation, standardized aptitude tests are seldom used today. Instead, attempts to measure language aptitude more often provide learners with information about their preferred styles and their potential strengths and weaknesses, with follow-up strategies for capitalizing on the strengths and overcoming the weaknesses. Any test that claims to predict success in learning a language is undoubtedly flawed because we now know that with appropriate self-knowledge, active strategic involvement in learning, and/or strategies-based instruction, virtually everyone can succeed eventually. To pigeon-hole learners *a priori,* before they have even attempted to learn a language, is to presuppose failure or success without substantial cause. (A further discussion of language aptitude can be found in *PLLT,* Chapter 4.)

Proficiency Tests

If your aim is to test global competence in a language, then you are, in conventional terminology, testing **proficiency**. A proficiency test is not limited to any one course, curriculum, or single skill in the language; rather, it tests overall ability. Proficiency tests have traditionally consisted of standardized multiple-choice items on grammar, vocabulary, reading comprehension, and aural comprehension. Sometimes a sample of writing is added, and more recent tests also include oral production performance. As noted in the previous chapter, such tests often have content validity weaknesses, but several decades of construct validation research have brought us much closer to constructing successful communicative proficiency tests.

Proficiency tests are almost always summative and norm-referenced. They provide results in the form of a single score (or at best two or three subscores, one for each section of a test), which is a sufficient result for the **gate-keeping** role they play of accepting or denying someone passage into the next stage of a journey. And because they measure performance against a norm, with equated scores and percentile ranks taking on paramount importance, they are usually not equipped to provide diagnostic feedback.

A typical example of a standardized proficiency test is the Test of English as a Foreign Language (TOEFL®) produced by the Educational Testing Service. The TOEFL is used by more than a thousand institutions of higher education in the United States as an indicator of a prospective student's ability to undertake academic work in an English-speaking milieu. The TOEFL consists of sections on listening comprehension, structure (or grammatical accuracy), reading comprehension, and written expression. The new computer-scored TOEFL announced for 2005 will also include an oral production component. With the exception of its writing section, the TOEFL (as well as many other large-scale proficiency tests) is machine-scorable for rapid turnaround and cost effectiveness (that is, for reasons of practicality). Research is in progress (Bernstein et al., 2000) to determine, through the technology of speech recognition, if oral production performance can be adequately machine-scored. (Chapter 4 provides a comprehensive look at the TOEFL and other standardized tests.)

A key issue in testing proficiency is how the *constructs* of language ability are specified. The tasks that test-takers are required to perform must be legitimate samples of English language use in a defined context. Creating these tasks and validating them with research is a time-consuming and costly process. Language teachers would be wise not to create an overall proficiency test on their own. A far more practical method is to choose one of a number of commercially available proficiency tests.

Placement Tests

Certain proficiency tests can act in the role of **placement** tests, the purpose of which is to place a student into a particular level or section of a language curriculum or school. A placement test usually, but not always, includes a sampling of the material to be covered in the various courses in a curriculum; a student's performance on the test should indicate the point at which the student will find material neither too easy nor too difficult but appropriately challenging.

The English as a Second Language Placement Test (ESLPT) at San Francisco State University has three parts. In Part I, students read a short article and then write a summary essay. In Part II, students write a composition in response to an article. Part III is multiple-choice: students read an essay and identify grammar errors in it. The maximum time allowed for the test is three hours. Justification for this three-part structure rests largely on the test's content validation. Most of the ESL courses at San Francisco State involve a combination of reading and writing, with a heavy emphasis on writing. The first part of the test acts as both a test of reading comprehension and a test of writing (a summary). The second part requires students to state opinions and to back them up, a task that forms a major component of the writing courses. Finally, proofreading drafts of essays is a useful academic skill, and the exercise in error detection simulates the proofreading process.

Teachers and administrators in the ESL program at SFSU are satisfied with this test's capacity to discriminate appropriately, and they feel that it is a more authentic test than its multiple-choice, discrete-point, grammar-vocabulary predecessor. The practicality of the ESLPT is relatively low: human evaluators are required for the first two parts, a process more costly in both time and money than running the multiple-choice Part III responses through a pre-programmed scanner. Reliability problems are also present but are mitigated by conscientious training of all evaluators of the test. What is lost in practicality and reliability is gained in the diagnostic information that the ESLPT provides. Statistical analysis of errors in the multiple-choice section furnishes data on each student's grammatical and rhetorical areas of difficulty, and the essay responses are available to teachers later as a preview of their students' writing.

Placement tests come in many varieties: assessing comprehension and production, responding through written and oral performance, open-ended and limited responses, selection (e.g., multiple-choice) and gap-filling formats, depending on the nature of a program and its needs. Some programs simply use existing standardized proficiency tests because of their obvious advantage in practicality—cost, speed in scoring, and efficient reporting of results. Others prefer the performance data available in more open-ended written and/or oral production. The ultimate objective of a placement test is, of course, to correctly place a student into a course or level. Secondary benefits to consider include face validity, diagnostic information on students' performance, and authenticity.

In a recent one-month special summer program in English conversation and writing at San Francisco State University, 30 students were to be placed into one of two sections. The ultimate objective of the placement test (consisting of a five-minute oral interview and an essay-writing task) was to find a performance-based means to divide the students evenly into two sections. This objective might have been achieved easily by administering a simple grid-scorable multiple-choice grammar-vocabulary test. But the interview and writing sample added some important face validity, gave a more personal touch in a small program, and provided some diagnostic information on a group of learners about whom we knew very little prior to their arrival on campus.

Diagnostic Tests

A **diagnostic test** is designed to diagnose specified aspects of a language. A test in pronunciation, for example, might diagnose the phonological features of English that are difficult for learners and should therefore become part of a curriculum. Usually, such tests offer a checklist of features for the administrator (often the teacher) to use in pinpointing difficulties. A writing diagnostic would elicit a writing sample from students that would allow the teacher to identify those rhetorical and linguistic features on which the course needed to focus special attention.

Diagnostic and placement tests, as we have already implied, may sometimes be indistinguishable from each other. The San Francisco State ESLPT serves dual purposes. Any placement test that offers information beyond simply designating a course level may also serve diagnostic purposes.

There is also a fine line of difference between a diagnostic test and a general achievement test. Achievement tests analyze the extent to which students have acquired language features that have *already* been taught; diagnostic tests should elicit information on what students need to work on in the future. Therefore, a diagnostic test will typically offer more detailed subcategorized information on the learner. In a curriculum that has a form-focused phase, for example, a diagnostic test might offer information about a learner's acquisition of verb tenses, modal auxiliaries, definite articles, relative clauses, and the like.

A typical diagnostic test of oral production was created by Clifford Prator (1972) to accompany a manual of English pronunciation. Test-takers are directed to read a 150-word passage while they are tape-recorded. The test administrator then refers to an inventory of phonological items for analyzing a learner's production. After multiple listenings, the administrator produces a checklist of errors in five separate categories, each of which has several subcategories. The main categories include

1. stress and rhythm,
2. intonation,
3. vowels,
4. consonants, and
5. other factors.

An example of subcategories is shown in this list for the first category (stress and rhythm):

a. stress on the wrong syllable (in multi-syllabic words)
b. incorrect sentence stress
c. incorrect division of sentences into thought groups
d. failure to make smooth transitions between words or syllables

(Prator, 1972)

Each subcategory is appropriately referenced to a chapter and section of Prator's manual. This information can help teachers make decisions about aspects of English phonology on which to focus. This same information can help a student become aware of errors and encourage the adoption of appropriate compensatory strategies.

Achievement Tests

An **achievement test** is related directly to classroom lessons, units, or even a total curriculum. Achievement tests are (or should be) limited to particular material addressed in a curriculum within a particular time frame and are offered after a course has focused on the objectives in question. Achievement tests can also serve the diagnostic role of indicating what a student needs to continue to work on in the future, but the primary role of an achievement test is to determine whether course objectives have been met—and appropriate knowledge and skills acquired—by the end of a period of instruction.

Achievement tests are often summative because they are administered at the end of a unit or term of study. They also play an important formative role. An effective achievement test will offer washback about the quality of a learner's performance in subsets of the unit or course. This washback contributes to the formative nature of such tests.

The specifications for an achievement test should be determined by

- the objectives of the lesson, unit, or course being assessed,
- the relative importance (or weight) assigned to each objective,
- the tasks employed in classroom lessons during the unit of time,
- practicality issues, such as the time frame for the test and turnaround time, and
- the extent to which the test structure lends itself to formative washback.

Achievement tests range from five- or ten-minute quizzes to three-hour final examinations, with an almost infinite variety of item types and formats. Here is the outline for a midterm examination offered at the high-intermediate level of an intensive English program in the United States. The course focus is on academic reading and writing; the structure of the course and its objectives may be implied from the sections of the test.

Midterm examination outline, high-intermediate

Section A. Vocabulary
    Part 1 (5 items): match words and definitions
    Part 2 (5 items): use the word in a sentence

Section B. Grammar
    (10 sentences): error detection (underline or circle the error)

Section C. Reading comprehension
    (2 one-paragraph passages): four short-answer items for each

Section D. Writing
    respond to a two-paragraph article on Native American culture

---

SOME PRACTICAL STEPS TO TEST CONSTRUCTION

The descriptions of types of tests in the preceding section are intended to help you understand how to answer the first question posed in this chapter: What is the purpose of the test? It is unlikely that you would be asked to design an aptitude test or a proficiency test, but for the purposes of interpreting those tests, it is important that you understand their nature. However, your opportunities to design placement, diagnostic, and achievement tests—especially the latter—will be plentiful. In the remainder of this chapter, we will explore the four remaining questions posed at the outset, and the focus will be on equipping you with the tools you need to create such classroom-oriented tests.

You may think that every test you devise must be a wonderfully innovative instrument that will garner the accolades of your colleagues and the admiration of your students. Not so. First, new and innovative testing formats take a lot of effort to design and a long time to refine through trial and error. Second, traditional testing techniques can, with a little creativity, conform to the spirit of an interactive, communicative language curriculum. Your best tack as a new teacher is to work within the guidelines of accepted, known, traditional testing techniques. Slowly, with experience, you can get bolder in your attempts. In that spirit, then, let us consider some practical steps in constructing classroom tests.

Assessing Clear, Unambiguous Objectives

In addition to knowing the purpose of the test you're creating, you need to know as specifically as possible what it is you want to test. Sometimes teachers give tests simply because it's Friday of the third week of the course, and after hasty glances at the chapter(s) covered during those three weeks, they dash off some test items so that students will have something to do during the class. This is no way to approach a test. Instead, begin by taking a careful look at everything that you think your students should "know" or be able to "do," based on the material that the students are responsible for. In other words, examine the **objectives** for the unit you are testing.

Remember that every curriculum should have appropriately framed assessable objectives, that is, objectives that are stated in terms of overt performance by students (see Chapter 2, page 32). Thus, an objective that states "Students will learn tag questions" or simply names the grammatical focus "Tag questions" is not testable. You don't know whether students should be able to understand them in spoken or written language, or whether they should be able to produce them orally or in writing. Nor do you know in what context (a conversation? an essay? an academic lecture?) those linguistic forms should be used. Your first task in designing a test, then, is to determine appropriate objectives.

If you're lucky, someone will have already stated those objectives clearly in performance terms. If you're a little less fortunate, you may have to go back through a unit and formulate them yourself. Let's say you have been teaching a unit in a low-intermediate integrated-skills class with an emphasis on social conversation, and involving some reading and writing, that includes the objectives outlined below, either stated already or as you have reframed them. Notice that each objective is stated in terms of the *performance* elicited and the target *linguistic domain.*

Selected objectives for a unit in a low-intermediate integrated-skills course

---

Form-focused objectives (listening and speaking)

Students will

1. recognize and produce tag questions, with the correct grammatical form and final intonation pattern, in simple social conversations.
2. recognize and produce *wh*-information questions with correct final intonation pattern.

Communication skills (speaking)

Students will

3. state completed actions and events in a social conversation.
4. ask for confirmation in a social conversation.
5. give opinions about an event in a social conversation.
6. produce language with contextually appropriate intonation, stress, and rhythm.

Reading skills (simple essay or story)

Students will

7. recognize irregular past tense of selected verbs in a story or essay.

Writing skills (simple essay or story)

Students will

8. write a one-paragraph story about a simple event in the past.
9. use conjunctions *so* and *because* in a statement of opinion.

You may find, in reviewing the objectives of a unit or a course, that you cannot possibly test each one. You will then need to choose a possible subset of the objectives to test.

Drawing Up Test Specifications

Test specifications for classroom use can be a simple and practical outline of your test. (For large-scale standardized tests [see Chapter 4] that are intended to be widely distributed and therefore are broadly generalized, test specifications are much more formal and detailed.) In the unit discussed above, your specifications will simply comprise (a) a broad outline of the test, (b) what skills you will test, and (c) what the items will look like. Let's look at the first two in relation to the midterm unit assessment already referred to above.

(a) Outline of the test and (b) skills to be included. Because of the constraints of your curriculum, your unit test must take no more than 30 minutes. This is an

integrated curriculum, so you need to test all four skills. Since you have the luxury of teaching a small class (only 12 students!), you decide to include an oral production component in the preceding period (taking students one by one into a separate room while the rest of the class reviews the unit individually and completes workbook exercises). You can therefore test oral production objectives directly at that time. You determine that the 30-minute test will be divided equally in time among listening, reading, and writing.

(c) Item types and tasks. The next and potentially more complex choices involve the item types and **tasks** to use in this test. It is surprising that there are a limited number of modes of **eliciting** responses (that is, prompting) and of **responding** on tests of any kind. Consider the options: the test prompt can be oral (student listens) or written (student reads), and the student can respond orally or in writing. It's that simple. But some complexity is added when you realize that the types of prompts in each case vary widely, and within each response mode, of course, there are a number of options, all of which are depicted in Figure 3.1.

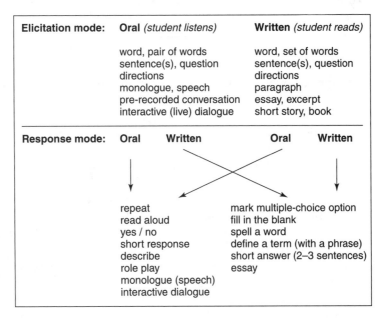

Figure 3.1. Elicitation and response modes in test construction

Granted, not all of the response modes correspond to all of the elicitation modes. For example, it is unlikely that directions would be read aloud, nor would spelling a word be matched with a monologue. A modicum of intuition will eliminate these non sequiturs.

Armed with a number of elicitation and response formats, you have decided to design your specs as follows, based on the objectives stated earlier:

Test specifications

Speaking (5 minutes per person, previous day)
Format: oral interview, T and S
Task: T asks questions of S (objectives 3, 5; emphasis on 6)

Listening (10 minutes)
Format: T makes audiotape in advance, with one other voice on it
Tasks: a. 5 minimal pair items, multiple-choice (objective 1)
b. 5 interpretation items, multiple-choice (objective 2)

Reading (10 minutes)
Format: cloze test items (10 total) in a story line
Tasks: fill-in-the-blanks (objective 7)

Writing (10 minutes)
Format: prompt for a topic: why I liked/didn't like a recent TV sitcom
Task: writing a short opinion paragraph (objective 9)

These informal, classroom-oriented specifications give you an indication of

- the topics (objectives) you will cover,
- the implied elicitation and response formats for items,
- the number of items in each section, and
- the time to be allocated for each.

Notice that three of the six possible speaking objectives are not directly tested. This decision may be based on the time you devoted to these objectives, but more likely on the feasibility of testing that objective or simply on the finite number of minutes available to administer the test. Notice, too, that objectives **4** and **8** are not assessed. Finally, notice that this unit was mainly focused on listening and speaking, yet 20 minutes of the 35-minute test is devoted to reading and writing tasks. Is this an appropriate decision?

One more test spec that needs to be included is a plan for scoring and assigning relative weight to each section and each item within. This issue will be addressed later in this chapter when we look at scoring, grading, and feedback.

Devising Test Tasks

Your oral interview comes first, and so you draft questions to conform to the accepted pattern of oral interviews (see Chapter 7 for information on constructing oral interviews). You begin and end with nonscored items (warm-up and wind-down) designed to set students at ease, and then sandwich between them items intended to test the objective (*level check*) and a little beyond (*probe*).

Oral interview format

A. Warm-up: questions and comments
B. Level-check questions (objectives 3, 5, and 6)
    1. Tell me about what you did last weekend.
    2. Tell me about an interesting trip you took in the last year.
    3. How did you like the TV show we saw this week?
C. Probe (objectives 5, 6)
    1. What is your opinion about _____ ? (news event)
    2. How do you feel about _____ ? (another news event)
D. Wind-down: comments and reassurance

You are now ready to draft other test items. To provide a sense of authenticity and interest, you have decided to conform your items to the context of a recent TV sitcom that you used in class to illustrate certain discourse and form-focused factors. The sitcom depicted a loud, noisy party with lots of small talk. As you devise your test items, consider such factors as how students will perceive them (face validity), the extent to which authentic language and contexts are present, potential difficulty caused by cultural schemata, the length of the listening stimuli, how well a story line comes across, how things like the cloze testing format will work, and other practicalities.

Let's say your first draft of items produces the following possibilities within each section:

Test items, first draft

Listening, part a. (sample item)

Directions: Listen to the sentence [on the tape]. Choose the sentence on your test page that is closest in meaning to the sentence you heard.

    Voice: They sure made a mess at that party, didn't they?
    S reads: a. They didn't make a mess, did they?
                  b. They <u>did</u> make a mess, didn't they?

Listening, part b. (sample item)

Directions: Listen to the question [on the tape]. Choose the sentence on your test page that is the best answer to the question.

    Voice: Where did George go after the party last night?
    S reads: a. Yes, he did.
                  b. Because he was tired.

> c. To Elaine's place for another party.
> d. He went home around eleven o'clock.
>
> **Reading** (sample items)
>
> *Directions: Fill in the correct tense of the verb (in parentheses) that should go in each blank.*
>
> Then, in the middle of this loud party they (hear) _____ the loudest thunder you have ever heard! And then right away lightning (strike) _____ right outside their house!
>
> **Writing**
>
> *Directions: Write a paragraph about what you liked or didn't like about <u>one</u> of the characters at the party in the TV sitcom we saw.*

As you can see, these items are quite traditional. You might self-critically admit that the format of some of the items is contrived, thus lowering the level of authenticity. But the thematic format of the sections, the authentic language within each item, and the contextualization add face validity, interest, and some humor to what might otherwise be a mundane test. All four skills are represented, and the tasks are varied within the 30 minutes of the test.

In revising your draft, you will want to ask yourself some important questions:

1. Are the directions to each section absolutely clear?
2. Is there an example item for each section?
3. Does each item measure a specified objective?
4. Is each item stated in clear, simple language?
5. Does each multiple-choice item have appropriate distractors; that is, are the wrong items clearly wrong and yet sufficiently "alluring" that they aren't ridiculously easy? (See below for a primer on creating effective distractors.)
6. Is the difficulty of each item appropriate for your students?
7. Is the language of each item sufficiently authentic?
8. Do the sum of the items and the test as a whole adequately reflect the learning objectives?

In the current example that we have been analyzing, your revising process is likely to result in at least four changes or additions:

1. In both interview and writing sections, you recognize that a scoring rubric will be essential. For the interview, you decide to create a holistic scale (see Chapter 7), and for the writing section you devise a simple analytic scale (see Chapter 9) that captures only the objectives you have focused on.
2. In the interview questions, you realize that follow-up questions may be needed for students who give one-word or very short answers.

3. In the listening section, part b, you intend choice "c" as the correct answer, but you realize that choice "d" is also acceptable. You need an answer that is unambiguously incorrect. You shorten it to "**d.** Around eleven o'clock." You also note that providing the prompts for this section on an audio recording will be logistically difficult, and so you opt to read these items to your students.

4. In the writing prompt, you can see how some students would not use the words *so* or *because,* which were in your objectives, so you reword the prompt: "Name one of the characters at the party in the TV sitcom we saw. Then, use the word *so* at least once and the word *because* at least once to tell why you liked or didn't like that person."

Ideally, you would try out all your tests on students not in your class before actually administering the tests. But in our daily classroom teaching, the tryout phase is almost impossible. Alternatively, you could enlist the aid of a colleague to look over your test. And so you must do what you can to bring to your students an instrument that is, to the best of your ability, practical and reliable.

In the final revision of your test, imagine that you are a student taking the test. Go through each set of directions and all items slowly and deliberately. Time yourself. (Often we underestimate the time students will need to complete a test.) If the test should be shortened or lengthened, make the necessary adjustments. Make sure your test is neat and uncluttered on the page, reflecting all the care and precision you have put into its construction. If there is an audio component, as there is in our hypothetical test, make sure that the script is clear, that your voice and any other voices are clear, and that the audio equipment is in working order before starting the test.

Designing Multiple-Choice Test Items

In the sample achievement test above, two of the five components (both of the listening sections) specified a multiple-choice format for items. This was a bold step to take. Multiple-choice items, which may appear to be the simplest kind of item to construct, are extremely difficult to design correctly. Hughes (2003, pp. 76–78) cautions against a number of weaknesses of multiple-choice items:

- The technique tests only recognition knowledge.
- Guessing may have a considerable effect on test scores.
- The technique severely restricts what can be tested.
- It is very difficult to write successful items.
- Washback may be harmful.
- Cheating may be facilitated.

The two principles that stand out in support of multiple-choice formats are, of course, practicality and reliability. With their predetermined correct responses and time-saving scoring procedures, multiple-choice items offer overworked teachers the tempting possibility of an easy and consistent process of scoring and grading. But is the preparation phase worth the effort? Sometimes it is, but you might spend even more time designing such items than you save in grading the test. Of course, if your objective is to design a large-scale standardized test for repeated administrations, then a multiple-choice format does indeed become viable.

First, a primer on terminology.

1. Multiple-choice items are all **receptive,** or **selective,** response items in that the test-taker chooses from a set of responses (commonly called a **supply** type of response) rather than creating a response. Other receptive item types include true-false questions and matching lists. (In the discussion here, the guidelines apply primarily to multiple-choice item types and not necessarily to other receptive types.)
2. Every multiple-choice item has a **stem,** which presents a stimulus, and several (usually between three and five) **options** or **alternatives** to choose from.
3. One of those options, the **key,** is the correct response, while the others serve as **distractors**.

Since there will be occasions when multiple-choice items are appropriate, consider the following four guidelines for designing multiple-choice items for both classroom-based and large-scale situations (adapted from Gronlund, 1998, pp. 60–75, and J. D. Brown, 1996, pp. 54–57).

1. Design each item to measure a specific objective.

Consider this item introduced, and then revised, in the sample test above:

Multiple-choice item, revised

> | *Voice:* | Where did George go after the party last night? |
> | *S reads:* | a. Yes, he did. |
> | | b. Because he was tired. |
> | | c. To Elaine's place for another party. |
> | | d. Around eleven o'clock. |

The specific objective being tested here is comprehension of *wh*-questions. Distractor (a) is designed to ascertain that the student knows the difference between an answer to a *wh*-question and a *yes/no* question. Distractors (b) and (d), as well as the key item (c), test comprehension of the meaning of *where* as opposed to *why* and *when*. The objective has been directly addressed.

On the other hand, here is an item that was designed to test recognition of the correct word order of indirect questions.

Multiple-choice item, flawed

Excuse me, do you know _____ ?
  a. where is the post office
  b. where the post office is
  c. where post office is

Distractor (a) is designed to lure students who don't know how to frame indirect questions and therefore serves as an efficient distractor. But what does distractor (c) actually measure? In fact, the missing definite article (*the*) is what J. D. Brown (1996, p. 55) calls an "unintentional clue"—a flaw that could cause the test-taker to eliminate (c) automatically. In the process, no assessment has been made of indirect questions in this distractor. Can you think of a better distractor for (c) that would focus more clearly on the objective?

2. State both stem and options as simply and directly as possible.

We are sometimes tempted to make multiple-choice items too wordy. A good rule of thumb is to get directly to the point. Here's an example.

Multiple-choice cloze item, flawed

My eyesight has really been deteriorating lately. I wonder if I need glasses. I think I'd better go to the _____ to have my eyes checked.
  a. pediatrician
  b. dermatologist
  c. optometrist

You might argue that the first two sentences of this item give it some authenticity and accomplish a bit of schema setting. But if you simply want a student to identify the type of medical professional who deals with eyesight issues, those sentences are superfluous. Moreover, by lengthening the stem, you have introduced a potentially confounding lexical item, *deteriorate,* that could distract the student unnecessarily.

Another rule of succinctness is to remove needless redundancy from your options. In the following item, *which were* is repeated in all three options. It should be placed in the stem to keep the item as succinct as possible.

Multiple-choice item, flawed

We went to visit the temples, _____ fascinating.

   a. which were beautiful

   b. which were especially

   c. which were holy

---

3. Make certain that the intended answer is clearly the only correct one.

In the proposed unit test described earlier, the following item appeared in the original draft:

Multiple-choice item, flawed

   Voice: Where did George go after the party last night?

  S reads: a. Yes, he did.

              b. Because he was tired.

              c. To Elaine's place for another party.

              d. He went home around eleven o'clock.

A quick consideration of the distractor (d) reveals that it is a plausible answer, along with the intended key, (c). Eliminating unintended possible answers is often the most difficult problem of designing multiple-choice items. With only a minimum of context in each stem, a wide variety of responses may be perceived as correct.

4. Use item indices to accept, discard, or revise items.

The appropriate selection and arrangement of suitable multiple-choice items on a test can best be accomplished by measuring items against three indices: item facility (or item difficulty), item discrimination (sometimes called item differentiation), and distractor analysis. Although measuring these factors on classroom tests would be useful, you probably will have neither the time nor the expertise to do this for every classroom test you create, especially one-time tests. But they are a must for standardized norm-referenced tests that are designed to be administered a number of times and/or administered in multiple forms.

*1. **Item facility** (or IF) is the extent to which an item is easy or difficult for the proposed group of test-takers. You may wonder why that is important if in your estimation the item achieves validity. The answer is that an item that is too easy (say 99 percent of respondents get it right) or too difficult (99 percent get it wrong) really does nothing to separate high-ability and low-ability test-takers. It is not really performing much "work" for you on a test.

IF simply reflects the percentage of students answering the item correctly. The formula looks like this:

$$IF = \frac{\text{\# of Ss answering the item correctly}}{\text{Total \# of Ss responding to that item}}$$

For example, if you have an item on which 13 out of 20 students respond correctly, your IF index is 13 divided by 20 or .65 (65 percent). There is no absolute IF value that must be met to determine if an item should be included in the test as is, modified, or thrown out, but appropriate test items will generally have IFs that range between .15 and .85. Two good reasons for occasionally including a very easy item (.85 or higher) are to build in some affective feelings of "success" among lower-ability students and to serve as warm-up items. And very difficult items can provide a challenge to the highest-ability students.

2. Item discrimination (ID) is the extent to which an item differentiates between high- and low-ability test-takers. An item on which high-ability students (who did well in the test) and low-ability students (who didn't) score equally well would have poor ID because it did not discriminate between the two groups. Conversely, an item that garners correct responses from most of the high-ability group and incorrect responses from most of the low-ability group has good discrimination power.

Suppose your class of 30 students has taken a test. Once you have calculated final scores for all 30 students, divide them roughly into thirds—that is, create three rank-ordered ability groups including the top 10 scores, the middle 10, and the lowest 10. To find out which of your 50 or so test items were most "powerful" in discriminating between high and low ability, eliminate the middle group, leaving two groups with results that might look something like this on a particular item:

Item #23	# Correct	# Incorrect
High-ability Ss (top 10)	7	3
Low-ability Ss (bottom 10)	2	8

Using the ID formula ($7-2 = 5 \div 10 = .50$), you would find that this item has an ID of .50, or a moderate level.

The formula for calculating ID is

$$ID = \frac{\text{high group \# correct } - \text{ low group \# correct}}{1/2 \times \text{total of your two comparison groups}} = \frac{7-2}{1/2 \times 20} = \frac{5}{10} = .50$$

The result of this example item tells you that the item has a moderate level of ID. High discriminating power would approach a perfect 1.0, and no discriminating power at all would be zero. In most cases, you would want to discard an item that scored near zero. As with IF, no absolute rule governs the establishment of acceptable and unacceptable ID indices.

One clear, practical use for ID indices is to select items from a test bank that includes more items than you need. You might decide to discard or improve some items with lower ID because you know they won't be as powerful an indicator of success on your test.

For most teachers who are using multiple-choice items to create a classroom-based unit test, juggling IF and ID indices is more a matter of intuition and "art" than a science. Your best calculated hunches may provide sufficient support for retaining, revising, and discarding proposed items. But if you are constructing a large-scale test, or one that will be administered multiple times, these indices are important factors in creating test forms that are comparable in difficulty. By engaging in a sophisticated procedure using what is called **item response theory** (IRT), professional test designers can produce test forms whose **equated** test scores are reliable measures of performance. (For more information on IRT, see Bachman, 1990, pp. 202–209.)

3. Distractor efficiency is one more important measure of a multiple-choice item's value in a test, and one that is related to item discrimination. The efficiency of distractors is the extent to which (a) the distractors "lure" a sufficient number of test-takers, especially lower-ability ones, and (b) those responses are somewhat evenly distributed across all distractors. Those of you who have a fear of mathematical formulas will be happy to read that there is no formula for calculating distractor efficiency and that an inspection of a distribution of responses will usually yield the information you need.

Consider the following. The same item (#23) used above is a multiple-choice item with five choices, and responses across upper- and lower-ability students are distributed as follows:

Choices	A	B	C*	D	E
High-ability Ss (10)	0	1	7	0	2
Low-ability Ss (10)	3	5	2	0	0

*Note: **C** is the correct response.

No mathematical formula is needed to tell you that this item successfully attracts seven of the ten high-ability students toward the correct response, while only two of the low-ability students get this one right. As shown above, its ID is .50, which is acceptable, but the item might be improved in two ways: (a) Distractor **D** doesn't fool anyone. No one picked it, and therefore it probably has no utility. A revision might provide a distractor that actually attracts a response or two. (b) Distractor **E** attracts more responses (2) from the high-ability group than the low-ability group (0). Why are good students choosing this one? Perhaps it includes a subtle reference that entices the high group but is "over the head" of the low group, and therefore the latter students don't even consider it.

The other two distractors (**A** and **B**) seem to be fulfilling their function of attracting some attention from lower-ability students.

SCORING, GRADING, AND GIVING FEEDBACK

Scoring

As you design a classroom test, you must consider how the test will be scored and graded. Your scoring plan reflects the relative weight that you place on each section and items in each section. The integrated-skills class that we have been using as an example focuses on listening and speaking skills with some attention to reading and writing. Three of your nine objectives target reading and writing skills. How do you assign scoring to the various components of this test?

Because oral production is a driving force in your overall objectives, you decide to place more weight on the speaking (oral interview) section than on the other three sections. Five minutes is actually a long time to spend in a one-on-one situation with a student, and some significant information can be extracted from such a session. You therefore designate 40 percent of the grade to the oral interview. You consider the listening and reading sections to be equally important, but each of them, especially in this multiple-choice format, is of less consequence than the oral interview. So you give each of them a 20 percent weight. That leaves 20 percent for the writing section, which seems about right to you given the time and focus on writing in this unit of the course.

Your next task is to assign scoring for each item. This may take a little numerical common sense, but it doesn't require a degree in math. To make matters simple, you decide to have a 100-point test in which

- the listening and reading items are each worth 2 points.
- the oral interview will yield four scores ranging from 5 to 1, reflecting fluency, prosodic features, accuracy of the target grammatical objectives, and discourse appropriateness. To weight these scores appropriately, you will double each individual score and then add them together for a possible total score of 40. (Chapters 4 and 7 will deal more extensively with scoring and assessing oral production performance.)
- the writing sample has two scores: one for grammar/mechanics (including the correct use of *so* and *because*) and one for overall effectiveness of the message, each ranging from 5 to 1. Again, to achieve the correct weight for writing, you will double each score and add them, so the possible total is 20 points. (Chapters 4 and 9 will deal in depth with scoring and assessing writing performance.)

Here are your decisions about scoring your test:

	Percent of Total Grade		Possible Total Correct
Oral Interview	40%	4 scores, 5 to 1 range × 2 =	40
Listening	20%	10 items @ 2 points each =	20
Reading	20%	10 items @ 2 points each =	20
Writing	20%	2 scores, 5 to 1 range × 2 =	20
Total			100

At this point you may wonder if the interview should carry less weight or the written essay more, but your intuition tells you that these weights are plausible representations of the relative emphases in this unit of the course.

After administering the test once, you may decide to shift some of these weights or to make other changes. You will then have valuable information about how easy or difficult the test was, about whether the time limit was reasonable, about your students' affective reaction to it, and about their general performance. Finally, you will have an intuitive judgment about whether this test correctly assessed your students. Take note of these impressions, however nonempirical they may be, and use them for revising the test in another term.

Grading

Your first thought might be that assigning grades to student performance on this test would be easy: just give an "A" for 90–100 percent, a "B" for 80–89 percent, and so on. Not so fast! Grading is such a thorny issue that all of Chapter 11 is devoted to the topic. How you assign letter grades to this test is a product of

- the country, culture, and context of this English classroom,
- institutional expectations (most of them unwritten),
- explicit and implicit definitions of grades that you have set forth,
- the relationship you have established with this class, and
- student expectations that have been engendered in previous tests and quizzes in this class.

For the time being, then, we will set aside issues that deal with grading this test in particular, in favor of the comprehensive treatment of grading in Chapter 11.

Giving Feedback

A section on scoring and grading would not be complete without some consideration of the forms in which you will offer feedback to your students, feedback that you want to become beneficial washback. In the example test that we have been referring to here—which is not unusual in the universe of possible formats for periodic classroom tests—consider the multitude of options. You might choose to return the test to the student with one of, or a combination of, any of the possibilities below:

1. a letter grade
2. a total score
3. four subscores (speaking, listening, reading, writing)
4. for the listening and reading sections
    a. an indication of correct/incorrect responses
    b. marginal comments
5. for the oral interview
    a. scores for each element being rated
    b. a checklist of areas needing work
    c. oral feedback after the interview
    d. a post-interview conference to go over the results
6. on the essay
    a. scores for each element being rated
    b. a checklist of areas needing work
    c. marginal and end-of-essay comments, suggestions
    d. a post-test conference to go over work
    e. a self-assessment
7. on all or selected parts of the test, peer checking of results
8. a whole-class discussion of results of the test
9. individual conferences with each student to review the whole test

Obviously, options 1 and 2 give virtually no feedback. They offer the student only a modest sense of where that student stands and a vague idea of overall performance, but the feedback they present does not become washback. Washback is achieved when students can, through the testing experience, identify their areas of success and challenge. When a test becomes a learning experience, it achieves washback.

Option 3 gives a student a chance to see the relative strength of each skill area and so becomes minimally useful. Options 4, 5, and 6 represent the kind of response a teacher can give (including stimulating a student self-assessment) that approaches maximum washback. Students are provided with individualized feedback that has good potential for "washing back" into their subsequent performance. Of course, time and the logistics of large classes may not permit 5d and 6d, which for many teachers may be going above and beyond expectations for a test like this. Likewise option 9 may be impractical. Options 6 and 7, however, are clearly viable possibilities that solve some of the practicality issues that are so important in teachers' busy schedules.

§   §   §   §   §

In this chapter, guidelines and tools were provided to enable you to address the five questions posed at the outset: (1) how to determine the purpose or criterion of the test, (2) how to state objectives, (3) how to design specifications, (4) how to select and arrange test tasks, including evaluating those tasks with item indices, and (5) how to ensure appropriate washback to the student. This five-part template can serve as a pattern as you design classroom tests.

In the next two chapters, you will see how many of these principles and guidelines apply to large-scale testing. You will also assess the pros and cons of what we've been calling standards-based assessment, including its social and political consequences. The chapters that follow will lead you through a wide selection of test tasks in the separate skills of listening, speaking, reading, and writing and provide a sense of how testing for form-focused objectives fits in to the picture. You will consider an array of possibilities of what has come to be called "alternative" assessment (Chapter 10), only because portfolios, conferences, journals, self- and peer-assessments are not always comfortably categorized among more traditional forms of assessment. And finally (Chapter 11) you will take a long, hard look at the dilemmas of grading students.

EXERCISES

[Note: (**I**) Individual work; (**G**) Group or pair work; (**C**) Whole-class discussion.]

1. (**I/C**) Consult the MLAT website address on page 44 and obtain as much information as you can about the MLAT. Aptitude tests propose to predict one's performance in a language course. Review the rationale supporting such testing, and then summarize the controversy surrounding aptitude tests. What can you say about the validity and the ethics of aptitude testing?

2. (**G**) In pairs, each assigned to one type of test (aptitude, proficiency, placement, diagnostic, or achievement), create a list of broad specifications for the test type you have been assigned: What are the test criteria? What kinds of items should be used? How would you sample among a number of possible objectives?

3. (**G**) Look again at the discussion of objectives (page 49). In a small group, discuss the following scenario: In the case that a teacher is faced with more objectives than are possible to sample in a test, draw up a set of guidelines for choosing which objectives to include on the test and which ones to exclude. You might start with considering the issue of the relative importance of all the objectives in the context of the course in question. How does one adequately sample objectives?

4. (**I/C**) Figure 3.1 depicts various modes of elicitation and response. Are there other modes of elicitation that could be included in such a chart? Justify your additions with an example of each.

5. (**G**) Select a language class in your immediate environment for the following project: In small groups, design an achievement test for a segment of the course (preferably a unit for which there is no current test or for which the present test is inadequate). Follow the guidelines in this chapter for

developing an assessment procedure. When it is completed, present your assessment project to the rest of the class.

6. **(G)** Find an existing, recently used standardized multiple-choice test for which there is accessible data on student performance. Calculate the item facility (IF) and item discrimination (ID) index for selected items. If there are no data for an existing test, select some items on the test and analyze the structure of those items in a distractor analysis to determine if they have (a) any bad distractors, (b) any bad stems, or (c) more than one potentially correct answer.

7. **(I/C)** On page 63, nine different options are listed for giving feedback to students on assessments. Review the practicality of each and determine the extent to which practicality (principally, more time expended) is justifiably sacrificed in order to offer better washback to learners.

FOR YOUR FURTHER READING

Carroll, John B. (1990). Cognitive abilities in foreign language aptitude: Then and now. In Thomas S. Parry & Charles W. Stansfield (Eds.), *Language aptitude reconsidered.* Englewood Cliffs, NJ: Prentice Hall Regents.

Carroll, the original developer of the MLAT, updates arguments for and against some of the original cognitive hypotheses underlying the MLAT. In the same volume, note articles by Oxford and by Ehrman contending that styles, strategies, and personality may be further factors in the construct of language aptitude.

Brown, James Dean. (1996). *Testing in language programs.* Upper Saddle River, NJ: Prentice Hall Regents.

Chapters 2 and 3 of this language testing manual offer some further information on developing tests and test items, including formulas for calculating item facility and item discrimination.

Gronlund, Norman E. (1998). *Assessment of student achievement.* Sixth Edition. Boston: Allyn and Bacon.

This widely used general manual of testing across educational subject matter provides useful information for language assessment. In particular, Chapters 3, 4, 5, and 6 describe detailed steps for designing tests and writing multiple-choice, true-false, and short-answer items.

CHAPTER 4

STANDARDIZED TESTING

Every educated person has at some point been touched—if not deeply affected—by a standardized test. For almost a century, schools, universities, businesses, and governments have looked to standardized measures for economical, reliable, and valid assessments of those who would enter, continue in, or exit their institutions. Proponents of these large-scale instruments make strong claims for their usefulness when great numbers of people must be measured quickly and effectively. Those claims are well supported by reams of research data that comprise construct validations of their efficacy. And so we have become a world that abides by the results of standardized tests as if they were sacrosanct.

The rush to carry out standardized testing in every walk of life has not gone unchecked. Some psychometricians have stood up in recent years to caution the public against reading too much into tests that require what may be a narrow band of specialized intelligence (Sternberg, 1997; Gardner, 2000; Kohn, 2000). Organizations such as the National Center for Fair and Open Testing (**www.fairtest.org**) have reminded us that standardization of assessment procedures creates an illusion of validity. Strong claims from the giants of the testing industry, they say, have pulled the collective wool over the public's eyes and in the process have incorrectly marginalized thousands, if not millions, of children and adults worldwide. These socioeconomic issues in standardized testing are discussed in Chapter 5.

Whichever side is "right"—and both sides have legitimate cases—it is important for teachers to understand the educational institutions they are working in, and an integral part of virtually all of those institutions is the use of standardized tests. So it is important for you to understand what standardized tests are, what they are not, how to interpret them, and how to put them into a balanced perspective in which we strive to accurately assess all learners on all proposed objectives. We can learn a great deal about many learners and their competencies through standardized forms of assessment. But some of those learners and some of those objectives may not be adequately measured by a sit-down, timed, multiple-choice format that is likely to be decontextualized.

This chapter has two goals: to introduce the process of constructing, validating, administering, and interpreting standardized tests of language; and to acquaint you with a variety of current standardized tests that claim to test overall language proficiency.

It should be clear from these goals that in this chapter we are not focusing centrally on classroom-based assessment. Don't forget, however, that standardized tests affect all classrooms, and some of the practical steps that are involved in creating standardized tests are directly transferable to designing classroom tests.

WHAT IS STANDARDIZATION?

A **standardized** test presupposes certain standard objectives, or criteria, that are held constant across one form of the test to another. The criteria in large-scale standardized tests are designed to apply to a broad band of competencies that are usually not exclusive to one particular curriculum. A good standardized test is the product of a thorough process of empirical research and development. It dictates standard procedures for administration and scoring. And finally, it is typical of a norm-referenced test, the goal of which is to place test-takers on a continuum across a range of scores and to differentiate test-takers by their relative ranking.

Most elementary and secondary schools in the United States have standardized achievement tests to measure children's mastery of the standards or competencies that have been prescribed for specified grade levels. These tests vary by states, counties, and school districts, but they all share the common objective of economical large-scale assessment. College entrance exams such as the Scholastic Aptitude Test (SAT®) are part of the educational experience of many high school seniors seeking further education. The Graduate Record Exam (GRE®) is a required standardized test for entry into many graduate school programs. Tests like the Graduate Management Admission Test (GMAT) and the Law School Aptitude Test (LSAT) specialize in particular disciplines. One genre of standardized test that you may already be familiar with is the Test of English as a Foreign Language (TOEFL®), produced by the Educational Testing Service (ETS) in the United States and/or its British counterpart, the International English Language Testing System (IELTS), which features standardized tests in affiliation with the University of Cambridge Local Examinations Syndicate (UCLES). They are all standardized because they specify a set of competencies (or standards) for a given domain, and through a process of construct validation they program a set of tasks that have been designed to measure those competencies.

Many people are under the incorrect impression that all standardized tests consist of items that have predetermined responses presented in a multiple-choice format. While it is true that many standardized tests conform to a multiple-choice format, by no means is multiple-choice a prerequisite characteristic. It so happens that a multiple-choice format provides the test producer with an "objective" means for determining correct and incorrect responses, and therefore is the preferred mode for large-scale tests. However, standards are equally involved in certain human-scored tests of oral production and writing, such as the Test of Spoken English (TSE®) and the Test of Written English (TWE®), both produced by ETS.

ADVANTAGES AND DISADVANTAGES OF STANDARDIZED TESTS

Advantages of standardized testing include, foremost, a ready-made previously validated product that frees the teacher from having to spend hours creating a test. Administration to large groups can be accomplished within reasonable time limits. In the case of multiple-choice formats, scoring procedures are streamlined (for either scannable computerized scoring or hand-scoring with a hole-punched grid) for fast turnaround time. And, for better or for worse, there is often an air of face validity to such authoritative-looking instruments.

Disadvantages center largely on the inappropriate use of such tests, for example, using an overall proficiency test as an achievement test simply because of the convenience of the standardization. A colleague told me about a course director who, after a frantic search for a last-minute placement test, administered a multiple-choice grammar achievement test, even though the curriculum was mostly listening and speaking and involved few of the grammar points tested. This instrument had the appearance and face validity of a good test when in reality it had no content validity whatsoever.

Another disadvantage is the potential misunderstanding of the difference between direct and indirect testing (see Chapter 2). Some standardized tests include tasks that do not directly specify performance in the target objective. For example, before 1996, the TOEFL included neither a written nor an oral production section, yet statistics showed a reasonably strong correspondence between performance on the TOEFL and a student's written and—to a lesser extent—oral production. The comprehension-based TOEFL could therefore be claimed to be an indirect test of production. A test of reading comprehension that proposes to measure ability to read extensively and that engages test-takers in reading only short one- or two-paragraph passages is an indirect measure of extensive reading.

Those who use standardized tests need to acknowledge both the advantages and limitations of indirect testing. In the pre-1996 TOEFL administrations, the expense of giving a direct test of production was considerably reduced by offering only comprehension performance and showing through construct validation the appropriateness of conclusions about a test-taker's production competence. Likewise, short reading passages are easier to administer, and if research validates the assumption that short reading passages indicate extensive reading ability, then the use of the shorter passages is justified. Yet the construct validation statistics that offer that support never offer a 100 percent probability of the relationship, leaving room for some possibility that the indirect test is not valid for its targeted use.

A more serious issue lies in the assumption (alluded to above) that standardized tests correctly assess all learners equally well. Well-established standardized tests usually demonstrate high correlations between performance on such tests and target objectives, but correlations are not sufficient to demonstrate unequivocally the acquisition of criterion objectives by *all* test-takers. Here is a non-language example. In the United States, some driver's license renewals require taking a paper-and-pencil multiple-choice test that covers signs, safe speeds and distances, lane changes, and other "rules of the road." Correlational statistics show a strong relationship between high scores on those tests and good driving records, so people who do well on these tests are a safe bet to relicense. Now, an extremely high correlation (of perhaps .80 or above) may be loosely interpreted to mean that a large majority of the drivers whose licenses are renewed by virtue of their having passed the little quiz are good behind-the-wheel drivers. What about those few who do not fit the model? That small minority of drivers could endanger the lives of the majority, and is that a risk worth taking? Motor vehicle registration departments in the United States seem to think so, and thus avoid the high cost of behind-the-wheel driving tests.

Are you willing to rely on a standardized test result in the case of *all* the learners in your class? Of an applicant to your institution, or of a potential degree candidate exiting your program? These questions will be addressed more fully in Chapter 5, but for the moment, think carefully about what has come to be known as **high-stakes** testing, in which standardized tests have become the *only* criterion for inclusion or exclusion. The widespread acceptance, and sometime misuse, of this **gate-keeping** role of the testing industry has created a political, educational, and moral maelstrom.

DEVELOPING A STANDARDIZED TEST

While it is not likely that a classroom teacher, with a team of test designers and researchers, would be in a position to develop a brand-new standardized test of large-scale proportions, it is a virtual certainty that some day you will be in a position (a) to revise an existing test, (b) to adapt or expand an existing test, and/or (c) to create a smaller-scale standardized test for a program you are teaching in. And even if none of the above three cases should ever apply to you, it is of paramount importance to understand the process of the development of the standardized tests that have become ingrained in our educational institutions.

How are standardized tests developed? Where do test tasks and items come from? How are they evaluated? Who selects items and their arrangement in a test? How do such items and tests achieve consequential validity? How are different forms of tests equated for difficulty level? Who sets norms and cut-off limits? Are security and confidentiality an issue? Are cultural and racial biases an issue in test development? All these questions typify those that you might pose in an attempt to understand the process of test development.

In the steps outlined below, three different standardized tests will be used to exemplify the process of standardized test design:

> (A) The Test of English as a Foreign Language (TOEFL), Educational Testing Service (ETS).
> (B) The English as a Second Language Placement Test (ESLPT), San Francisco State University (SFSU).
> (C) The Graduate Essay Test (GET), SFSU.

The first is a test of general language ability or proficiency. The second is a placement test at a university. And the third is a gate-keeping essay test that all prospective students must pass in order to take graduate-level courses. As we look at the steps, one by one, you will see patterns that are consistent with those outlined in the previous two chapters for evaluating and developing a classroom test.

1. Determine the purpose and objectives of the test.

Most standardized tests are expected to provide high practicality in administration and scoring without unduly compromising validity. The initial outlay of time and money for such a test is significant, but the test would be used repeatedly. It is therefore important for its purpose and objectives to be stated specifically. Let's look at the three tests.

(A) The purpose of the TOEFL is "to evaluate the English proficiency of people whose native language is not English" (*TOEFL Test and Score Manual*, 2001, p. 9). More specifically, the TOEFL is designed to help institutions of higher learning make "valid decisions concerning English language proficiency in terms of [their] own requirements" (p. 9). Most colleges and universities in the United States use TOEFL scores to admit or refuse international applicants for admission. Various cut-off scores apply, but most institutions require scores from 475 to 525 (paper-based) or from 150 to 195 (computer-based) in order to consider students for admission. The high-stakes, gate-keeping nature of the TOEFL is obvious.

(B) The ESLPT, referred to in Chapter 3, is designed to place already admitted students at San Francisco State University in an appropriate course in academic writing, with the secondary goal of placing students into courses in oral production and grammar-editing. While the test's primary purpose is to make placements, another desirable objective is to provide teachers with some diagnostic information about their students on the first day or two of class. The ESLPT is locally designed by university faculty and staff.

(C) The GET, another test designed at SFSU, is given to prospective graduate students—both native and non-native speakers—in all disciplines to determine whether their writing ability is sufficient to permit them to enter graduate-level courses in their programs. It is offered at the beginning of each term. Students who fail or marginally pass the GET are technically ineligible to take graduate courses in their field. Instead, they may elect to take a course in graduate-level writing of research papers. A pass in that course is equivalent to passing the GET.

As you can see, the objectives of each of these tests are specific. The content of each test must be designed to accomplish those particular ends. This first stage of goal-setting might be seen as one in which the consequential validity of the test is foremost in the mind of the developer: each test has a specific gate-keeping function to perform; therefore the criteria for entering those gates must be specified accurately.

2. Design test specifications.

Now comes the hard part. Decisions need to be made on how to go about structuring the specifications of the test. Before specs can be addressed, a comprehensive program of research must identify a set of constructs underlying the test itself. This stage of laying the foundation stones can occupy weeks, months, or even years of effort. Standardized tests that don't work are often the product of short-sighted construct validation. Let's look at the three tests again.

(A) Construct validation for the TOEFL is carried out by the TOEFL staff at ETS under the guidance of a Policy Council that works with a Committee of Examiners that is composed of appointed external university faculty, linguists, and assessment specialists. Dozens of employees are involved in a complex process of reviewing current TOEFL specifications, commissioning and developing test tasks and items, assembling forms of the test, and performing ongoing exploratory research related to formulating new specs. Reducing such a complex process to a set of simple steps runs the risk of gross overgeneralization, but here is an idea of how a TOEFL is created.

Because the TOEFL is a proficiency test, the first step in the developmental process is to define the construct of **language proficiency**. First, it should be made clear that many assessment specialists such as Bachman (1990) and Palmer (Bachman & Palmer, 1996) prefer the term *ability* to *proficiency* and thus speak of **language ability** as the overarching concept. The latter phrase is more consistent, they argue, with our understanding that the specific *components* of language ability must be assessed separately. Others, such as the American Council on Teaching Foreign Languages (ACTFL), still prefer the term *proficiency* because it connotes more of a holistic, unitary trait view of language ability (Lowe, 1988). Most current views accept the *ability* argument and therefore strive to specify and assess the many components of language. For the purposes of consistency in this book, the term *proficiency* will nevertheless be retained, with the above caveat.

How you view language will make a difference in how you assess language proficiency. After breaking language competence down into subsets of listening, speaking, reading, and writing, each performance mode can be examined on a continuum of linguistic units: phonology (pronunciation) and orthography (spelling), words (lexicon), sentences (grammar), discourse, and pragmatic (sociolinguistic, contextual, functional, cultural) features of language.

How will the TOEFL sample from all these possibilities? Oral production tests can be tests of overall conversational fluency or pronunciation of a particular subset of phonology, and can take the form of imitation, structured responses, or free responses. Listening comprehension tests can concentrate on a particular feature of language or on overall listening for general meaning. Tests of reading can cover the range of language units and can aim to test comprehension of long or short passages, single sentences, or even phrases and words. Writing tests can take on an open-ended form with free composition, or be structured to elicit anything from correct spelling to discourse-level competence. Are you overwhelmed yet?

From the sea of potential performance modes that could be sampled in a test, the developer must select a subset on some systematic basis. To make a very long story short (and leaving out numerous controversies), the TOEFL had for many years included three types of performance in its organizational specifications: listening, structure, and reading, all of which tested comprehension through standard multiple-choice tasks. In 1996 a major step was taken to include written production in the computer-based TOEFL by adding a slightly modified version of the already existing Test of Written English (TWE). In doing so, some face validity and content validity were improved along with, of course, a significant increase in administrative expense! Each of these four major sections is capsulized in the box below (adapted from the description of the current computer-based TOEFL at **www.toefl.org**). Such descriptions are not, strictly speaking, specifications, which are kept confidential by ETS. Nevertheless, they can give a sense of many of the constraints that are placed on the design of actual TOEFL specifications.

TOEFL® specifications

Listening Section. The listening section measures the examinee's ability to understand English as it is spoken in North America. Conversational features of the language are stressed, and the skills tested include vocabulary and idiomatic expression as well as special grammatical constructions that are frequently used in spoken English. The stimulus material and questions are recorded in standard North American English.

The listening section includes various stimuli, such as dialogues, short conversations, academic discussions, and mini-lectures, and poses questions that test comprehension of main ideas, the order of a process, supporting ideas, important details, and inferences, as well as the ability to categorize topics/objects.

The test developers have taken advantage of the multimedia capability of the computer by using photos and graphics to create context and support the content of the lectures, producing stimuli that more closely approximate "real-world" situations in which people do more than just listen to voices. The listening stimuli are often accompanied by either context-setting or content-based visuals. All dialogues, conversations, academic discussions, and mini-lectures include context visuals to establish the setting and role of the speakers. Content-based visuals are often used to complement the topics of the mini-lectures.

Structure Section. The structure section measures an examinee's ability to recognize language that is appropriate for standard written English. The language tested is formal rather than conversational. The topics of the sentences are associated with general academic discourse so that individuals in specific fields of study or from specific national or linguistic groups have no particular advantage.

Two types of questions are used: questions in which examinees must (1) complete an incomplete sentence using one of four answers provided and (2) identify one of four underlined words or phrases that would not be accepted in English. The two question types are mixed randomly rather than being separated into two subsections as in the paper-based TOEFL test.

Reading Section. The reading section measures the ability to read and understand short passages similar in topic and style to academic texts used in North American colleges and universities. Examinees read a variety of short passages on academic subjects and answer several questions about each passage. Test items refer to what is stated or implied in the passage, as well as to words used in the passage. To avoid creating an advantage for individuals in any one field of study, sufficient context is provided so that no specific familiarity with the subject matter is required to answer the questions.

The reading section consists of four to five passages of 250–350 words, with 10–14 questions per passage. This section is not computer-adaptive, so examinees can skip questions and return to previous questions. The questions in this section assess the comprehension of main ideas, inferences, factual information stated in a passage, pronoun referents, and vocabulary (direct meaning, synonym, antonym). In all cases, the questions can be answered by reading and understanding the passages. This section consists of (1) traditional multiple-choice questions, (2) questions that require examinees to click on a word, phrase, sentence, or paragraph to answer, and (3) questions that ask examinees to "insert a sentence" where it fits best.

Writing Section. The writing section measures the ability to write in English, including the ability to generate, organize, and develop ideas, to support those ideas with examples or evidence, and to compose a response to one assigned topic in standard written English. Because some examinees may not be accustomed to composing an essay on computer, they are given the choice of handwriting or typing the essay in the 30-minute time limit. The rating scale for scoring the essay, ranging from 0 to 6, is virtually the same as that of the Test of Written English [see Chapter 9 of this book]. A score of 0 is given to papers that are blank, simply copy the topic, are written in a language other than English, consist only of random keystroke characters, or are written on a topic different from the one assigned.

Each essay is rated independently by two trained, certified readers. Neither reader knows the rating assigned by the other. An essay will receive the average of the two ratings unless there is a discrepancy of more than one point: in that case, a third reader will independently rate the essay. The essay rating is incorporated into the Structure/Writing scaled score, and constitutes approximately 50 percent of that combined score.

(B) The designing of the test specs for the ESLPT was a somewhat simpler task because the purpose is placement and the construct validation of the test consisted of an examination of the content of the ESL courses. In fact, in a recent revision of the ESLPT (Imao et al., 2000; Imao, 2001), content validity (coupled with its attendant face validity) was the central theoretical issue to be considered. The major issue centered on designing practical and reliable tasks and item response formats. Having established the importance of designing ESLPT tasks that simulated classroom tasks used in the courses, the designers ultimately specified two writing production tasks (one a response to an essay that students read, and the other a summary of another essay) and one multiple-choice grammar-editing task. These specifications mirrored the reading-based, process writing approach used in the courses.

(C) Specifications for the GET arose out of the perceived need to provide a threshold of acceptable writing ability for all prospective graduate students at SFSU, both native and non-native speakers of English. The specifications for the GET are the skills of writing grammatically and rhetorically acceptable prose on a topic of some interest, with clearly produced organization of ideas and logical development. The GET is a direct test of writing ability in which test-takers must, in a two-hour time period, write an essay on a given topic.

3. Design, select, and arrange test tasks/items.

Once specifications for a standardized test have been stipulated, the sometimes never-ending task of designing, selecting, and arranging items begins. The specs act much like a blueprint in determining the number and types of items to be created. Let's look at the three examples.

(A) TOEFL test design specifies that each item be coded for content and statistical characteristics. Content coding ensures that each examinee will receive test questions that assess a variety of skills (reading, comprehending the main idea, or understanding inferences) and cover a variety of subject matter without unduly biasing the content toward a subset of test-takers (for example, in the listening section involving an academic lecture, the content must be universal enough for students from many different academic fields of study). Statistical characteristics, including the IRT equivalents of estimates of item facility (IF) and the ability of an item to discriminate (ID) between higher or lower ability levels, are also coded.

Items are then designed by a team who select and adapt items solicited from a bank of items that have been "deposited" by free-lance writers and ETS staff. Probes for the reading section, for example, are usually excerpts from authentic general or academic reading that are edited for linguistic difficulty, culture bias, or other topic biases. Items are designed to test overall comprehension, certain specific information, and inference.

Consider the following sample of a reading selection and ten items based on it, from a practice TOEFL (Phillips, 2001, pp.423–424):

For hundreds of years in the early history of America, pirates sailed through coastal waters, pillaging and plundering all in their path. They stole from other ships and stole from coastal towns; not content only to steal, they destroyed everything they could not carry away. Some of the pirate ships amassed large treasures, the fates of which are unknown, leaving people of today to wonder at their whereabouts and to dream of one day coming across some lost treasure.

One notoriously large treasure was on the pirate ship *Whidah,* which sank in the waters off Cape Cod during a strong storm in 1717. A hundred of the crew members went down with the ship, along with its treasure of coins, gold, silver, and jewels. The treasure on board had an estimated value, on today's market, of more than 100 million dollars.

The remains of the *Whidah* were discovered in 1984 by Barry Clifford, who had spent years of painstaking research and tireless searching, only finally to locate the ship about 500 yards from shore. A considerable amount of treasure from the centuries-old ship has been recovered from its watery grave, but there is clearly still a lot more out there. Just as a reminder of what the waters off the coast have been protecting for hundreds of years, occasional pieces of gold, or silver, or jewels still wash up on the beaches, and lucky beach-goers find pieces of the treasure.

11. The passage mainly discusses
    (A) early pirates
    (B) a large pirate treasure

(C) what really happened to the *Whidah's* pirates
(D) why people go to the beach

12. It is NOT mentioned in the passage that pirates did which of the following?
(A) They killed lots of people.
(B) They robbed other ships.
(C) They took things from towns.
(D) They gathered big treasures.

13. The word "amassed" in line 4 is closest in meaning to
(A) sold   (C) transported
(B) hid   (D) gathered

14. It is implied in the passage that the *Whidah's* crew
(A) died
(B) went diving
(C) searched for the treasure
(D) escaped with parts of the treasure

15. Which of the following is NOT mentioned as part of the treasure of the *Whidah?*
(A) Art objects
(B) Coins
(C) Gold and silver
(D) Jewels

16. The word "estimated" in line 10 is closest in meaning to which of the following?
(A) Known   (C) Approximate
(B) Sold   (D) Decided

17. The passage indicates that the cargo of the *Whidah* is worth about
(A) $100,000
(B) $1,000,000
(C) $10,000,000
(D) $100,000,000

18. The work that Barry Clifford did to locate the *Whidah* was NOT
(A) successful
(B) effortless
(C) detailed
(D) lengthy

19. It is mentioned in the passage that the treasure of the *Whidah*
(A) is not very valuable
(B) is all in museums
(C) has not all been found
(D) was taken to share by the pirates

20. The paragraph following the passage most likely discusses
(A) what Barry Clifford is doing today
(B) the fate of the *Whidah's* crew
(C) other storms in the area of Cape Cod
(D) additional pieces that turn up from the *Whidah's* treasure

As you can see, items target the assessment of comprehension of the main idea (item #11), stated details (#17, 19), unstated details (#12, 15, 18), implied details (#14, 20), and vocabulary in context (#13, 16). An argument could be made about the cultural schemata implied in a passage about pirate ships, and you could engage in an "angels on the head of a pin" argument about the importance of picking certain vocabulary for emphasis, but every test item is a sample of a larger domain, and each of these fulfills its designated specification.

Before any such items are released into a form of the TOEFL (or any validated standardized test), they are piloted and scientifically selected to meet difficulty specifications within each subsection, section, and the test overall. Furthermore, those items are also selected to meet a desired discrimination index. Both of these indices are important considerations in the design of a computer-adaptive test, where performance on one item determines the next one to be presented to the test-taker. (See Chapter 3 for a complete treatment of multiple-choice item design.)

(B) The selection of items in the ESLPT entailed two entirely different processes. In the two subsections of the test that elicit writing performance (summary of reading; response to reading), the main hurdles were (a) selecting appropriate passages for test-takers to read, (b) providing appropriate prompts, and (c) processing data from pilot testing. Passages have to conform to standards of content validity by being within the genre and the difficulty of the material used in the courses. The prompt in each case (the section asking for a summary and the section asking for a response) has to be tailored to fit the passage, but a general template is used.

In the multiple-choice editing test that seeks to test grammar proofreading ability, the first and easier task is to choose an appropriate essay within which to embed errors. The more complicated task is to embed a specified number of errors from a previously determined taxonomy of error categories. Those error categories came directly from student errors as perceived by their teachers (verb tenses, verb agreement, logical connectors, articles, etc.). The distractors for each item were selected from actual errors that students make. Items in pilot versions were then coded for difficulty and discrimination indices, after which final assembly of items could occur.

(C) The GET prompts are designed by a faculty committee of examiners who are specialists in the field of university academic writing. The assumption is made that the topics are universally appealing and capable of yielding the intended product of an essay that requires an organized logical argument and conclusion. No pilot testing of prompts is conducted. The conditions for administration remain constant: two-hour time limit, sit-down context, paper and pencil, closed-book format. Consider the following recent prompt:

Graduate Essay Test, sample prompt

In the Middletown Elementary School District, the assistant superintendent has just been made superintendent in another district. Her resignation leaves vacant the district's only administrative position ever held by a woman. The School Board, in response to strong arguments from the Teachers' Association, has urged that a woman be hired to replace her. As a member of the hiring committee, you must help choose her successor.

Only one woman applicant meets the written qualifications for the job; the two top male applicants are both more experienced than she.

The hiring committee has asked each committee member to prepare a written statement to distribute before meeting together to discuss the issue. Write a report that represents your position, making it as logical and persuasive as possible.

Some facts you may wish to draw on:

1. Women make up more than 75 percent of classroom teachers, but hold fewer than 10 percent of administrative positions in education. Administrators' salaries average 30 percent more than teachers' salaries.

2. The local Teachers' Association is 89 percent women, mostly under 40. In a heated debate on television, a member of the National Organization of Women (NOW) and the chair of the Teachers' Association threatened, if a man is hired, to bring a class-action suit against the district on behalf of all women teachers who cannot expect advancement because of discriminatory hiring practices.

3. The local Lions Club, which contributes heavily to school sports, says hiring the less experienced woman would not be in the best interests of the school, the children, or the teachers.

The finalists for the position:

1. Carole Gates. Classroom teacher, 10 years; "Teacher of the Year," 1985; supervisor of practice teachers at Teacher's College; former president of Teachers' Association; Administrative Credential, 1984; Ed.D. degree, 1986; assistant principal of Hoptown Elementary School, 2 years.

2. "Spud" Stonewall. Principal of Middletown Elementary, 15 years; Ph.D. in educational administration; State Board of Education Committee for Improving Elementary School Curriculum, 1982–present.

3. Jim Henderson. School Administrator, 22 years, grades K–9; supports innovation in education; "Fair Bargaining" Award, 1981; former coach for winning collegiate basketball team, 10 years.

It is clear from such a prompt that the problem the test-takers must address is complex, that there is sufficient information here for writing an essay, and that test-takers will be reasonably challenged to write a clear statement of opinion. What also emerges from this prompt (and virtually any prompt that one might propose) is the potential cultural effect on the numerous international students who must take the GET. Is it possible that such students, who are not familiar with school systems in the United States, with hiring procedures, and perhaps with the "politics" of school board elections, might be at a disadvantage in mounting their arguments within a two-hour time frame? Some (such as Hosoya, 2001) have strongly claimed such a bias.

4. Make appropriate evaluations of different kinds of items.

In Chapter 3 the concepts of item facility (IF), item discrimination (ID), and distractor analysis were introduced. As the discussion there showed, such calculations provide useful information for classroom tests, but sometimes the time and effort involved in performing them may not be practical, especially if the classroom-based test is a one-time test. Yet for a standardized multiple-choice test that is designed to be marketed commercially, and/or administered a number of times, and/or administered in a different form, these indices are a must.

For other types of response formats, namely, production responses, different forms of evaluation become important. The principles of practicality and reliability are prominent, along with the concept of facility. Practicality issues in such items include the clarity of directions, timing of the test, ease of administration, and how much time is required to score responses. Reliability is a major player in instances where more than one scorer is employed, and to a lesser extent when a single scorer has to evaluate tests over long spans of time that could lead to deterioration of standards. Facility is also a key to the validity and success of an item type: unclear directions, complex language, obscure topics, fuzzy data, and culturally biased information may all lead to a higher level of difficulty than one desires.

(A) The IF, ID, and efficiency statistics of the multiple-choice items of current forms of the TOEFL are not publicly available information. For reasons of security and protection of patented, copyrighted materials, they must remain behind the closed doors of the ETS development staff. Those statistics remain of paramount importance in the ongoing production of TOEFL items and forms and are the foundation stones for demonstrating the equatability of forms. Statistical indices on retired forms of the TOEFL are available on request for research purposes.

The essay portion of the TOEFL undergoes scrutiny for its practicality, reliability, and facility. Special attention is given to reliability since two human scorers must read each essay, and every time a third reader becomes necessary (when the two readers disagree by more than one point), it costs ETS more money.

(B) In the case of the open-ended responses on the two written tasks on the ESLPT, a similar set of judgments must be made. Some evaluative impressions of the effectiveness of prompts and passages are gained from informal student and scorer feedback. In the developmental stage of the newly revised ESLPT, both types of feedback were formally solicited through questionnaires and interviews. That information proved to be invaluable in the revision of prompts and stimulus reading passages. After each administration now, the teacher-scorers provide informal feedback on their perceptions of the effectiveness of the prompts and readings.

The multiple-choice editing passage showed the value of statistical findings in determining the usefulness of items and pointing administrators toward revisions. Following is a sample of the format used:

Multiple-choice editing passage

---

(1) <u>Ever</u> since supermarkets first <u>appeared</u>, they have been <u>take</u> over <u>the</u> world.
    A   B   C   D

(2) <u>Supermarkets</u> have changed people's life <u>styles</u>, yet <u>and</u> at the same time, changes in
       A   B   C

people's life <u>styles</u> have encouraged the opening of supermarkets.
             D

The task was to locate the error in each sentence. Statistical tests on the experimental version of this section revealed that a number of the 45 items were found to be of zero IF (no difficulty whatsoever) and of inconsequential discrimination power (some IDs of .15 and lower). Many distractors were of no consequence because they lured no one. Such information led to a revision of numerous items and their options, eventually strengthening the effectiveness of this section.

(C) The GET, like its written counterparts in the ESLPT, is a test of written ability with a single prompt, and therefore questions of practicality and facility are also largely observational. No data are collected from students on their perceptions, but the scorers have an opportunity to reflect on the validity of a given topic. After one sitting, a topic is retired, which eliminates the possibility of improving a specific topic, but future framing of topics might benefit from scorers' evaluations. Inter-rater reliability is checked periodically, and reader training sessions are modified if too many instances of unreliability appear.

5. Specify scoring procedures and reporting formats.

A systematic assembly of test items in pre-selected arrangements and sequences, all of which are validated to conform to an expected difficulty level, should yield a test that can then be scored accurately and reported back to test-takers and institutions efficiently.

(A) Of the three tests being exemplified here, the most straightforward scoring procedure comes from the TOEFL, the one with the most complex issues of validation, design, and assembly. Scores are calculated and reported for (a) three sections of the TOEFL (the essay ratings are combined with the Structure and Written Expression score) and (b) a total score (range 40 to 300 on the computer-based TOEFL and 310 to 677 on the paper-and-pencil TOEFL). A separate score (c) for the Essay (range 0 to 6) is also provided on the examinee's score record (see simulation of a score record on page 80).

Facsimile of a TOEFL® score report

TOEFL Scaled Scores: Claudia Y. Estudiante, Peru _____			
19	17	17	177
Listening	Structure / Writing	Reading	Total Score
Essay rating: 3.0			

The rating scale for the essay is virtually the same one that is used for the Test of Written English (see Chapter 9 for details), with a "zero" level added for no response, copying the topic only, writing completely off topic, or not writing in English.

(B) The ESLPT reports a score for each of the essay sections, but the rating scale differs between them because in one case the objective is to write a summary, and in the other to write a response to a reading. Each essay is read by two readers; if there is a discrepancy of more than one level, a third reader resolves the difference. The editing section is machine-scanned and -scored with a total score and with part-scores for each of the grammatical/rhetorical sections. From these data, placement administrators have adequate information to make placements, and teachers receive some diagnostic information on each student in their classes. Students do not receive their essays back.

(C) Each GET is read by two trained readers, who give a score between 1 and 4 according to the following scale:

Graduate Essay Test: Scoring Guide

Please make no marks on the writer's work. Write your reader number and score on the front cover of each test booklet.

4 **Superior.** The opening establishes context, purpose and point of view; the body of the essay develops recommendations logically and coherently. The writer demonstrates awareness of the complexities in the situation and provides analysis of the problem, offers compelling or common-sense reasons for recommendations made, makes underlying assumptions explicit.

The writer uses fluent and idiomatic English with few mechanical errors. Style reveals syntactic maturity, is clear and direct, is not choppy or over-colloquial nor over-formal, stuffy or unfocused. Occasional spelling or punctuation errors may be easily attributed to hasty transcription under pressure.

3 **Competent.** After an opening that establishes context and purpose, the paper unfolds with few lapses in coherence, but may have somewhat less clear organization of less explicit transitions than a top-score paper. It may have somewhat less compelling logic or slightly less-well-reasoned suggestions than a 4 paper, though it will provide reasons for the recommendations made.

The writer uses clear, fluent and generally idiomatic English, but may make minor or infrequent ESL errors (preposition errors, dropped articles or verb endings, etc.), or repeat a single error (e.g., not punctuate possessive nouns). Occasional lapses of style are offset by demonstrated mastery of syntax.

2   Weak. The writer makes somewhat simplistic suggestions not fully supported with reasons, fails to cite key facts, offers little analysis of the problem or shows a limited grasp of the situation; the given information is copied or listed, with little integration into argument. Points may be random or repetitious. Writing may be badly focused, with careless use of abstract language resulting in predication errors or illogical sentences.

ESL and/or careless mechanical errors are frequent enough to be distracting OR sentences may be choppy, style over-casual, usage occasionally unidiomatic.

1   Inadequate. The essay may be disjointed, incoherent, or minimally developed. The writer shows little grasp of the complex issues involved, is unable to establish context, point of view or purpose in opening of paper, or has a poor sense of audience. Mechanical and/or ESL errors or unidiomatic usages are frequent; sentences may be ungrammatical OR correct but short and very simple.

The two readers' scores are added to yield a total possible score of 2 to 8. Test administrators recommend a score of 6 as the threshold for allowing a student to pursue graduate-level courses. Anything below that is accompanied by a recommendation that the student either repeat the test or take a "remedial" course in graduate writing offered in one of several different departments. Students receive neither their essays nor any feedback other than the final score.

6. Perform ongoing construct validation studies.

From the above discussion, it should be clear that no standardized instrument is expected to be used repeatedly without a rigorous program of ongoing construct validation. Any standardized test, once developed, must be accompanied by systematic periodic corroboration of its effectiveness and by steps toward its improvement. This rigor is especially true of tests that are produced in **equated** forms; that is, forms must be reliable across tests such that a score on a subsequent form of a test has the same validity and interpretability as its original.

(A) The TOEFL program, in cooperation with other tests produced by ETS, has an impressive program of research. Over the years dozens of TOEFL-sponsored research studies have appeared in the *TOEFL Monograph Series.* An early example of such a study was the seminal Duran et al. (1985) study, *TOEFL from a Communicative Viewpoint on Language Proficiency,* which examined the content characteristics of the TOEFL from a communicative perspective based on current research in applied linguistics and language proficiency assessment. More recent studies (such as Ginther, 2001; Leacock & Chodorow, 2001; Powers et al., 2002) demonstrate an impressive array of scrutiny.

(B) For approximately 20 years, the ESLPT appeared to be placing students reliably by means of an essay and a multiple-choice grammar and vocabulary test. Over the years the security of the latter became suspect, and the faculty administrators wished to see some content validity achieved in the process. In the year 2000 that process began with a group of graduate students (Imao et al., 2000) in consultation with faculty members, and continued to fruition in the form of a new ESLPT, reported in Imao (2002). The development of the new ESLPT involved a lengthy process of both content and construct validation, along with facing such practical issues as scoring the written sections and a machine-scorable multiple-choice answer sheet.

The process of ongoing validation will no doubt continue as new forms of the editing section are created and as new prompts and reading passages are created for the writing section. Such a validation process should also include consistent checks on placement accuracy and on face validity.

(C) At this time there is little or no research to validate the GET itself. For its construct validation, its administrators rely on a stockpile of research on university-level academic writing tests such as the TWE. The holistic scoring rubric and the topics and administrative conditions of the GET are to some extent patterned after that of the TWE. In recent years some criticism of the GET has come from international test-takers (Hosoya, 2001) who posit that the topics and time limits of the GET, among other factors, work to the disadvantage of writers whose native language is not English. These validity issues remain to be fully addressed in a comprehensive research study.

STANDARDIZED LANGUAGE PROFICIENCY TESTING

Tests of language proficiency presuppose a comprehensive definition of the specific competencies that comprise overall language ability. The specifications for the TOEFL provided an illustration of an operational definition of ability for assessment purposes. This is not the only way to conceptualize the concept. Swain (1990) offered a multidimensional view of proficiency assessment by referring to three linguistic traits (grammar, discourse, and sociolinguistics) that can be assessed by means of oral, multiple-choice, and written responses (see Table 4.1). Swain's conception was not meant to be an exhaustive analysis of ability, but rather to serve as an operational framework for constructing proficiency assessments.

Another definition and conceptualization of proficiency is suggested by the ACTFL association, mentioned earlier. ACTFL takes a holistic and more unitary view of proficiency in describing four levels: superior, advanced, intermediate, and novice. Within each level, descriptions of listening, speaking, reading, and writing are provided as guidelines for assessment. For example, the ACTFL Guidelines describe the superior level of speaking as follows:

ACTFL speaking guidelines, summary, superior-level

Superior-level speakers are characterized by the ability to

- participate fully and effectively in conversations in formal and informal settings on topics related to practical needs and areas of professional and/or scholarly interests.
- provide a structured argument to explain and defend opinions and develop effective hypotheses within extended discourse.
- discuss topics concretely and abstractly.
- deal with a linguistically unfamiliar situation.
- maintain a high degree of linguistic accuracy.
- satisfy the linguistic demands of professional and/or scholarly life.

The other three ACTFL levels use the same parameters in describing progressively lower proficiencies across all four skills. Such taxonomies have the advantage of considering a number of functions of linguistic discourse, but the disadvantage, at the lower levels, of overly emphasizing test-takers' deficiencies.

Table 4.1. Traits of second language proficiency (Swain, 1990, p. 403)

Trait	Grammar	Discourse	Sociolinguistic
Method	focus on grammatical accuracy within sentences	focus on textual cohesion and coherence	focus on social appropriateness of language use
Oral	*structured interview*	*story telling and argumentation/persuasion*	*role-play of speech acts: requests, offers, complaints*
	scored for accuracy of verbal morphology, prepositions, syntax	detailed rating for identification, logical sequence, and time orientation, and global ratings for coherence	scored for ability to distinguish formal and informal register
Multiple-choice	*sentence-level 'select the correct form' exercise*	*paragraph-level 'select the coherent sentence' exercise*	*speech act-level 'select the appropriate utterance' exercise*
	(45 items)	(29 items)	(28 items)
	involving verb morphology, prepositions, and other items		
Written composition	*narrative and letter of persuasion*	*narrative and letter of persuasion*	*formal request letter and informal note*
	scored for accuracy of verb morphology, prepositions, syntax	detailed ratings much as for oral discourse and global rating for coherence	scored for the ability to distinguish formal and informal register

FOUR STANDARDIZED LANGUAGE PROFICIENCY TESTS

We now turn to some of the better-known standardized tests of overall language ability, or proficiency, to examine some of the typical formats used in commercially available tests. We will not look at standardized tests of other specific skills here, but that should not lead you to think, by any means, that proficiency is the only kind of test in the field that is standardized. Three standardized oral production tests, the

Test of Spoken English (TSE), the Oral Proficiency Inventory (OPI), and PhonePass® are discussed in Chapter 7, and the Test of Written English (TWE) is covered in Chapter 8.

Four commercially produced standardized tests of English language proficiency are described briefly in this section: the TOEFL, the Michigan English Language Assessment Battery (MELAB), the International English Language Testing System (IELTS), and the Test of English for International Communication (TOEIC®). In an appendix to this chapter are sample items from each section of each test. When you turn to that appendix, use the following questions to help you evaluate these four tests and their subsections:

1. What item types are included?
2. How practical and reliable does each subsection of each test appear to be?
3. Do the item types and tasks appropriately represent a conceptualization of language proficiency (ability)? That is, can you evaluate their construct validity?
4. Do the tasks achieve face validity?
5. Are the tasks authentic?
6. Is there some washback potential in the tasks?

Test of English as a Foreign Language (TOEFL®)

Producer:	Educational Testing Service (ETS)
Objective:	To test overall proficiency (language ability)
Primary market:	Almost exclusively U.S. universities and colleges for admission purposes
Type:	Computer-based (CB) (and two sections are computer-adaptive). A traditional paper-based (PB) version is also available.
Response modes:	Multiple-choice responses; essay
Specifications:	See the box on pp. 72–73
Time allocation:	Up to 4 hours (CB); 3 hours (PB)
Internet access:	**www.toefl.org**

Comments: In the North American context, the TOEFL is the most widely used commercially available standardized test of proficiency. Each year the TOEFL test is administered to approximately 800,000 candidates in more than 200 countries. It is highly respected because of the thorough program of ongoing research and development conducted by ETS. The TOEFL's primary use is to set proficiency standards for international students seeking admission to English-speaking universities. More than 4,200 academic institutions, government agencies, scholarship programs, and licensing/certification agencies in more than 80 countries use TOEFL scores. By 2004, the TOEFL will include a section on oral production.

Michigan English Language Assessment Battery (MELAB)

Producer:	English Language Institute, University of Michigan
Objective:	To test overall proficiency (language ability)
Primary market:	Mostly U.S. and Canadian language programs and colleges; some worldwide educational settings as well
Type:	Paper-based
Response modes:	Multiple-choice responses; essay
Time allocation:	2.5 to 3.5 hours
Internet access:	**www.lsa.umich.edu/eli/melab.htm**

Specifications: The MELAB consists of three sections. Part 1, a 30-minute impromptu essay, is written on an assigned topic. Part 2, a 25-minute multiple-choice listening comprehension test, is delivered via tape recorder. Part 3 is a 100-item, 75-minute, multiple-choice test containing grammar, cloze reading, vocabulary, and reading comprehension. An oral interview (speaking test) is optional.

Comments: The ELI at the University of Michigan has been producing the MELAB and its earlier incarnation (Michigan Test of English Language Proficiency) since 1961. Like the TOEFL, it serves a North American audience but is also used internationally. While its use is not as widespread as the TOEFL, its validity is widely respected. Because it is cheaper than the TOEFL and more easily obtained, it is popular among language schools and institutes. Many institutions and companies accept MELAB scores in lieu of TOEFL scores.

International English Language Testing System (IELTS)

Producer:	Jointly managed by The University of Cambridge Local Examinations Syndicate (UCLES), The British Council, and IDP Education Australia
Objective:	To test overall proficiency (language ability)
Primary market:	Australian, British, Canadian, and New Zealand academic institutions and professional organizations. American academic institutions are increasingly accepting IELTS for admissions purposes.
Type:	Computer-based (for the Reading and Writing sections); paper-based for the Listening and Speaking modules
Response modes:	Multiple-choice responses; essay; oral production
Time allocation:	2 hours, 45 minutes
Internet access:	**http://www.ielts.org/** **http://www.ucles.org.uk** **http://www.britishcouncil.org**

Specifications: Reading: candidates choose between academic reading or general training reading (60 minutes). Writing: the same option, academic writing or general training writing (60 minutes). Listening: four sections, for all candidates (30 minutes). Speaking: five sections, for all candidates (10–15 minutes).

Comments: The University of Cambridge Local Examinations Syndicate (UCLES) has been producing English language tests since 1858. Now, with three organizations cooperating to form the IELTS, more than a million examinations are administered every year. In 2002, a computer-based version of the Reading and Writing modules of the IELTS became available at selected centers around the world. The other sections are administered locally by an examiner. The paper-based IELTS remains an option for candidates. The IELTS retains the distinct advantage of requiring all four skills in the test-taker's performance.

Test of English for International Communication (TOEIC®)

Producer:	The Chauncey Group International, a subsidiary of Educational Testing Service
Objective:	To test overall proficiency (language ability)
Primary market:	Worldwide; business, commerce, and industry contexts (workplace settings)
Type:	Computer-based and paper-based versions
Response modes:	Multiple-choice responses
Time allocation:	2 hours
Internet access:	**http://www.toeic.com**

Specifications: Listening Comprehension: 100 items administered by audiocassette. Four types of task: statements, questions, short conversations, and short talks (approximately 45 minutes). Reading: 100 items. Three types of task: cloze sentences, error recognition, and reading comprehension (75 minutes).

Comments: The TOEIC has become a very widely used international test of English proficiency in workplace settings where English is required for job performance. The content includes many different employment settings such as conferences, presentations, sales, ordering, shipping, schedules, reservations, letters, and memoranda. It is appropriate to use in educational settings where vocational or workplace English courses are being offered.

§ § § § §

The construction of a valid standardized test is no minor accomplishment, whether the instrument is large- or small-scale. The designing of specifications alone, as this chapter illustrates, requires a sophisticated process of construct validation coupled with considerations of practicality. Then, the construction of items and scoring/interpretation procedures may require a lengthy period of trial and error with prototypes of the final form of the test. With painstaking attention to all the details of construction, the end product can result in a cost-effective, time-saving, accurate instrument. Your use of the results of such assessments can provide useful data on learners' language abilities. But your caution is warranted as well, for all the reasons discussed in this chapter. The next chapter will elaborate on what lies behind that need for a cautious approach to standardized assessment.

EXERCISES

[Note: (**I**) Individual work; (**G**) Group or pair work; (**C**) Whole-class discussion.]

1. (**C**) Tell the class about the worst test experience you've ever had. Briefly analyze what made the experience so unbearable, and try to come up with suggestions for improvement of the test and/or its administrative conditions.
2. (**G**) In pairs or small groups, compile a brief list of pros and cons of standardized testing. Cite illustrations of as many items in each list as possible. Report your lists and examples to the rest of the class.
3. (**I**) Select a standardized test that you are quite familiar with (probably a recent experience). Mentally evaluate that test using the five principles of practicality, reliability, validity, authenticity, and washback. Report your evaluation to the class.
4. (**G**) The appendix to this chapter provides sample items from four different tests of language proficiency. In groups, one test for each group, analyze your test for (a) content validity, (b) face validity, and (c) authenticity.
5. (**C**) Do you think that the sample TOEFL reading passage about pirates (pages 74–75) and the Graduate Essay Test prompt (pages 76–77) about a school board hiring committee have any culture bias? Discuss this and other cultural biases you have noticed in tests. Is it possible to design a test that is completely free of culture bias?
6. (**C/G**) Compare the differences in conceptualization of language proficiency represented by Swain's model, the TOEFL, and the ACTFL philosophy. Which one best represents current thinking about communicative language ability? What are the strengths and weaknesses of each approach?

FOR YOUR FURTHER READING

Gronlund, Norman E. (1998). *Assessment of student achievement.* Sixth Edition. Boston: Allyn and Bacon.

> Gronlund's classic, also mentioned in Chapter 3, offers a concise overview of features of standardized tests, offering definitions and examples of the statistical considerations in interpreting scores. His approach is unbiased, clearly written, and accessible to those who might "fear" the mathematics of standardized testing.

Phillips, Deborah. 2001. *Longman introductory course for the TOEFL test.* White Plains, NY: Pearson Education.

> A careful examination of this or any other reputable preparation course for a standardized language test is well worth a student's time. Note especially how the book acquaints the user with the specifications of the test and offers a number of useful strategies that can be used in preparation for the test and during its administration.

APPENDIX TO CHAPTER 4

Commercial Proficiency Tests: Sample Items and Tasks

Test of English as a Foreign Language (TOEFL®)

Listening

Part A

In this section, you will hear short conversations between two people. In some of the conversations, each person speaks only once. In other conversations, one or both of the people speak more than once. Each conversation is followed by one question about it. Each question in this part has four answer choices. You should click on the best answer to each question. Answer the questions on the basis of what is stated or implied by the speakers. Here is an example. On the computer screen, you will see:

   [man and woman talking]

On the recording, you will hear:

(woman)	Hey, where's your sociology book?
(man)	At home. Why carry it around when we're just going to be taking a test?
(woman)	Don't you remember? Professor Smith said we could us it during the test.
(man)	Oh, no! Well, I've still got an hour, right? I'm so glad I ran into you!

You will then see and hear the question before the answer choices appear:

What will the man probably do next?

- ○ Begin studying for the sociology test
- ○ Explain the problem to his professor
- ○ Go home to get his textbook
- ○ Borrow the woman's book

To choose an answer, you will click on an oval. The oval next to that answer will darken. After you click on Next and Confirm Answer, the next conversation will be presented.

Part B

In this section, you will hear several longer conversations and talks. Each conversation or talk is followed by several questions. The conversations, talks, and questions will not be repeated. The conversations and talks are about a variety of topics. You do not need special knowledge of the topics to answer the questions correctly. Rather, you should answer each question on the basis of what is stated or implied by the speakers in the conversations or talks.

For most of the questions, you will need to click on the best of four possible answers. Some questions will have special directions. The special directions will appear in a box on the computer screen. Here is an example of a conversation and some questions:

Marine Biology

(narrator)	Listen to part of a discussion in a marine biology class.
(professor)	A few years ago, our local government passed a number of strict environmental laws. As a result, Sunrise Beach looks nothing like it did ten years ago. The water is cleaner, and there's been a tremendous increase in all kinds of marine life, which is why we're going there on Thursday.
(woman)	I don't know if I agree that the water quality has improved. I mean, I was out there last weekend, and it looked all brown. It didn't seem too clean to me.
(professor)	Actually, the color of the water doesn't always indicate whether it's polluted. The brown color you mentioned might be a result of pollution, or it can mean a kind of brown algae is growing there. It's called "devil's apron," and it actually serves as food for whales.
(man)	So when does the water look blue?
(professor)	Well, water that's completely unpolluted is actually colorless. But it often looks bluish-green because the sunlight can penetrate deep down and that's the color that's reflected.
(woman)	But sometimes it looks really green. What's that about?
(professor)	Ok, well, it's the same principle as with "devil's apron": the water might be green because of different types of green algae there—gulfweed, phytoplankton. You all should finish reading about algae and plankton before we go. In fact, those are the types of living things I'm going to ask you to be looking for when we're there.

Now get ready to answer the questions.

What is the discussion mainly about?

- The importance of protecting ocean environments
- The reasons why ocean water appears to be different colors
- The survival of whales in polluted water
- The effect that colored ocean water has on algae

To choose an answer, click on an oval. The oval next to that answer will darken. After you click on Next and Confirm Answer, the next question will be presented:

According to the professor, what can make ocean water look brown?

- ☐ Pollution
- ☐ Cloudy Skies
- ☐ Sand
- ☐ Algae

Click on 2 answers.

To choose your answers, you will click on the squares. An "X" will appear in each square.

Structure and Written Expression

This section measures the ability to recognize language that is appropriate for standard written English. There are two types of questions in this section. In the first type of question, there are incomplete sentences. Beneath each sentence, there are four words or phrases.

Directions: Click on the one word or phrase that best completes the sentence.

The columbine flower, _____ to nearly all of the United States, can be raised from seed in almost any garden.

    native
    how native is
    how native is it
    is native

Time   Help   Confirm

After you click on <u>Next</u> and <u>Confirm Answer</u>, the next question will be presented.

The second type of question has four underlined words or phrases. You will choose the one underlined word or phrase that must be changed for the sentence to be correct.

Directions: Click on the one underlined word or phrase that must be changed for the sentence to be correct.

One of the <u>most</u> difficult problems <u>in understanding</u> sleep is <u>determining</u> what the functions of sleep <u>is</u>.

Time   Help   Confirm

Clicking on an underlined word or phrase will darken it.

Reading

This section measures the ability to read and understand short passages similar in topic and style to those that students are likely to encounter in North American universities and colleges. This section contains reading passages and questions about the passages. There are several different types of questions in this section. In the Reading section, you will first have the opportunity to read the passage.

●●●●●●●

    The temperature of the Sun is over 10,000 degrees Fahrenheit at the surface, but it rises perhaps more than 27,000,000° at the center. The Sun is so much hotter than the Earth that matter can exist only as a gas, except perhaps at the core. In the core of the Sun, the pressures are so great that, despite the high temperature, there may be a small solid core. However, no one really knows, since the center of the Sun can never be directly observed.
→ Solar astronomers do know that the Sun is divided into five general layers or zones. Starting at the outside and going down into the Sun, the zones are the corona, chromosphere, hotosphere, convection zone, and finally the core. The first three zones are regarded as the Sun's atmosphere. But since the Sun has no solid surface, it is hard to tell where the atmosphere ends and the main body of the Sun begins.
    The Sun's outermost layer begins about 10,000 miles above the visible surface and goes outward for millions of miles. This is the only part of the Sun that can be seen during an eclipse such as the one in February 1979. At any other time, the corona can be seen

only when special instruments are used on cameras and telescopes to block the light from the photosphere.

The corona is a brilliant, pearly white filmy light, about as bright as the full Moon. Its beautiful rays are a sensational sight during an eclipse. The corona's rays flash out in a brilliant fan that has wispy spikelike rays near the Sun's north and south poles. The corona is generally thickest at the Sun's equator. The corona is made up of gases streaming outward at tremendous speeds that reach a temperature of more than 2 million degrees Fahrenheit. The gas thins out as it reaches the space around the planets. By the time the gas of the corona reaches the Earth, it has a relatively low density.

● ● ● ● ● ● ●

When you have finished reading the passage, you will use the mouse to click on <u>Proceed</u>. Then the questions about the passage will be presented. You are to choose the one best answer to each question. Answer all questions about the information in a passage on the basis of what is stated or implied in that passage. Most of the questions will be multiple-choice questions. To answer these questions, you will click on a choice below the question.

With what topic is paragraph 2 mainly concerned?

○ How the Sun evolved
○ The structure of the Sun
○ Why scientists study the Sun
○ The distance of the Sun from the planets

Paragraph 2 is marked with an arrow (→).

You will see the next question after you click on <u>Next</u>.

To answer some questions you will click on a word or phrase. Here is an example:

*Look at the word <u>one</u> in the passage. Click on the word or phrase in the **bold** text that <u>one</u> refers to. To answer, you can click on any part of the word or phrase in the passage. Your choice will darken to show which word you have chosen.*

The Sun's outermost layer begins about 10,000 miles above the visible surface and goes outward for millions of miles. This is the only part of the Sun that can be seen during an eclipse such as the <u>one</u> in February 1979. At any other time, the corona can be seen only when special instruments are used on cameras and telescopes to block the light from the photosphere.

● ● ● ● ● ● ●

You will see the next question after you click on <u>Next</u>. To answer some questions, you will click on a sentence in the passage. Here is an example:

→ The corona is a brilliant, pearly white, filmy light about as bright as the full Moon. Its beautiful rays are a sensational sight during an eclipse. The corona's rays flash out in a brilliant fan that has wispy spikelike rays near the Sun's north and south poles. The corona is generally thickest at the Sun's equator.

→ The corona is made up of gases streaming outward at tremendous speeds that reach a temperature of more than 2 million degrees Fahrenheit. The gas thins out as it reaches the space around the planets. By the time the gas of the corona reaches the Earth, it has a relatively low density.

Click on the sentence in paragraph 4 or 5 in which the author compares the light of the Sun's outermost layer to that of another astronomical body. Paragraphs 4 and 5 are marked with arrows (→).

● ● ● ● ● ● ●

To answer some questions, you will click on a square to add a sentence to the passage. Here is an example:

The following sentence can be added to paragraph 1.

At the center of the Earth's solar system lies the Sun.

Where would it best fit in paragraph 1? Click on the square to add the sentence to the paragraph.

☐ The temperature of the Sun is over 10,000 degrees Fahrenheit at the surface, but it rises to perhaps more than 27,000,000° at the center. ☐ The Sun is so much hotter than the Earth that matter can exist only as a gas, except perhaps at the core. In the core of the Sun, the pressures are so great that, despite the high temperature, there may be a small solid core. ☐ However, no one really knows, since the center of the Sun can never be directly observed. ☐
01:00

When you click on a square, the sentence will appear in the passage at the place you have chosen. You can read the sentence added to the paragraph to see if this is the best place to add it. You can click on another square to change your answer. The sentence will be added and shown in a dark box.

Writing

In this section, you will have an opportunity to demonstrate your ability to write in English. This includes the ability to generate and organize ideas, to support those ideas with examples or evidence, and to compose in standard written English in response to an assigned topic. You will have 30 minutes to write your essay on that topic. You must write on the topic you are assigned. An essay on any other topic will receive a score of "0." Read the topic below and then make any notes that will help you plan your response. Begin typing your response in the box at the bottom of the screen, or write your answer on the answer sheet provided to you.

Following is a sample topic:

Do you agree or disagree with the following statement?

   "Teachers should make learning enjoyable and fun for their students."

Use specific reasons and examples to support your opinion.

Michigan English Language Assessment Battery (MELAB)

Composition

*The time limit for the composition is 30 minutes. You must write on only **one** of the topics below. If you write about something else, your composition paper will not be graded, and you cannot be given a final score. If you do not understand the topics, ask the examiner to explain or to translate them. You may be asked to give your opinion of something and explain why you believe this, to describe something from your experience, or to explain a problem and offer possible solutions. You should write at least one page. Some sample topics are:*

1. What do you think is your country's greatest problem? Explain in detail and tell what you think can be done about it.
2. What are the characteristics of a good teacher? Explain and give examples.
3. An optimist is someone who sees the good side of things. A pessimist sees the bad side. Are you an optimist or a pessimist? Relate a personal experience that shows this.
4. In your opinion, are the benefits of space exploration really worth the enormous costs? Discuss.

*Most MELAB compositions are one or two pages long (about 200–300 words). If your paper is **extremely** short (less than 150 words), your composition will be given a lower score. Before you begin writing, you might want to take 2 or 3 minutes to plan your composition and to make a short outline to organize your thoughts. Such outlines will not be graded; they are only to help you. You should use the last 5 minutes to read through your composition and to make changes or corrections.*

Your composition will be graded on how clearly you express yourself in English, and on the range of English you are able to use and your control in doing so. This means your composition should be well organized, your arguments should be fully developed, and you should show a range of grammatical structures and broad vocabulary. Compositions that consist only of very short sentences and very simple vocabulary cannot be given the highest scores. If errors are not frequent and if they do not confuse your meaning, they will not lower your score very much.

Listening

Now you will hear a short lecture. You may take notes during the lecture. Following the lecture, you will be asked some questions about it.

There'll be a two-week exhibit of the paintings of the little-known master Laura Bernhart at the Claire Osmond Galleries starting on the fifteenth of the month and running through the thirtieth. Bernhart's known for her innovative designs in abstract expressionism. Though a true original, she declared a spiritual heritage from Salvador Dali, the famous Spanish painter. Since Bernhart lived a rather solitary life and died while only in her twenties, few people are aware of her works. This showing at the Osmond Galleries will provide many with an introduction to her works.

10. Where is the exhibit?
    a. the Art Museum
    b. the Dali Galleries
    c. the Osmond Galleries

11. What is Bernhart known for?
   a. her copies of Dali's paintings
   b. the originality of her designs
   c. her exhibitions

12. What will going to the exhibit allow most people to do?
   a. to see Salvador Dali's paintings
   b. to see Bernhart's works for the first time
   c. to learn about Spanish art

Grammar

1. "What did the teacher just tell you?"

"She reminded _____ our notebooks."
   a. us to bring
   b. that we bring
   c. our bringing
   d. we should bring

2. "Is Bill a good dancer?"

"Not really, _____ he tries very hard."
   a. in spite of
   b. despite
   c. even though
   d. while

3. "Your clothes are all wet!"

"Yes, I didn't come _____ the rain soon enough."
   a. away to
   b. over to
   c. down with
   d. in from

Cloze

In years to come, zoos will not only be places where animals are exhibited to the public, but repositories where rare species can be saved from extinction (7) captive breeding. The most powerful force (8) the future of many animals—and of zoos—is the decline of the wild. (9) even zoo directors would argue that (10) are better places for animals than the fields and forest of their native (11), yet zoos may be the last chance for some creatures that would otherwise pass quietly into oblivion.

7. a. through   c. from
   b. of   d. damage

8. a. bringing   c. to
   b. that   d. influencing

9. a. But   c. Not
   b. So   d. Then

10. a. where   c. even
   b. zoos   d. wilds

11. a. lands   c. residence
   b. life   d. field

Vocabulary

12. Mark has a <u>flair</u> for writing.
  a. need
  b. purpose
  c. talent
  d. dislike

13. Bill Collins <u>launched </u>his restaurant last June.
  a. moved
  b. started
  c. sold
  d. bought

14. John will not accept the <u>censure</u>.
  a. burden
  b. blame
  c. credit
  d. decision

15. I can't think of the answer. Can you give me a _____?
  a. hint
  b. token
  c. taste
  d. gaze

16. Because fewer people are taking expensive vacations, the tourist industry is in a _____.
  a. choke
  b. grope
  c. grumble
  d. slump

17. I disagree with a few of his opinions, but _____ we agree.
  a. deliberately
  b. conclusively
  c. essentially
  d. immensely

Reading

The influenza virus is a single molecule built from many millions of single atoms. You must have heard of the viruses, which are sometimes called "living molecules." While bacteria can be considered as a type of plant, secreting poisonous substances into the body of the organism they attack, viruses are living organisms themselves. We may consider them as regular chemical molecules, since they have a strictly defined atomic structure, but on the other hand we must also consider them as being alive, since they are able to multiply in unlimited quantities.

18. According to the passage, bacteria are . . .
  a. poisons.
  b. larger than viruses.
  c. very small
  d. plants.

19. The writer says that viruses are alive because they . . .
   a. have a complex atomic structure.
   b. move.
   c. multiply.
   d. need warmth and light.

20. The atomic structure of viruses . . .
   a. is variable.
   b. is strictly defined.
   c. cannot be analyzed chemically.
   d. is more complex than that of bacteria.

International English Language Testing System (IELTS)

Listening

The Listening Module has four sections. The first two sections are concerned with social needs. There is a conversation between two speakers and then a monologue. For example: a conversation about travel arrangements or decisions on a night out, and a speech about student services on a university campus or arrangements for meals during a conference. The final two sections are concerned with situations related more closely to educational or training contexts. For example: conversation between a tutor and a student about an assignment or between three students planning a research project, and a lecture or talk of general academic interest. All the topics are of general interest, and it makes no difference what subjects candidates study. Tests and tasks become more difficult as the sections progress. A range of English accents and dialects are used in the recording, which reflects the international usage of IELTS.

Academic Reading

[A 750-word article on the topic of "Wind Power in the US" with a short glossary at the end]

Questions 1–5

Complete the summary below.

Choose your answers from the box below the summary and write them in boxes 1–5 on your answer sheet. Note: There are more words or phrases than you will need to fill the gaps. You may use any word or phrase more than once.

Example

The failure during the late 1970s and early 1980s of an attempt to establish a widespread wind power industry in the United States resulted largely from the . . . (1) . . . in oil prices during this period. The industry is now experiencing a steady . . . (2) . . . due to improvements in technology and an increased awareness of the potential in the power of wind. The wind turbines that are now being made, based in part on the . . . (3) . . . of wide-ranging research in Europe, are easier to manufacture and maintain than their predecessors. This has led wind-turbine makers to be able to standardise and thus minimize . . . (4) . . . There has been growing . . . (5) . . . of the importance of wind power as an energy source.

criticism	stability	skepticism
success	operating costs	decisions
design costs	fall	effects
production costs	growth	decline
failure	recognition	results

Questions 6–10

Look at the following list of issues (Questions 6–10) and implications (A–C). Match each issue with one implication. Write the appropriate letters A–C in boxes 6–10 on your answer sheet.

Example:
The current price of one wind-generated kilowatt . . .
Answer:

6. The recent installation of systems taking advantage of economies of scale . . .
7. The potential of meeting one fifth of current U.S. energy requirements by wind power . . .
8. The level of acceptance of current wind turbine technology . . .
9. A comparison of costs between conventional and wind power sources . . .
10. The view of wind power in the European Union . . .

Implications

A. provides evidence against claims that electricity produced from wind power is relatively expensive.
B. supports claims that wind power is an important source of energy.
C. opposes the view that wind power technology requires further development.

General Training Reading

Read the passage on Daybreak trips by coach and look at the statements below. On your answer sheet write:

TRUE	if the statement is true
FALSE	if the statement is false
NOT GIVEN	if the information is not given in the leaflet

1. Millers Coaches owns Cambridge's Cambus fleet.
2. Premier is an older company than Millers.
3. Most of the Daybreak coaches are less than 5 years old.
4. Daybreak fares are more expensive than most of their competitors.
5. Soft drinks and refreshments are served on most longer journeys.
6. Smoking is permitted at the rear of the coach on longer journeys.
7. Tickets must be bought in advance from an authorised Daybreak agent.
8. Tickets and seats can be reserved by phoning the Daybreak Hotline.
9. Daybreak passengers must join their coach at Cambridge Drummer Street.
10. Daybreak cannot guarantee return times.

FROM CAMBRIDGE AND SURROUNDING AREA

SPRING IS IN THE AIR!

Welcome to our Spring Daybreak programme, which continues the tradition of offering unbeatable value for money daytrips and tours. All the excursions in this brochure will be operated by Premier Travel Services Limited or Millers Coaches; both companies are part of the CHL Group, owners of Cambridge's Cambus fleet.

WE'RE PROUD OF OUR TRADITION

Premier was established in 1936; the Company now offers the highest standards of coaching in today's competitive operating environment. Miller has an enviable reputation stretching back over the past 20 years, offering coach services at realistic prices. We've traveled a long way since our early days of pre-war seaside trips. Now our fleet of 50 modern coaches (few are more than five years old) operate throughout Britain and Europe, but we're pleased to still maintain the high standards of quality and service, the trademark of our founders nearly sixty years ago.

EXCLUSIVE FEATURES

Admission—inclusive fares:
All Daybreak fares (unless specifically otherwise stated) include admission charges to the attractions, shows and exhibits we visit. Many full-day scenic tours are accompanied by a fully trained English Tourist Board 'Blue Badge' guide or local experienced driver/guide. Some Daybreaks include lunch or afternoon tea. Compare our admission inclusive fares and see how much you save. Cheapest is not the best, and value for money is guaranteed. If you compare our bargain Daybreak fares, beware—most of our competitors do not offer an all-inclusive fare.

SEAT RESERVATIONS

We value the freedom of choice, so you can choose your seat when you book. The seat reservation is guaranteed and remains yours at all times when aboard the coach.

NO SMOKING COMFORT

With the comfort of our passengers in mind, coaches on all our Daybreaks are no smoking throughout. In the interests of fellow passengers' comfort, we kindly ask that smokers observe our 'no smoking' policy. On scenic tours and longer journeys, ample refreshment stops are provided when, of course, smoking is permitted.

YOUR QUESTIONS ANSWERED

Do I need to book?
Booking in advance is strongly recommended as all Daybreak tours are subject to demand. Subject to availability, stand-by tickets can be purchased from the driver.

What time does the coach leave?
The coach departs from Cambridge Drummer Street (Bay 12, adjacent to public toilets) at the time shown. There are many additional joining points indicated by departure codes in the brochure. If you are joining at one of our less popular joining points, you will be advised of your pick-up time (normally by telephone) not less than 48 hours before departure. In this way, we can minimize the length of pick-up routes and reduce journey times for the majority of passengers.

What time do we get back?
An approximate return time is shown for each excursion. The times shown serve as a guide, but road conditions can sometimes cause delay. If your arrival will be later than advertised, your driver will try to allow for a telephone call during the return journey.

Where can I board the coach?
All the Daybreaks in the brochure leave from Cambridge Drummer Street (Bay 12, adjacent to public toilets) at the time shown. Many Daybreaks offer additional pick-ups for pre-booked passengers within Cambridge and the surrounding area. This facility must be requested at the time of booking.

Academic Writing

Writing Task 1
You should spend about 20 minutes on this task.

The graph below shows the different modes of transport used to travel to and from work in one European city in 1950, 1970 and 1990.

[graph shown here]

Write a report for a university lecturer describing the information shown below. You should write at least 150 words.

Writing Task 2
You should spend about 40 minutes on this task.

Present a written argument or case to an educated reader with no specialist knowledge of the following topic.

It is inevitable that as technology develops, so traditional cultures must be lost. Technology and tradition are incompatible—you cannot have both together.

To what extent do you agree or disagree with this statement? Give reasons for your answer. You should write at least 250 words. You should use your own ideas, knowledge and experience and support your arguments with examples and relevant evidence.

General Training Writing

Writing Task 1
You should spend about 20 minutes on this task. You rent a house through an agency. The heating system has stopped working. You phoned the agency a week ago but it has still not been mended. Write a letter to the agency. Explain the situation and tell them what you want them to do about it.

You should write at least 150 words. You do NOT need to write your own address.

Begin your letter as follows:

Dear _____,

Writing Task 2
You should spend about 40 minutes on this task. As part of a class assignment, you have to write about the following topic:

Some businesses now say that no one can smoke cigarettes in any of their offices. Some governments have banned smoking in all public places. This is a good idea, but it takes away some of our freedom.

Do you agree or disagree? Give reasons for your answer. You should write at least 250 words.

Speaking

In each of the three parts of the speaking module, a specific function is fulfilled. In Part 1, the candidates answer general questions about themselves, their homes or families, their jobs or studies, their interests, and a range of similar familiar topic areas. This part lasts between four and five minutes. In Part 2, the candidate is given a verbal prompt on a card and is asked to talk on a particular topic. The candidate has one minute to prepare before speaking at length, for between one and two minutes. The examiner then asks one or two wind-down questions. In Part 3, the examiner and candidate engage in a discussion of more abstract issues and concepts which are thematically linked to the topic prompt in Part 2. The discussion lasts between four and five minutes.
    All interviews are recorded on audiocassette. Here is a sample of a Part 2 topic:

Describe a teacher who has greatly influenced you in your education.

You should say:

> where you met them
> what subject they taught
> what was special about them

and explain why this person influenced you so much.

You will have to talk about the topic for 1 to 2 minutes. You have 1 minute to think about what you are going to say. You can make some notes if you wish.

Test of English for International Communication (TOEIC®)

Listening

Part 1: Photographs
Directions: For each question, you will see a picture in your test book and you will hear four short statements. The statements will be spoken just one time. They will not be printed in your test book, so you must listen carefully to understand what the speaker says. When you hear the four statements, look at the picture in your test book and choose the statement that best describes what you see in the picture. Then, on your answer sheet find the number of the question and mark your answer.

[photograph of a scientist looking through a microscope]

You will hear: "Look at the picture marked number 1 in your test book."

> (A) She's speaking into a microphone.
> (B) She's put on her glasses.
> (C) She has both eyes open.
> (D) She's using a microscope.

Part 2: Question–Response

Directions: In this part of the test, you will hear a question or statement spoken in English, followed by three responses, also spoken in English. The question or statement and the responses will be spoken just one time. They will not be printed in your test book, so you must listen carefully to understand what the speakers say. You are to choose the best response to each question or statement.

Question 1. You will hear: "Ms. Morikawa has worked here for a long time, hasn't she?"

(A) At three o'clock.
(B) No, I've lost my watch.
(C) More than ten years.

Question 2. You will hear: "Which of these papers has a wider circulation?"

(A) The morning edition.
(B) Get more exercise.
(C) By messenger.

Part 3: Short Conversations

Directions: In this part of the test, you will hear short conversations between two people. The conversations will not be printed in your test book. You will hear the conversations only once, so you must listen carefully to understand what the speakers say. In your test book, you will read a question about each conversation. The question will be followed by four answers. You are to choose the best answer to each question and mark it on your answer sheet.

Question 1.   (Man)   We should think about finding another restaurant for lunch.
      (Woman)   Why? The food and service here are great.
      (Man)   Yes, but the prices are going up every week.

You will read: Why is this man unhappy with the restaurant?

(A) It is too noisy.
(B) It is too expensive.
(C) It is too crowded
(D) It is too difficult to find.

Question 2.   (Woman A)   How was Dr. Borg's recent trip to Singapore?
      (Woman B)   She enjoyed the tour of the port very much.
      (Woman A)   They say it's one of the most active in Asia.

You will read: 2. What did Dr. Borg find interesting?

(A) The tourist center.
(B) The airport.
(C) The musical performance.
(D) The harbor.

Part 4: Short Talks

Directions: In this part of the test, you will hear several short talks. Each will be spoken just one time. They will not be printed in your test book, so you must listen carefully to understand and remember what is said. In your test book, you will read two or more questions about each short talk. The questions will be followed by four answers. You are to choose the best answer to each question and mark it on your answer sheet.

You will hear: Questions 1 and 2 refer to the following announcement:

Good afternoon and welcome aboard Nordair Flight 857 from Copenhagen to Bangkok, with intermediate stops in Dubai and Calcutta. We are preparing for departure in a few minutes. At this time your seat back should be returned to its full upright position and your seat belt should be fastened. Our anticipated total flying time to Dubai is six hours and twenty-five minutes. I hope you enjoy the flight.
You will hear: Now read question 1 in your test book and answer it.
You will read: 1. What is the final destination of the flight?

  (A) Bangkok.
  (B) Copenhagen.
  (C) Dubai.
  (D) Calcutta.

You will hear: Now read question 2 in your test book and answer it.
You will read: 2. What will happen in a few minutes?

  (A) The flight will land in Dubai.
  (B) The passengers will board the plane.
  (C) The plane will take off.
  (D) The gate number will be announced.

Reading

In this section of the test you will have the chance to show how well you understand written English. There are three parts to this section, with special directions for each part.

Part 4. Incomplete Sentences
Directions: This part of the test has incomplete sentences. Four words or phrases, marked (A), (B), (C), (D), are given beneath each sentence. You are to choose the one word or phrase that best completes the sentence. Then, on your answer sheet, find the number of the question and mark your answer.

1. Mr. Yang's trip will _____ him away from the office for ten days.
   (A) withdraw
   (B) continue
   (C) retain
   (D) keep

2. The company that Marie DuBois started now sells _____ products throughout the world.
   (A) its
   (B) it
   (C) theirs
   (D) them

3. If your shipment is not delivered _____ Tuesday, you can request a full refund for the merchandise.
   (A) at
   (B) by
   (C) within
   (D) while

Part 6. Error Recognition
Directions: In this part of the test, each sentence has four words or phrases underlined. The four underlined parts of the sentence are marked (A), (B), (C), (D). You are to identify the one underlined word or phrase that should be corrected or rewritten. Then, on your answer sheet, find the number of the question and mark your answer.

1. The <u>pamphlet</u> <u>contains</u> some <u>importance</u> information about the <u>current</u> exhibit.
     A   B   C   D

2. <u>No matter</u> how long it <u>taking to</u> finish the <u>annual report</u>, it <u>must be</u> done properly.
     A   B   C   D

3. The <u>popularity</u> of jogging <u>appears</u> to have decreased <u>since</u> the past <u>couple</u> of years.
        A   B   C   D

Part 7. Reading Comprehension
Directions: The questions in this part of the test are based on a selection of reading materials, such as notices, letters, forms, newspaper and magazine articles, and advertisements. You are to choose the one best answer, (A), (B), (C), or (D), to each question. Then, on your answer sheet, find the number of the question and mark your answer. Answer all questions following each reading selection on the basis of what is stated or implied in that selection.

The Museum of Technology is a "hands-on" museum, designed for people to experience science at work. Visitors are encouraged to use, test, and handle the objects on display. Special demonstrations are scheduled for the first and second Wednesdays of each month at 13:30. Open Tuesday–Friday 12:00–16:30, Saturday 10:00–17:30, and Sunday 11:00–16:30.

1. When during the month can visitors see special demonstrations?
   (A) Every weekend.
   (B) The first two Wednesdays.
   (C) One afternoon a week.
   (D) Every other Wednesday.

Questions 2 and 3 refer to the following notice:

NOTICE
If you are unable to work because of an extended illness or injury that is not work-related, you may be entitled to receive weekly benefits from your employer or the firm's insurance company. To claim benefits, you must file a claim form within thirty days of the first day of your disability. Before filing the claim, you must ask your doctor to fill in the Doctor's Statement on the claim form, stating the period of disability.

3. To whom is this notice addressed?
   (A) Employers
   (B) Doctors
   (C) Employees
   (D) When paying the bill

4. When must the claim form be filed?
   (A) On the first of the month
   (B) On the thirtieth of the month
   (C) On the first day of disability
   (D) Within 30 days of the start of disability

CHAPTER 5

STANDARDS-BASED

ASSESSMENT

In the previous chapter, you saw that a standardized test is an assessment instrument for which there are uniform procedures for administration, design, scoring, and reporting. It is also a procedure that, through repeated administrations and ongoing research, demonstrates criterion and construct validity. But a third, and perhaps the most important, element of standardized testing is the presupposition of an accepted set of **standards** on which to base the procedure. This feature of an educational and business world caught up in a frenzy of standardized measurement is perhaps the most complex, and is the subject of this chapter.

A history of standardized testing in the United States reveals that during most of the decades in the middle of the twentieth century, standardized tests enjoyed a popularity and growth that was almost unchallenged. Standardized instruments brought with them convenience, efficiency, and an air of empirical science. In schools, for example, millions of children could be led into a room, seated, armed with a lead pencil and a score sheet, and almost instantly assessed on their achievement in subject-matter areas in their curricula. Standardized test advocates' utopian dream of quickly and cheaply assessing students across the country soon became a political issue, and would-be office holders to this day promise to "reform" education with tests, tests, and more tests.

Toward the end of the twentieth century, such claims began to be challenged on all fronts (see Medina & Neill, 1990; Kohn, 2000), and at the vanguard of those challenges were the teachers of those millions of children. Teachers saw not only possible inequity in such tests but a disparity between the content and tasks of the tests and what they were teaching in their classes. Were those tests accurate measures of achievement and success in the specified domains? Were those efficient, well-researched instruments based on carefully framed, comprehensive, validated standards of achievement?

For the most part, they were not. As educators became aware of this weakness, we saw the advent of a movement to establish standards on which students of all ages and subject-matter areas might be assessed. Appropriately, the last 20 years have seen a mushrooming of efforts on the part of educational leaders to base the plethora of school-administered standardized tests on clearly specified criteria within each content area being measured. For example, most departments of education at the state level in the United States have now specified (or are in the process of specifying) the appropriate standards (that is, criteria or objectives) for each grade level (kindergarten to grade 12) and each content area (math, language, sciences, arts).

The construction of such standards makes possible a concordance between standardized test specifications and the goals and objectives of educational programs. And so, in the broad domain of language arts, teachers and educational administrators began the painstaking process of carefully examining existing curricular goals, conducting needs assessments among students, and designing appropriate assessments of those standards. A subfield of language arts that is of increasing importance in the United States, with its millions of non-native users of English, is English as a Second Language (ESL), also known as English for Speakers of Other Languages (ESOL), English Language Learners (ELLs), and English Language Development (ELD). (Note: The once-popular term Limited English Proficient [LEP] has now been discarded because of the negative connotation of the word *limited*.)

ELD STANDARDS

The process of designing and conducting appropriate periodic reviews of ELD standards involves dozens of curriculum and assessment specialists, teachers, and researchers (Fields, 2000; Kuhlman, 2001). In creating such "benchmarks for accountability" (O'Malley & Valdez Pierce, 1996), there is a tremendous responsibility to carry out a comprehensive study of a number of domains:

- literally thousands of *categories of language* ranging from phonology at one end of a continuum to discourse, pragmatics, functional, and sociolinguistic elements at the other end;
- specification of what ELD *students' needs* are, at thirteen different grade levels, for succeeding in their academic and social development;
- a consideration of what is a realistic *number and scope of standards* to be included within a given curriculum;
- a separate set of *standards* (qualifications, expertise, training) *for teachers* to teach ELD students successfully in their classrooms; and
- a thorough analysis of the *means available* to assess student attainment of those standards.

Standards-setting is a global challenge. In many non-English-speaking countries, English is now a required subject starting as early as the first grade in some countries and by the seventh grade in virtually every country worldwide. In Japan and Korea, for example, a "communicative" curriculum in English is required from third grade onward. Such mandates from ministries of education require the specification of standards on which to base curricular objectives, the teachability of which has been met with only limited success in some areas (Chinen, 2000; Yoshida, 2001; Sakamoto, 2002).

California, with one of the largest populations of second language learners in the United States, was one of the first states to generate standards. Other states follow similar sets of standards. To view the standards developed by the California Department of Education, visit the website at **http://www.cde.ca.gov/standards/**. The preamble to about 70 pages of "strategies and applications" of the California standards sets the tone:

> The Listening and Speaking standards for English-language learners (ELLs) identify a student's competency to understand the English language and to produce the language orally. Students must be prepared to use English effectively in social and academic settings. Listening and speaking skills provide one of the most important building blocks for the foundation of second language acquisition. These skills are essential for developing reading and writing skills in English; however, to ensure that ELLs acquire proficiency in English listening, speaking, reading, and writing, it is important that students receive reading and writing instruction in English while they are developing fluency in oral English.
>
> To ensure that ELLs develop the skills and concepts needed to demonstrate proficiency on the English-Language Arts (ELA) Listening and Speaking standards, teachers must concurrently use both the ELD and the ELA standards. ELLs achieving at the Advanced ELD proficiency level should demonstrate proficiency on the ELA standards for their own and all prior grade levels. This means that all prerequisite skills needed to achieve the ELA standards must be learned by the Early Advanced ELD proficiency level. ELLs must develop both fluency in English and proficiency on the ELA standards. Teachers must ensure that ELLS receive instruction in listening and speaking that will enable them to demonstrate proficiency on the ELA Speaking Applications standards.

An example of standards for listening and speaking, beginning level, is reproduced in Table 5.1.

ELD ASSESSMENT

The development of standards obviously implies the responsibility for correctly assessing their attainment. As standards-based education became more accepted in the 1990s, many school systems across the United States found that the standardized tests of past decades were not in line with newly developed standards. Thus began the interactive process not only of developing standards but also of creating **standards-based assessments**. The comprehensive process of developing such assessment in California still continues as curriculum and assessment specialists design, revise, and validate numerous tests (Morgan & Kuhlman, 2001; Stack et al., 2002; see also the website **http://www.cde.ca.gov/statetests/celdt/celdt.html**). Between 1999 and 2002,

Table 5.1. California English language development standards for listening and speaking
(© 1999, California Department of Education, p. 21)

Listening and Speaking

ELA Categories	Grades K–2	Grades 3–5	Grades 6–8	Grades 9–12
Comprehension	Begin to speak with a few words or sentences, using some English phonemes and rudimentary English grammatical forms (e.g., single words or phrases).	Begin to speak with a few words or sentences, using some English phonemes and rudimentary English grammatical forms (e.g., single words or phrases).	Begin to speak with a few words or sentences, using some English phonemes and rudimentary English grammatical forms (e.g., single words or phrases).	Begin to speak with a few words or sentences, using some English phonemes and rudimentary English grammatical forms (e.g., single words or phrases).
	Answer simple questions with one- to two-word responses.	Answer simple questions with one- to two-word responses.	Ask and answer questions using simple sentences or phrases.	Ask and answer questions using simple sentences or phrases.
	Respond to simple directions and questions using physical actions and other means of nonverbal communication (e.g., matching objects, pointing to an answer, drawing pictures).	Retell familiar stories and participate in short conversations by using appropriate gestures, expressions, and illustrative objects.	Demonstrate comprehension of oral presentations and instructions through nonverbal responses (e.g., gestures, pointing, drawing).	Demonstrate comprehension of oral presentations and instructions through non-verbal responses.
Comprehension, Organization & Delivery of Oral Communication	Independently use common social greetings and simple repetitive phrases (e.g., "Thank you." "You're welcome.").	Independently use common social greetings and simple repetitive phrases (e.g., "May I go and play?").	Independently use common social greetings and simple repetitive phrases (e.g., "Good Morning. Ms. _____.").	
Analysis & Evaluation of Oral & Media Communications, Comprehension				Respond with simple words or phrases to questions about simple written texts.
				Orally identify types of media by name (e.g., magazine, documentary film, news report).

the California English Language Development Test (CELDT) was developed. The CELDT is a battery of instruments designed to assess the attainment of ELD standards across grade levels. (For reasons of test security, specifications for this test are not available to the public.)

The process of administering a comprehensive, valid, and fair assessment of ELD students continues to be perfected. Stringent budgets within departments of education worldwide predispose many in decision-making positions to rely on traditional standardized tests for ELD assessment, but rays of hope lie in the exploration of more student-centered approaches to learner assessment. Stack, Stack, and Fern (2002), for example, reported on a portfolio assessment system in the San Francisco Unified School District called the Language and Literacy Assessment Rubric (LALAR), in which multiple forms of evidence of students' work are collected. Teachers observe students year-round and record their observations on scannable forms. The use of the LALAR system provides useful data on students' performance at all grade levels for oral production, and for reading and writing performance in elementary and middle school grades (1–8). Further research is ongoing for high school levels (grades 9–12).

CASAS AND SCANS

At the higher levels of education (colleges, community colleges, adult schools, language schools, and workplace settings), standards-based assessment systems have also had an enormous impact. The Comprehensive Adult Student Assessment System (CASAS), for example, is a program designed to provide broadly based assessments of ESL curricula across the United States. The system includes more than 80 standardized assessment instruments used to place learners in programs, diagnose learners' needs, monitor progress, and certify mastery of functional basic skills. CASAS assessment instruments are used to measure functional reading, writing, listening, and speaking skills, and higher-order thinking skills. CASAS scaled scores report learners' language ability levels in employment and adult life skills contexts. Further information about CASAS may be found on the website **http://www.ed.gov/pubs/EPTW/eptw14/eptw14a.html**.

A similar set of standards compiled by the U. S. Department of Labor, now known as the Secretary's Commission in Achieving Necessary Skills (SCANS), outlines competencies necessary for language in the workplace. The competencies cover language functions in terms of

- resources (allocating time, materials, staff, etc.),
- interpersonal skills, teamwork, customer service, etc.,
- information processing, evaluating data, organizing files, etc.,
- systems (e.g., understanding social and organizational systems), and
- technology use and application.

These five competencies are acquired and maintained through training in the basic skills (reading, writing, listening, speaking); thinking skills such as reasoning and creative problem solving; and personal qualities, such as self-esteem and sociability. For more information on SCANS, consult **http://wdr.doleta.gov/SCANS/teaching/**.

TEACHER STANDARDS

In addition to the movement to create standards for learning, an equally strong movement has emerged to design standards for teaching. Cloud (2001, p. 3) noted that a student's "performance [on an assessment] depends on the quality of the instructional program provided, . . . which depends on the quality of professional development." Kuhlman (2001) emphasized the importance of teacher standards in three domains:

1. linguistics and language development
2. culture and the interrelationship between language and culture
3. planning and managing instruction

Professional teaching standards have also been the focus of several committees in the international association of Teachers of English to Speakers of Other Languages (TESOL). For more information, consult **http://www.tesol.org/assoc/alstandards/index.html**.

How to assess whether teachers have met standards remains a complex issue. Can pedagogical expertise be assessed through a traditional standardized test? In the first of Kuhlman's domains—linguistics and language development—knowledge can perhaps be so evaluated, but the cultural and interactive characteristics of effective teaching are less able to be appropriately assessed in such a test. TESOL's standards committee advocates performance-based assessment of teachers for the following reasons:

- Teachers can demonstrate the standards in their teaching.
- Teaching can be assessed through what teachers do with their learners in their classrooms or virtual classrooms (their performance).
- This performance can be detailed in what are called "indicators": examples of evidence that the teacher can meet a part of a standard.
- The processes used to assess teachers need to draw on complex evidence of performance. In other words, indicators are more than simple "how to" statements.
- Performance-based assessment of the standards is an integrated system. It is neither a checklist nor a series of discrete assessments.
- Each assessment within the system has performance criteria against which the performance can be measured.
- Performance criteria identify to what extent the teacher meets the standard.
- Student learning is at the heart of the teacher's performance.

The standards-based approach to teaching and assessment presents the profession with many challenges. However thorny those issues are, the social consequences of this movement cannot be ignored, especially in terms of student assessment.

THE CONSEQUENCES OF STANDARDS-BASED AND STANDARDIZED TESTING

A couple of decades ago I had the pleasure and challenge of serving on the TOEFL® Research Committee. Among other things, it was a good opportunity to hear some of the "inside" stories about the TOEFL. One of those stories, as told by Russell Webster (personal communication), illustrates the high-stakes nature of this globally marketed standardized test.

A ring of enterprising "business" persons organized a group of pretend test-takers to take the TOEFL in an early time zone on a given day. (In those days the tests were administered everywhere on the same day across a number of time zones. So TOEFL administrations *ended* in some East Asian countries as much as 8 to 14 hours before they began in the United States.)

The task of each test-taking "spy" was not to pass the TOEFL, but to memorize a subset of items, including the stimulus and all of the multiple-choice options, and immediately upon leaving the exam to telephone those items to the central organizers. As the memorized subsections were called in, a complete form of the TOEFL was quickly reconstructed. The organizers had employed expert consultants to generate the correct response for each item, thereby re-creating the test items and their correct answers! For an outrageous price of many thousands of dollars, prearranged buyers of the results were given copies of the test items and correct responses with a few hours to spare before entering a test administration in the Western Hemisphere.

The story of how this underhanded group of entrepreneurs were caught and brought to justice is a long tale of blockbuster spy-novel proportions involving the FBI and, eventually, international investigators. But the story shows the huge **gate-keeping** role of tests like the TOEFL and the high price that some were willing to pay to gain access to a university in the United States and the visa that accompanied it.

The widespread global acceptance of standardized tests as valid procedures for assessing individuals in many walks of life brings with it a set of consequences that fall under the category of **consequential validity** discussed in Chapter 2. Some of those consequences are positive. Standardized tests offer high levels of practicality and reliability and are often supported by impressive construct validation studies. They are therefore capable of accurately placing tens and hundreds of thousands of test-takers onto a norm-referenced scale with high reliability ratios (most ranging between 80 and 90 percent). For decades, university admissions offices around the world have relied on the results of tests such as the Scholastic Aptitude Test (SAT®), the Graduate Record Exam (GRE®), and the TOEFL to screen applicants. The respectably moderate correlations between these tests and academic performance are used to justify determining the future of students' lives on the basis of one relatively inexpensive sit-down multiple-choice test. Thus has emerged the term **high-stakes** testing, based on the gate-keeping function that standardized tests perform.

Are the institutions that produce and utilize high-stakes standardized tests justified in their decisions? An impressive array of research would seem to say yes. Consider the fact that correlations between TOEFL scores and academic performance in the first year of college are impressively high (Henning & Cascallar, 1992). Are tests that lack a high level of content validity appropriate assessments of ability? A good deal of research says yes to this question as well. A study of the correlation of TOEFL results with oral and written production, for example, showed that years before TOEFL's current use of an essay and oral production section, significant positive correlations were obtained between *all* subsections of the TOEFL and independent direct measures of oral and written production (Henning & Cascallar, 1992). Test promoters commonly use such findings to support their claims for the efficacy of their tests.

But several nagging, persistent issues emerge from the arguments about the consequences of standardized testing. Consider the following interrelated questions:

1. Should the educational and business world be satisfied with high but not perfect probabilities of accurately assessing test-takers on standardized instruments? In other words, what about the small minority who are *not* fairly assessed?
2. Regardless of construct validation studies and correlation statistics, should further types of performance be elicited in order to get a more comprehensive picture of the test-taker?
3. Does the proliferation of standardized tests throughout a young person's life give rise to test-driven curricula, diverting the attention of students from creative or personal interests and in-depth pursuits?
4. Is the standardized test industry in effect promoting a cultural, social, and political agenda that maintains existing power structures by assuring opportunity to an elite (wealthy) class of people?

Test Bias

It is no secret that standardized tests involve a number of types of test bias. That bias comes in many forms: language, culture, race, gender, and learning styles (Medina & Neill, 1990). The National Center for Fair and Open Testing, in its bimonthly newsletter *Fair Test,* every year offers dozens of instances of claims of test bias from teachers, parents, students, and legal consultants (see their website: **www.fairtest. org**). For example, reading selections in standardized tests may use a passage from a literary piece that reflects a middle-class, white, Anglo-Saxon norm. Lectures used for listening stimuli can easily promote a biased sociopolitical view. Consider the following prompt for an essay in "general writing ability" on the IELTS:

> You rent a house through an agency. The heating system has stopped working. You phoned the agency a week ago, but it has still not been mended. Write a letter to the agency. Explain the situation and tell them what you want them to do about it.

While this task favorably illustrates the principle of authenticity, a number of cultural and economic presuppositions are evident in such a prompt, calling into question its potential cultural bias.

In an era when we seek to recognize the multiple intelligences present within every student (Gardner, 1983, 1999), is it not likely that standardized tests promote logical-mathematical and verbal-linguistic intelligences to the virtual exclusion of the other contextualized, integrative intelligences? Only very recently have traditionally receptive tests begun to include written and oral production in their test battery—a positive sign. But is it enough? It is also clear that many otherwise "smart" people do not perform well on standardized tests. They may excel in cognitive styles that are not amenable to a standardized format. Perhaps they need to be assessed by such performance-based evaluation as interviews, portfolios, samples of work, demonstrations, and observation reports? Perhaps, as Weir (2001, p. 122) suggested, learners and teachers need to be given the freedom to choose more formative assessment rather than the summative assessment inherent in standardized tests.

Expanding test batteries to include such measures would help to solve the problem of test bias (which is extremely difficult to control for in standardized items) and to account for the small but significant number of test-takers who are not accurately assessed by standardized tests. Those who are using the tests for gate-keeping purposes, with few if any other assessments, would do well to consider multiple measures before attributing infallible predictive power to standardized tests.

Test-Driven Learning and Teaching

Yet another consequence of standardized testing is the danger of test-driven learning and teaching. When students and other test-takers know that one single measure of performance will determine their lives, they are less likely to take a positive attitude toward learning. The motives in such a context are almost exclusively extrinsic, with little likelihood of stirring intrinsic interests. Test-driven learning is a worldwide issue. In Japan, Korea, and Taiwan, to name just a few countries, students approaching their last year of secondary school focus obsessively on passing the year-end college entrance examination, a major section of which is English (Kuba, 2002). Little attention is given to any topic or task that does not directly contribute to passing that one exam. In the United States, high school seniors are forced to give almost as much attention to SAT scores.

Teachers also get caught up in the wave of test-driven systems. In Florida, elementary school teachers were recently promised cash bonuses of $100 per student as a reward for their schools' high performance on the state-mandated grade-level test, the Florida Comprehensive Achievement Exam (*Fair Test,* 2000). The effect of this policy was undue pressure on teachers to make sure their students excelled in the exam, possibly at the risk of ignoring other objectives in their curricula. But a further, ultimately more serious effect was to punish schools in lower-socioeconomic neighborhoods. A teacher in such a school might actually be a superb teacher, and that teacher's students might make excellent progress through the school year, but because of the test-driven policy, the teacher would receive no reward at all.

ETHICAL ISSUES: CRITICAL LANGUAGE TESTING

One of the by-products of a rapidly growing testing industry is the danger of an abuse of power. In a special report on "fallout from the testing explosion," Medina and Neill (1990, p. 36) noted:

> Unfortunately, too many policymakers and educators have ignored the complexities of testing issues and the obvious limitations they should place on standardized test use. Instead, they have been seduced by the promise of simplicity and objectivity. The price which has been paid by our schools and our children for their infatuation with tests is high.

Shohamy (1997, p. 2) further defines the issue: "Tests represent a social technology deeply embedded in education, government, and business; as such they provide the mechanism for enforcing power and control. Tests are most powerful as they are often the single indicators for determining the future of individuals." Test designers, and the corporate sociopolitical infrastructure that they represent, have an obligation to maintain certain standards as specified by their client educational institutions. These standards bring with them certain ethical issues surrounding the gate-keeping nature of standardized tests.

Shohamy (1997) and others (such as Spolsky, 1997; Hamp-Lyons, 2001) see the ethics of testing as an extension of what educators call **critical pedagogy,** or more precisely in this case, **critical language testing** (see *TBP,* Chapter 23, for some comments on critical language pedagogy in general). Proponents of a critical approach to language testing claim that large-scale standardized testing is not an unbiased process, but rather is the "agent of cultural, social, political, educational, and ideological agendas that shape the lives of individual participants, teachers, and learners" (Shohamy, 1997, p. 3). The issues of critical language testing are numerous:

- Psychometric traditions are challenged by interpretive, individualized procedures for predicting success and evaluating ability.
- Test designers have a responsibility to offer multiple modes of performance to account for varying styles and abilities among test-takers.

- Tests are deeply embedded in culture and ideology.
- Test-takers are political subjects in a political context.

These issues are not new. More than a century ago, British educator F. Y. Edgeworth (1888) challenged the potential inaccuracy of contemporary qualifying examinations for university entrance. In recent years, the debate has heated up. In 1997, an entire issue of the journal *Language Testing* was devoted to questions about ethics in language testing.

One of the problems highlighted by the push for critical language testing is the widespread conviction, already alluded to above, that carefully constructed standardized tests designed by reputable test manufacturers are infallible in their predictive validity. One standardized test is deemed to be sufficient; follow-up measures are considered to be too costly.

A further problem with our test-oriented culture lies in the agendas of those who design and those who utilize the tests. Tests are used in some countries to deny citizenship (Shohamy, 1997, p. 10). Tests may by nature be culture-biased and therefore may disenfranchise members of a nonmainstream value system. Test givers are always in a position of power over test-takers and therefore can impose social and political ideologies on test-takers through standards of acceptable and unacceptable items. Tests promote the notion that answers to real-world problems have unambiguous right and wrong answers with no shades of gray. A corollary to the latter is that tests presume to reflect an appropriate core of common knowledge, such as the competencies reflected in the standards discussed earlier in this chapter. Logic would therefore dictate that the test-taker must buy in to such a system of beliefs in order to make the cut.

Language tests, some may argue, are less susceptible than general-knowledge tests to such sociopolitical overtones. The research process that undergirds the TOEFL goes to great lengths to screen out Western cultural bias, monocultural belief systems, and other potential agendas. Nevertheless, even the process of the selection of content alone for the TOEFL involves certain standards that may not be universal, and the very fact that the TOEFL is used as an absolute standard of English proficiency by most universities does not exonerate this particular standardized test.

As a language teacher, you might be able to exercise some influence in the ways tests are used and interpreted in your own milieu. If you are offered a variety of choices in standardized tests, you could choose a test that offers the least degree of cultural bias. Better yet, you might encourage the use of multiple measures of performance (varying item types, oral and written production, and other alternatives to traditional assessment) even though this might cost more money. Further, you and your co-teachers might help establish an institutional system of evaluation that places less emphasis on standardized tests and more emphasis on an ongoing process of formative evaluation. In so doing, you might be offering educational opportunity to a few more people who would otherwise be eliminated from contention.

EXERCISES

[Note: **(I)** Individual work; **(G)** Group or pair work; **(C)** Whole-class discussion.]

1. **(C)** Evaluate the standards-based assessment movement. What are its advantages and disadvantages? How might one compensate for potential disadvantages?
2. **(I)** Consult the California English Language Development Test websites listed. From what you can glean from that information, how would you evaluate the CELDT in terms of content validity, face validity, and authenticity?
3. **(I)** Consult the TESOL website on teacher standards (page 109). What would you say are a few minimal standards that language teachers should measure up to? In your own institutional context, or one that you are familiar with, how would you assess a teacher's attainment of those standards?
4. **(G/C)** Look at the four questions posed on page 111 regarding the consequences of standardized testing. In groups, one question for each group, or as a whole class, respond to those questions.
5. **(I)** Log on to the website for the National Center for Fair and Open Testing (see page 111). Report back to the class on the topics and issues sponsored by that organization.
6. **(C)** Explain the claim that "test-takers are political subjects in a political context" (page 113) and Shohamy's assertion that large-scale standardized testing is the "agent of cultural, social, political, educational, and ideological agendas." Draw up a list of DOs and DON'Ts through which teachers might overcome the potential political agendas in the use of standardized tests.

FOR YOUR FURTHER READING

Kohn, Alfie. 2000. *The case against standardized testing.* Westport, CT: Heinemann.

Kohn makes a strong case for the unfairness of the widespread exclusive use of standardized testing in elementary and secondary schools in the United States. His arguments may be appropriate for any other test-driven educational institution in any country.

Hamp-Lyons, Liz. (2001). Ethics, fairness(es), and developments in language testing. In Catherine Elder (Ed.), *Experimenting with uncertainty: Essays in honour of Alan Davies* (pp. 222–227). (Studies in Language Testing #11). Cambridge: Cambridge University Press.

The political and ethical issues in testing are capsulized in this brief article. The author addresses the question of what "fairness" is and how one might discern when a test is unfair.

CHAPTER 6

ASSESSING LISTENING

In earlier chapters, a number of foundational principles of language assessment were introduced. Concepts like practicality, reliability, validity, authenticity, washback, direct and indirect testing, and formative and summative assessment are by now part of your vocabulary. You have become acquainted with some tools for evaluating a "good" test, examined procedures for designing a classroom test, and explored the complex process of creating different kinds of test items. You have begun to absorb the intricate psychometric, educational, and political issues that intertwine in the world of standardized and standards-based testing.

Now our focus will shift away from the standardized testing juggernaut to the level at which you will usually work: the day-to-day classroom assessment of listening, speaking, reading, and writing. Since this is the level at which you will most frequently have the opportunity to apply principles of assessment, the next four chapters of this book will provide guidelines and hands-on practice in testing within a curriculum of English as a second or foreign language.

But first, two important caveats. The fact that the four language skills are discussed in four separate chapters should in no way predispose you to think that those skills are or should be assessed in isolation. Every TESOL professional (see *TBP,* Chapter 15) will tell you that the *integration of skills is of paramount importance in language learning.* Likewise, assessment is more authentic and provides more washback when skills are integrated. Nevertheless, the skills are treated independently here in order to identify principles, test types, tasks, and issues associated with each one.

Second, you may already have scanned through this book to look for a chapter on assessing grammar and vocabulary, or something in the way of a **focus on form** in assessment. The treatment of form-focused assessment is not relegated to a separate chapter here for a very distinct reason: there is no such thing as a test of grammar or vocabulary that does not invoke one or more of the separate skills of listening, speaking, reading, or writing! It's not uncommon to find little "grammar tests" and "vocabulary tests" in textbooks, and these may be perfectly useful instruments. But responses on these quizzes are usually written, with multiple-choice selection or fill-in-the-blank items. In this book, we treat the various linguistic forms (phonology, morphology, lexicon, grammar, and discourse) within the context of skill areas. That way, we don't perpetuate the myth that grammar and vocabulary and other linguistic forms can somehow be disassociated from a mode of performance.

OBSERVING THE PERFORMANCE OF THE FOUR SKILLS

Before focusing on listening itself, think about the two interacting concepts of **performance** and **observation**. All language users perform the acts of listening, speaking, reading, and writing. They of course rely on their underlying competence in order to accomplish these performances. When you propose to assess someone's ability in one or a combination of the four skills, you assess that person's *competence,* but you observe the person's *performance.* Sometimes the performance does not indicate true competence: a bad night's rest, illness, an emotional distraction, test anxiety, a memory block, or other student-related reliability factors could affect performance, thereby providing an unreliable measure of actual competence.

So, one important principle for assessing a learner's competence is to consider the fallibility of the results of a single performance, such as that produced in a test. As with any attempt at measurement, it is your obligation as a teacher to **triangulate** your measurements: consider at least two (or more) performances and/or contexts before drawing a conclusion. That could take the form of one or more of the following designs:

- several tests that are combined to form an assessment
- a single test with multiple test tasks to account for learning styles and performance variables
- in-class and extra-class graded work
- alternative forms of assessment (e.g., journal, portfolio, conference, observation, self-assessment, peer-assessment).

Multiple measures will always give you a more reliable and valid assessment than a single measure.

A second principle is one that we teachers often forget. We must rely as much as possible on *observable* performance in our assessments of students. Observable means being able to see or hear the performance of the learner (the senses of touch, taste, and smell don't apply very often to language testing!). What, then, is observable among the four skills of listening, speaking, reading, and writing? Table 6.1 offers an answer.

Isn't it interesting that in the case of the receptive skills, we can observe neither the process of performing nor a product? I can hear your argument already: "But I can *see* that she's listening because she's nodding her head and frowning and smiling and asking relevant questions." Well, you're not observing the listening performance; you're observing the *result* of the listening. You can no more observe listening (or reading) than you can see the wind blowing. The process of

Table 6.1. *Observable performance of the four skills*

	Can the teacher directly observe . . .	
	the process?	**the product?**
Listening	No	No
Speaking	Yes	No*
Reading	No	No
Writing	Yes	Yes

*Except in the case of an audio or video recording that preserves the output.

the listening performance itself is the *invisible, inaudible* process of internalizing meaning from the auditory signals being transmitted to the ear and brain. Or you may argue that the product of listening is a spoken or written response from the student that indicates correct (or incorrect) auditory processing. Again, the product of listening and reading is not the spoken or written response. The product is within the structure of the brain, and until teachers carry with them little portable MRI scanners to detect meaningful intake, it is impossible to observe the product. You observe only the result of the meaningful input in the form of spoken or written output, just as you observe the result of the wind by noticing trees waving back and forth.

The productive skills of speaking and writing allow us to hear and see the process as it is performed. Writing gives a permanent product in the form of a written piece. But unless you have recorded speech, there is no *permanent* observable product for speaking performance because all those words you just heard have vanished from your perception and (you hope) have been transformed into meaningful intake somewhere in your brain.

Receptive skills, then, are clearly the more enigmatic of the two modes of performance. You cannot observe the actual act of listening or reading, nor can you see or hear an actual product! You can observe learners only *while* they are listening or reading. The upshot is that all assessment of listening and reading must be made on the basis of observing the test-taker's speaking or writing (or nonverbal response), and not on the listening or reading itself. So, all assessment of receptive performance must be made by inference!

How discouraging, right? Well, not necessarily. We have developed reasonably good assessment tasks to make the necessary jump, through the process of inference, from unobservable reception to a conclusion about comprehension competence. And all this is a good reminder of the importance not just of triangulation but of the potential fragility of the assessment of comprehension ability. The actual performance is made "behind the scenes," and those of us who propose to make reliable assessments of receptive performance need to be on our guard.

THE IMPORTANCE OF LISTENING

Listening has often played second fiddle to its counterpart, speaking. In the standardized testing industry, a number of separate oral production tests are available (Test of Spoken English, Oral Proficiency Inventory, and PhonePass®, to name several that are described Chapter 7 of this book), but it is rare to find just a listening test. One reason for this emphasis is that listening is often implied as a component of speaking. How could you speak a language without also listening? In addition, the overtly observable nature of speaking renders it more empirically measurable then listening. But perhaps a deeper cause lies in universal biases toward speaking. A good speaker is often (unwisely) valued more highly than a good listener. To determine if someone is a proficient user of a language, people customarily ask, "Do you speak Spanish?" People rarely ask, "Do you *understand* and speak Spanish?"

Every teacher of language knows that one's oral production ability—other than monologues, speeches, reading aloud, and the like—is only as good as one's listening comprehension ability. But of even further impact is the likelihood that *input* in the aural-oral mode accounts for a large proportion of successful language acquisition. In a typical day, we do measurably more listening than speaking (with the exception of one or two of your friends who may be nonstop chatterboxes!). Whether in the workplace, educational, or home contexts, aural comprehension far outstrips oral production in quantifiable terms of time, number of words, effort, and attention.

We therefore need to pay close attention to listening as a mode of performance for assessment in the classroom. In this chapter, we will begin with basic principles and types of listening, then move to a survey of tasks that can be used to assess listening. (For a review of issues in teaching listening, you may want to read Chapter 16 of *TBP*.)

BASIC TYPES OF LISTENING

As with all effective tests, designing appropriate assessment tasks in listening begins with the specification of objectives, or criteria. Those objectives may be classified in terms of several types of listening performance. Think about what you do when you listen. Literally in nanoseconds, the following processes flash through your brain:

1. You recognize speech sounds and hold a temporary "imprint" of them in short-term memory.
2. You simultaneously determine the type of speech event (monologue, interpersonal dialogue, transactional dialogue) that is being processed and attend to its context (who the speaker is, location, purpose) and the content of the message.
3. You use (bottom-up) linguistic decoding skills and/or (top-down) background schemata to bring a plausible interpretation to the message, and assign a *literal* and *intended meaning* to the utterance.

4. In most cases (except for repetition tasks, which involve short-term memory only), you delete the exact linguistic form in which the message was originally received in favor of conceptually retaining important or relevant information in long-term memory.

Each of these stages represents a potential assessment objective:

- comprehending of surface structure elements such as phonemes, words, intonation, or a grammatical category
- understanding of pragmatic context
- determining meaning of auditory input
- developing the gist, a global or comprehensive understanding

From these stages we can derive four commonly identified types of listening performance, each of which comprises a category within which to consider assessment tasks and procedures.

1. *Intensive.* Listening for perception of the components (phonemes, words, intonation, discourse markers, etc.) of a larger stretch of language.
2. *Responsive.* Listening to a relatively short stretch of language (a greeting, question, command, comprehension check, etc.) in order to make an equally short response.
3. *Selective.* Processing stretches of discourse such as short monologues for several minutes in order to "scan" for certain information. The purpose of such performance is not necessarily to look for global or general meanings, but to be able to comprehend designated information in a context of longer stretches of spoken language (such as classroom directions from a teacher, TV or radio news items, or stories). Assessment tasks in selective listening could ask students, for example, to listen for names, numbers, a grammatical category, directions (in a map exercise), or certain facts and events.
4. *Extensive.* Listening to develop a top-down, global understanding of spoken language. Extensive performance ranges from listening to lengthy lectures to listening to a conversation and deriving a comprehensive message or purpose. Listening for the gist, for the main idea, and making inferences are all part of extensive listening.

For full comprehension, test-takers may at the extensive level need to invoke **interactive** skills (perhaps note-taking, questioning, discussion): listening that includes all four of the above types as test-takers actively participate in discussions, debates, conversations, role plays, and pair and group work. Their listening performance must be intricately integrated with speaking (and perhaps other skills) in the authentic give-and-take of communicative interchange. (Assessment of interactive skills will be embedded in Chapter 7.)

MICRO- AND MACROSKILLS OF LISTENING

A useful way of synthesizing the above two lists is to consider a finite number of micro- and macroskills implied in the performance of listening comprehension. Richards' (1983) list of microskills has proven useful in the domain of specifying objectives for learning and may be even more useful in forcing test makers to carefully identify specific assessment objectives. In the following box, the skills are subdivided into what I prefer to think of as microskills (attending to the smaller bits and chunks of language, in more of a bottom-up process) and macroskills (focusing on the larger elements involved in a top-down approach to a listening task). The micro- and macroskills provide 17 different objectives to assess in listening.

Micro- and macroskills of listening (adapted from Richards, 1983)

Microskills

1. Discriminate among the distinctive sounds of English.
2. Retain chunks of language of different lengths in short-term memory.
3. Recognize English stress patterns, words in stressed and unstressed positions, rhythmic structure, intonation contours, and their role in signaling information.
4. Recognize reduced forms of words.
5. Distinguish word boundaries, recognize a core of words, and interpret word order patterns and their significance.
6. Process speech at different rates of delivery.
7. Process speech containing pauses, errors, corrections, and other performance variables.
8. Recognize grammatical word classes (nouns, verbs, etc.), systems (e.g., tense, agreement, pluralization), patterns, rules, and elliptical forms.
9. Detect sentence constituents and distinguish between major and minor constituents.
10. Recognize that a particular meaning may be expressed in different grammatical forms.
11. Recognize cohesive devices in spoken discourse.

Macroskills

12. Recognize the communicative functions of utterances, according to situations, participants, goals.
13. Infer situations, participants, goals using real-world knowledge.
14. From events, ideas, and so on, described, predict outcomes, infer links and connections between events, deduce causes and effects, and detect such relations as main idea, supporting idea, new information, given information, generalization, and exemplification.

---

15. Distinguish between literal and implied meanings.
16. Use facial, kinesic, body language, and other nonverbal clues to decipher meanings.
17. Develop and use a battery of listening strategies, such as detecting key words, guessing the meaning of words from context, appealing for help, and signaling comprehension or lack thereof.

Implied in the taxonomy above is a notion of what makes many aspects of listening difficult, or why listening is not simply a linear process of recording strings of language as they are transmitted into our brains. Developing a sense of which aspects of listening performance are predictably difficult will help you to challenge your students appropriately and to assign weights to items. Consider the following list of what makes listening difficult (adapted from Richards, 1983; Ur, 1984; Dunkel, 1991):

1. *Clustering:* attending to appropriate "chunks" of language—phrases, clauses, constituents
2. *Redundancy:* recognizing the kinds of repetitions, rephrasing, elaborations, and insertions that unrehearsed spoken language often contains, and benefiting from that recognition
3. *Reduced forms:* understanding the reduced forms that may not have been a part of an English learner's past learning experiences in classes where only formal "textbook" language has been presented
4. *Performance variables:* being able to "weed out" hesitations, false starts, pauses, and corrections in natural speech
5. *Colloquial language:* comprehending idioms, slang, reduced forms, shared cultural knowledge
6. *Rate of delivery:* keeping up with the speed of delivery, processing automatically as the speaker continues
7. *Stress, rhythm, and intonation:* correctly understanding prosodic elements of spoken language, which is almost always much more difficult than understanding the smaller phonological bits and pieces
8. *Interaction:* managing the interactive flow of language from listening to speaking to listening, etc.

DESIGNING ASSESSMENT TASKS: INTENSIVE LISTENING

Once you have determined objectives, your next step is to design the tasks, including making decisions about how you will elicit performance and how you will expect the test-taker to respond. We will look at tasks that range from intensive listening performance, such as minimal phonemic pair recognition, to extensive comprehension of language in communicative contexts. The focus in this section is on the microskills of intensive listening.

Recognizing Phonological and Morphological Elements

A typical form of intensive listening at this level is the assessment of recognition of phonological and morphological elements of language. A classic test task gives a spoken stimulus and asks test-takers to identify the stimulus from two or more choices, as in the following two examples:

Phonemic pair, consonants

Test-takers hear:	He's from California.
Test-takers read:	(a) He's from California.
	(b) She's from California.

Phonemic pair, vowels

Test-takers hear:	Is he living?
Test-takers read:	(a) Is he leaving?
	(b) Is he living?

In both cases above, minimal phonemic distinctions are the target. If you are testing recognition of morphology, you can use the same format:

Morphological pair, -ed ending

Test-takers hear:	I missed you very much.
Test-takers read:	(a) I missed you very much.
	(b) I miss you very much.

Hearing the past tense morpheme in this sentence challenges even advanced learners, especially if no context is provided. Stressed and unstressed words may also be tested with the same rubric. In the following example, the reduced form (contraction) of *can not* is tested:

Stress pattern in can't

Test-takers hear:	My girlfriend can't go to the party.
Test-takers read:	(a) My girlfriend can't go to the party.
	(b) My girlfriend can go to the party.

Because they are decontextualized, these kinds of tasks leave something to be desired in their authenticity. But they are a step better than items that simply provide a one-word stimulus:

One-word stimulus

Test-takers hear:	vine
Test-takers read:	(a) vine
	(b) wine

Paraphrase Recognition

The next step up on the scale of listening comprehension microskills is words, phrases, and sentences, which are frequently assessed by providing a stimulus sentence and asking the test-taker to choose the correct paraphrase from a number of choices.

Sentence paraphrase

Test-takers hear:	Hellow, my name's Keiko. I come from Japan.
Test-takers read:	(a) Keiko is comfortable in Japan.
	(b) Keiko wants to come to Japan.
	(c) Keiko is Japanese.
	(d) Keiko likes Japan.

In the above item, the idiomatic *come from* is the phrase being tested. To add a little context, a conversation can be the stimulus task to which test-takers must respond with the correct paraphrase:

Dialogue paraphrase

Test-takers hear:	Man:	Hi, Maria, my name's George.
	Woman:	Nice to meet you, George. Are you American?
	Man:	No, I'm Canadian.
Test-takers read:		(a) George lives in the United States.
		(b) George is American.
		(c) George comes from Canada.
		(d) Maria is Canadian.

Here, the criterion is recognition of the adjective form used to indicate country of origin: Canadian, American, Brazilian, Italian, etc.

DESIGNING ASSESSMENT TASKS: RESPONSIVE LISTENING

A question-and-answer format can provide some interactivity in these lower-end listening tasks. The test-taker's response is the appropriate answer to a question.

Appropriate response to a question

Test-takers hear:	How much time did you take to do your homework?
Test-takers read:	(a) In about an hour.
	(b) About an hour.
	(c) About $10.
	(d) Yes, I did.

The objective of this item is recognition of the *wh*-question *how much* and its appropriate response. Distractors are chosen to represent common learner errors: (a) responding to *how much* vs. *how much longer;* (c) confusing *how much* in reference to time vs. the more frequent reference to money; (d) confusing a *wh*-question with a *yes/no* question.

None of the tasks so far discussed have to be framed in a multiple-choice format. They can be offered in a more open-ended framework in which test-takers write or speak the response. The above item would then look like this:

Open-ended response to a question

Test-takers hear:	How much time did you take to do your homework?
Test-takers write or speak:	_____.

If open-ended response formats gain a small amount of authenticity and creativity, they of course suffer some in their practicality, as teachers must then read students' responses and judge their appropriateness, which takes time.

DESIGNING ASSESSMENT TASKS: SELECTIVE LISTENING

A third type of listening performance is **selective** listening, in which the test-taker listens to a limited quantity of aural input and must discern within it some specific information. A number of techniques have been used that require selective listening.

Listening Cloze

Listening cloze tasks (sometimes called **cloze dictations** or **partial dictations**) require the test-taker to listen to a story, monologue, or conversation and simultaneously read the written text in which selected words or phrases have been deleted. **Cloze procedure** is most commonly associated with reading only (see Chapter 9). In its generic form, the test consists of a passage in which every *n*th word (typically every seventh word) is deleted and the test-taker is asked to supply an appropriate word. In a listening cloze task, test-takers see a transcript of the passage that they are listening to and fill in the blanks with the words or phrases that they hear.

One potential weakness of listening cloze techniques is that they may simply become reading comprehension tasks. Test-takers who are asked to listen to a story with periodic deletions in the written version may not need to listen at all, yet may still be able to respond with the appropriate word or phrase. You can guard against this eventuality if the blanks are items with high information load that cannot be easily predicted simply by reading the passage. In the example below (adapted from Bailey, 1998, p. 16), such a shortcoming was avoided by focusing only on the criterion of numbers. Test-takers hear an announcement from an airline agent and see the transcript with the underlined words deleted:

Listening cloze

Test-takers hear:
Ladies and gentlemen, I now have some connecting gate information for those of you making connections to other flights out of San Francisco.

Flight *seven-oh-six* to Portland will depart from gate *seventy-three* at *nine-thirty* P.M.
Flight *ten-forty-five* to Reno will depart at *nine-fifty* P.M. from gate *seventeen*.
Flight *four-forty* to Monterey will depart at *nine-thirty-five* P.M. from gate *sixty*.
And flight *sixteen-oh-three* to Sacramento will depart from gate *nineteen* at *ten-fifteen* P.M.

Test-takers write the missing words or phrases in the blanks.

Other listening cloze tasks may focus on a grammatical category such as verb tenses, articles, two-word verbs, prepositions, or transition words/phrases. Notice two important structural differences between listening cloze tasks and standard reading cloze. In a listening cloze, deletions are governed by the objective of the test, not by mathematical deletion of every *n*th word; and more than one word may be deleted, as in the above example.

Listening cloze tasks should normally use an **exact word** method of scoring, in which you accept as a correct response only the actual word or phrase that was spoken and consider other **appropriate words** as incorrect. (See Chapter 8 for further discussion of these two methods.) Such stringency is warranted; your objective is, after all, to test listening comprehension, not grammatical or lexical expectancies.

Information Transfer

Selective listening can also be assessed through an **information transfer** technique in which aurally processed information must be transferred to a visual representation, such as labeling a diagram, identifying an element in a picture, completing a form, or showing routes on a map.

At the lower end of the scale of linguistic complexity, simple **picture-cued** items are sometimes efficient rubrics for assessing certain selected information. Consider the following item:

Information transfer: multiple-picture–cued selection

Test-takers hear:

Choose the correct picture. In my back yard I have a bird feeder. Yesterday, there were two birds and a squirrel fighting for the last few seeds in the bird feeder. The squirrel was on top of the bird feeder while the larger bird sat at the bottom of the feeder screeching at the squirrel. The smaller bird was flying around the squirrel, trying to scare it away.

Test-takers see:

The preceding example illustrates the need for test-takers to focus on just the relevant information. The objective of this task is to test prepositions and prepositional phrases of location (*at the bottom, on top of, around,* along with *larger, smaller*), so other words and phrases such as *back yard, yesterday, last few seeds,* and *scare away* are supplied only as context and need not be tested. (The task also presupposes, of course, that test-takers are able to identify the difference between a bird and a squirrel!)

In another genre of picture-cued tasks, a number of people and/or actions are presented in one picture, such as a group of people at a party. Assuming that all the items, people, and actions are clearly depicted and understood by the test-taker, assessment may take the form of

- questions: "Is the tall man near the door talking to a short woman?"
- true/false: "The woman wearing a red skirt is watching TV."
- identification: "Point to the person who is standing behind the lamp." "Draw a circle around the person to the left of the couch."

In a third picture-cued option used by the Test of English for International Communication (TOEIC®), one single photograph is presented to the test-taker, who then hears four different statements and must choose one of the four to describe the photograph. Here is an example.

Information transfer: single-picture–cued verbal multiple-choice

Test-takers see:	a photograph of a woman in a laboratory setting, with no glasses on, squinting through a microscope with her right eye, and with her left eye closed.
Test-takers hear:	(a) She's speaking into a microphone. (b) She's putting on her glasses. (c) She has both eyes open. (d) She's using a microscope.

Information transfer tasks may reflect greater authenticity by using charts, maps, grids, timetables, and other artifacts of daily life. In the example below, test-takers hear a student's daily schedule, and the task is to fill in the partially completed weekly calendar.

Information transfer: chart-filling

Test-takers hear:

Now you will hear information about Lucy's daily schedule. The information will be given twice. The first time just listen carefully. The second time, there will be a pause after each sentence. Fill in Lucy's blank daily schedule with the correct information. The example has already been filled in.

You will hear: Lucy gets up at eight o'clock every morning except on weekends.

You will fill in the schedule to provide the information.

Now listen to the information about Lucy's schedule. Remember, you will first hear all the sentences; then you will hear each sentence separately with time to fill in your chart.

Lucy gets up at 8:00 every morning except on weekends. She has English on Monday, Wednesday, and Friday at ten o'clock. She has History on Tuesdays and Thursdays at two o'clock. She takes Chemistry on Monday from two o'clock to six o'clock. She plays tennis on weekends at four o'clock. She eats lunch at twelve o'clock every day except Saturday and Sunday.

Now listen a second time. There will be a pause after each sentence to give you time to fill in the chart. (Lucy's schedule is repeated with a pause after each sentence).

Test-takers see the following weekly calendar grid:

	Monday	Tuesday	Wednesday	Thursday	Friday	Weekends
8:00	get up	get up	get up	get up	get up	
10:00						
12:00						
2:00						
4:00						
6:00						

Such chart-filling tasks are good examples of aural **scanning** strategies. A listener must discern from a number of pieces of information which pieces are relevant. In the above example, virtually all of the stimuli are relevant, and very few words can be ignored. In other tasks, however, much more information might be presented than is needed (as in the birdfeeder item on page 127), forcing the test-taker to select the correct bits and pieces necessary to complete a task.

Chart-filling tasks increase in difficulty as the linguistic stimulus material becomes more complex. In one task described by Ur (1984, pp. 108–112), test-takers listen to a very long description of animals in various cages in a zoo. While they listen, they can look at a map of the layout of the zoo with unlabeled cages. Their task is to fill in the correct animal in each cage, but the complexity of the language used to describe the positions of cages and their inhabitants is very challenging. Similarly, Hughes (1989, p. 138) described a map-marking task in which test-takers must process around 250 words of colloquial language in order to complete the tasks of identifying names, positions, and directions in a car accident scenario on a city street.

Sentence Repetition

The task of simply repeating a sentence or a partial sentence, or **sentence repetition,** is also used as an assessment of listening comprehension. As in a dictation (discussed below), the test-taker must retain a stretch of language long enough to reproduce it, and then must respond with an oral repetition of that stimulus. Incorrect listening comprehension, whether at the phonemic or discourse level, may be manifested in the correctness of the repetition. A miscue in repetition is scored as a miscue in listening. In the case of somewhat longer sentences, one could argue that the ability to recognize and retain chunks of language as well as threads of meaning might be assessed through repetition. In Chapter 7, we will look closely at PhonePass, a commercially produced test that relies largely on sentence repetition to assess both oral production and listening comprehension.

Sentence repetition is far from a flawless listening assessment task. Buck (2001, p. 79) noted that such tasks "are not just tests of listening, but tests of general oral skills." Further, this task may test only recognition of sounds, and it can easily be contaminated by lack of short-term memory ability, thus invalidating it as an assessment of comprehension alone. And the teacher may never be able to distinguish a listening comprehension error from an oral production error. Therefore, sentence repetition tasks should be used with caution.

DESIGNING ASSESSMENT TASKS: EXTENSIVE LISTENING

Drawing a clear distinction between any two of the categories of listening referred to here is problematic, but perhaps the fuzziest division is between selective and extensive listening. As we gradually move along the continuum from smaller to larger stretches of language, and from micro- to macroskills of listening, the probability of using more extensive listening tasks increases. Some important questions about designing assessments at this level emerge.

1. Can listening performance be distinguished from cognitive processing factors such as memory, associations, storage, and recall?
2. As assessment procedures become more communicative, does the task take into account test-takers' ability to use grammatical expectancies, lexical collocations, semantic interpretations, and pragmatic competence?
3. Are test tasks themselves correspondingly content valid and authentic—that is, do they mirror real-world language and context?
4. As assessment tasks become more and more open-ended, they more closely resemble pedagogical tasks, which leads one to ask what the difference is between assessment and teaching tasks. The answer is *scoring:* the former imply specified scoring procedures, while the latter do not.

We will try to address these questions as we look at a number of extensive or quasi-extensive listening comprehension tasks.

Dictation

Dictation is a widely researched genre of assessing listening comprehension. In a dictation, test-takers hear a passage, typically of 50 to 100 words, recited three times: first, at normal speed; then, with long pauses between phrases or natural word groups, during which time test-takers write down what they have just heard; and finally, at normal speed once more so they can check their work and proofread. Here is a sample dictation at the intermediate level of English.

Dictation

First reading (natural speed, no pauses, test-takers listen for gist):

The state of California has many geographical areas. On the western side is the Pacific Ocean with its beaches and sea life. The central part of the state is a large fertile valley. The southeast has a hot desert, and north and west have beautiful mountains and forests. Southern California is a large urban area populated by millions of people.

Second reading (slowed speed, pause at each // break, test-takers write):

The state of California // has many geographical areas. // On the western side // is the Pacific Ocean // with its beaches and sea life. // The central part of the state // is a large fertile valley. // The southeast has a hot desert, // and north and west // have beautiful mountains and forests. // Southern California // is a large urban area // populated by millions of people.

Third reading (natural speed, test-takers check their work).

Dictations have been used as assessment tools for decades. Some readers still cringe at the thought of having to render a correctly spelled, verbatim version of a paragraph or story recited by the teacher. Until research on integrative testing was published (see Oller, 1971), dictations were thought to be not much more than glorified spelling tests. However, the required integration of listening and writing in a dictation, along with its presupposed knowledge of grammatical and discourse expectancies, brought this technique back into vogue. Hughes (1989), Cohen (1994), Bailey (1998), and Buck (2001) all defend the plausibility of dictation as an integrative test that requires some sophistication in the language in order to process and write down all segments correctly. Thus, I include dictation here under the rubric of extensive tasks, although I am more comfortable with labeling it quasi-extensive.

The difficulty of a dictation task can be easily manipulated by the length of the word groups (or **bursts,** as they are technically called), the length of the pauses, the speed at which the text is read, and the complexity of the discourse, grammar, and vocabulary used in the passage.

Scoring is another matter. Depending on your context and purpose in administering a dictation, you will need to decide on scoring criteria for several possible kinds of errors:

- spelling error only, but the word appears to have been heard correctly
- spelling and/or obvious misrepresentation of a word, illegible word
- grammatical error (For example, test-taker hears *I can't do it*, writes *I can do it*.)
- skipped word or phrase
- permutation of words
- additional words not in the original
- replacement of a word with an appropriate synonym

Determining the weight of each of these errors is a highly idiosyncratic choice; specialists disagree almost more than they agree on the importance of the above categories. They do agree (Buck, 2001) that a dictation is not a spelling test, and that the first item in the list above should not be considered an error. They also suggest that point systems be kept simple (for maintaining practicality and reliability) and that a deductible scoring method, in which points are subtracted from a hypothetical total, is usually effective.

Dictation seems to provide a reasonably valid method for integrating listening and writing skills and for tapping into the cohesive elements of language implied in short passages. However, a word of caution lest you assume that dictation provides a quick and easy method of assessing extensive listening comprehension. If the bursts in a dictation are relatively long (more than five-word segments), this method places a certain amount of load on memory and processing of meaning (Buck, 2001, p. 78). But only a moderate degree of cognitive processing is required, and claiming that dictation fully assesses the ability to comprehend pragmatic or illocutionary elements of language, context, inference, or semantics may be going too far. Finally, one can easily question the authenticity of dictation: it is rare in the real world for people to write down more than a few chunks of information (addresses, phone numbers, grocery lists, directions, for example) at a time.

Despite these disadvantages, the practicality of the administration of dictations, a moderate degree of reliability in a well-established scoring system, and a strong correspondence to other language abilities speaks well for the inclusion of dictation among the possibilities for assessing extensive (or quasi-extensive) listening comprehension.

Communicative Stimulus-Response Tasks

Another—and more authentic—example of extensive listening is found in a popular genre of assessment task in which the test-taker is presented with a stimulus monologue or conversation and then is asked to respond to a set of comprehension questions. Such tasks (as you saw in Chapter 4 in the discussion of standardized testing) are commonly used in commercially produced proficiency tests. The monologues, lectures, and brief conversations used in such tasks are sometimes a little contrived, and certainly the subsequent multiple-choice questions don't mirror communicative, real-life situations. But with some care and creativity, one can create reasonably authentic stimuli, and in some rare cases the response mode (as shown in one example below) actually approaches complete authenticity. Here is a typical example of such a task.

Dialogue and multiple-choice comprehension items

Test-takers hear:

Directions: Now you will hear a conversation between Lynn and her doctor. You will hear the conversation two times. After you hear the conversation the second time, choose the correct answer for questions 11–15 below. Mark your answers on the answer sheet provided.

Doctor:	Good morning, Lynn. What's the problem?
Lynn:	Well, you see, I have a terrible headache, my nose is running, and I'm really dizzy.
Doctor:	Okay. Anything else?
Lynn:	I've been coughing, I think I have a fever, and my stomach aches.
Doctor:	I see. When did this start?
Lynn:	Well, let's see, I went to the lake last weekend, and after I returned home I started sneezing.
Doctor:	Hmm. You must have the flu. You should get lots of rest, drink hot beverages, and stay warm. Do you follow me?
Lynn:	Well, uh, yeah, but . . . shouldn't I take some medicine?
Doctor:	Sleep and rest are as good as medicine when you have the flu.
Lynn:	Okay, thanks, Dr. Brown.

Test-takers read:

11. What is Lynn's problem?
    (A) She feels horrible.
    (B) She ran too fast at the lake.
    (C) She's been drinking too many hot beverages.

12. When did Lynn's problem start?
    (A) When she saw her doctor.
    (B) Before she went to the lake.
    (C) After she came home from the lake.

13. The doctor said that Lynn _____.
    (A) flew to the lake last weekend
    (B) must not get the flu
    (C) probably has the flu

---

14. The doctor told Lynn _____.
    (A) to rest
    (B) to follow him
    (C) to take some medicine

15. According to Dr. Brown, sleep and rest are _____ medicine when you have the flu.
    (A) more effective than
    (B) as effective as
    (C) less effective than

Does this meet the criterion of authenticity? If you want to be painfully fussy, you might object that it is rare in the real world to eavesdrop on someone else's doctor–patient conversation. Nevertheless, the conversation itself is relatively authentic; we all have doctor–patient exchanges like this. Equally authentic, if you add a grain of salt, are monologues, lecturettes, and news stories, all of which are commonly utilized as listening stimuli to be followed by comprehension questions aimed at assessing certain objectives that are built into the stimulus.

Is the task itself (of responding to multiple-choice questions) authentic? It's plausible to assert that *any task* of this kind following a one-way listening to a conversation is artificial: we simply don't often encounter little quizzes about conversations we've heard (unless it's your parent, spouse, or best friend who wants to get in on the latest gossip!). The questions posed above, with the possible exception of #14, are unlikely to appear in a lifetime of doctor visits. Yet the ability to respond correctly to such items can be construct validated as an appropriate measure of field-independent listening skills: the ability to remember certain details from a conversation. (As an aside here, many highly proficient native speakers of English might miss some of the above questions if they heard the conversation only once and if they had no visual access to the items until after the conversation was done!)

To compensate for the potential inauthenticity of post-stimulus comprehension questions, you might, with a little creativity, be able to find contexts where questions that probe understanding are more appropriate. Consider the following situation:

Dialogue and authentic questions on details

Test-takers hear:
You will hear a conversation between a detective and a man. The tape will play the conversation twice. After you hear the conversation a second time, choose the correct answers on your test sheet.

Detective:	Where were you last night at eleven P.M., the time of the murder?
Man:	Uh, let's see, well, I was just starting to see a movie.
Detective:	Did you go alone?
Man:	No, uh, well, I was with my friend, uh, Bill. Yeah, I was with Bill.

Detective: What did you do after that?
Man: We went out to dinner, then I dropped her off at her place.
Detective: Then you went home?
Man: Yeah.
Detective: When did you get home?
Man: A little before midnight.

Test-takers read:

7. Where was the man at 11:00 P.M.?
   (A) In a restaurant.
   (B) In a theater.
   (C) At home.

8. Was he with someone?
   (A) He was alone.
   (B) He was with his wife.
   (C) He was with a friend.

9. Then what did he do?
   (A) He ate out.
   (B) He made dinner.
   (C) He went home.

10. When did he get home?
    (A) About 11:00.
    (B) Almost 12:00.
    (C) Right after the movie.

11. The man is probably lying because (name two clues):
    1. _____
    2. _____

   In this case, test-takers are brought into a little scene in a crime story. The questions following are plausible questions that might be asked to review fact and fiction in the conversation. Question #11, of course, provides an extra shot of reality: the test-taker must name the probable lies told by the man (he referred to Bill as "her"; he saw a movie and ate dinner in the space of one hour), which requires the process of inference.

Authentic Listening Tasks

Ideally, the language assessment field would have a stockpile of listening test types that are cognitively demanding, communicative, and authentic, not to mention interactive by means of an integration with speaking. However, the nature of a test as a *sample* of performance and a set of tasks with limited time frames implies an equally limited capacity to mirror all the real-world contexts of listening performance. "There is no such thing as a communicative test," stated Buck (2001, p. 92). "Every test requires some components of communicative language ability, and no test covers them all. Similarly, with the notion of authenticity, every task shares some characteristics with target-language tasks, and no test is completely authentic."

Beyond the rubrics of intensive, responsive, selective, and quasi-extensive communicative contexts described above, can we assess aural comprehension in a truly communicative context? Can we, at this end of the range of listening tasks, ascertain from test-takers that they have processed the main idea(s) of a lecture, the gist of a story, the pragmatics of a conversation, or the unspoken inferential data present in most authentic aural input? Can we assess a test-taker's comprehension of humor, idiom, and metaphor? The answer is a cautious yes, but not without some concessions to practicality. And the answer is a more certain yes if we take the liberty of stretching the concept of assessment to extend beyond tests and into a broader framework of alternatives. Here are some possibilities.

1. Note-taking. In the academic world, classroom lectures by professors are common features of a non-native English-user's experience. One form of a midterm examination at the American Language Institute at San Francisco State University (Kahn, 2002) uses a 15-minute lecture as a stimulus. One among several response formats includes note-taking by the test-takers. These notes are evaluated by the teacher on a 30-point system, as follows:

Scoring system for lecture notes

0–15 points
Visual representation: Are your notes clear and easy to read? Can you easily find and retrieve information from them? Do you use the space on the paper to visually represent ideas? Do you use indentation, headers, numbers, etc.?

0–10 points
Accuracy: Do you accurately indicate main ideas from lectures? Do you note important details and supporting information and examples? Do you leave out unimportant information and tangents?

0–5 points
Symbols and abbreviations: Do you use symbols and abbreviations as much as possible to save time? Do you avoid writing out whole words, and do you avoid writing down every single word the lecturer says?

The process of scoring is time consuming (a loss of practicality), and because of the subjectivity of the point system, it lacks some reliability. But the gain is in offering students an authentic task that mirrors exactly what they have been focusing on in the classroom. The notes become an indirect but arguably valid form of assessing global listening comprehension. The task fulfills the criteria of cognitive demand, communicative language, and authenticity.

2. *Editing.* Another authentic task provides both a written and a spoken stimulus, and requires the test-taker to listen for discrepancies. Scoring achieves relatively high reliability as there are usually a small number of specific differences that must be identified. Here is the way the task proceeds.

Editing a written version of an aural stimulus

> *Test-takers read:* the written stimulus material (a news report, an email from a friend, notes from a lecture, or an editorial in a newspaper).
>
> *Test-takers hear:* a spoken version of the stimulus that deviates, in a finite number of facts or opinions, from the original written form.
>
> *Test-takers mark:* the written stimulus by circling any words, phrases, facts, or opinions that show a discrepancy between the two versions.

One potentially interesting set of stimuli for such a task is the description of a political scandal first from a newspaper with a political bias, and then from a radio broadcast from an "alternative" news station. Test-takers are not only forced to listen carefully to differences but are subtly informed about biases in the news.

3. *Interpretive tasks.* One of the intensive listening tasks described above was paraphrasing a story or conversation. An interpretive task extends the stimulus material to a longer stretch of discourse and forces the test-taker to infer a response. Potential stimuli include

- song lyrics,
- [recited] poetry,
- radio/television news reports, and
- an oral account of an experience.

Test-takers are then directed to interpret the stimulus by answering a few questions (in open-ended form). Questions might be:

- "Why was the singer feeling sad?"
- "What events might have led up to the reciting of this poem?"
- "What do you think the political activists might do next, and why?"
- "What do you think the storyteller felt about the mysterious disappearance of her necklace?"

This kind of task moves us away from what might traditionally be considered a test toward an informal assessment, or possibly even a pedagogical technique or activity. But the task conforms to certain time limitations, and the questions can be quite specific, even though they ask the test-taker to use inference. While reliable scoring may be an issue (there may be more than one correct interpretation), the authenticity of the interaction in this task and potential washback to the student surely give it some prominence among communicative assessment procedures.

4. Retelling. In a related task, test-takers listen to a story or news event and simply retell it, or summarize it, either orally (on an audiotape) or in writing. In so doing, test-takers must identify the gist, main idea, purpose, supporting points, and/or conclusion to show full comprehension. Scoring is partially predetermined by specifying a minimum number of elements that must appear in the retelling. Again reliability may suffer, and the time and effort needed to read and evaluate the response lowers practicality. Validity, cognitive processing, communicative ability, and authenticity are all well incorporated into the task.

§   §   §   §   §

A fifth category of listening comprehension was hinted at earlier in the chapter: **interactive** listening. Because such interaction presupposes a process of *speaking* in concert with listening, the interactive nature of listening will be addressed in the next chapter. Don't forget that a significant proportion of real-world listening performance is interactive. With the exception of media input, speeches, lectures, and eavesdropping, many of our listening efforts are directed toward a two-way process of speaking and listening in face-to-face conversations.

EXERCISES

[Note: **(I)** Individual work; **(G)** Group or pair work; **(C)** Whole-class discussion.]

1. **(C)** In Table 6.1 on page 118, it is noted that one cannot actually observe listening and reading performance. Do you agree? And do you agree that there isn't even a product to observe for speaking, listening, and reading? How, then, can one infer the competence of a test-taker to speak, listen, and read a language?
2. **(C)** Given that we spend much more time listening than we do speaking, why are there many more tests of speaking than listening?
3. **(G)** Look at the list of micro- and macroskills of listening on pages 121–122. In pairs, each assigned to a different skill (or two), brainstorm some tasks that assess those skills. Present your findings to the rest of the class.
4. **(G)** Eight characteristics of listening that make listening "difficult" are listed on page 122. In pairs, each assigned to an assessment task itemized in this chapter, decide which of the eight factors, in order of significance, contribute to the potential difficulty of the items. Report back to the class.
5. **(G)** Divide the basic types of listening among groups or pairs, one type for each. Look at the sample assessment techniques provided and evaluate them

according the five principles (practicality, reliability, validity [face and content], authenticity, and washback). Present your critique to the rest of the class.

6. **(G)** In the same groups as in #5 above and with the same type of listening, design some other item types, different from the one(s) provided here, that assess the same type of listening performance.

7. **(G)** With a linguistic objective assigned to each pair or group, construct a listening cloze test for two-word verbs, verb tenses, prepositions, transition words, articles, and/or other grammatical categories.

8. **(I/C)** On page 131, you are reminded that dictations are considered by some assessment specialists to be integrative (requiring the integration of listening, writing, reading [proofreading], along with attendant grammatical and discourse abilities). Is this a valid claim? Justify your response.

9. **(I/C)** On page 136 is Buck's claim that "no test is completely authentic." Discuss the extent to which you agree or disagree with this assertion and justify your own conclusion.

FOR YOUR FURTHER READING

Buck, Gary. (2001). *Assessing listening.* Cambridge: Cambridge University Press.

One of a series of very useful reference books on assessing specific skill areas published by Cambridge University Press, this one gives an overview of research and pedagogy on listening comprehension and demonstrates many different assessment procedures in common use.

Richards, Jack C. (1983). Listening comprehension: Approach, design, procedure. *TESOL Quarterly, 17,* 219–239.

Even though Richards published this article in 1983, it still provides a standard backdrop for teaching listening skills. While formal assessment is not directly addressed, informal assessment is implied in its pedagogical focus on practical classroom techniques.

Mendelsohn, David J. (1998). Teaching listening. *Annual Review of Applied Linguistics, 18,* 81–101.

Mendelsohn's overview of research on teaching listening provides an excellent foundation for understanding assessment tasks. He focuses on a strategy-based approach to teaching listening and adds an annotated bibliography of professional resource books.

CHAPTER 7

ASSESSING SPEAKING

From a pragmatic view of language performance, listening and speaking are almost always closely interrelated. While it is possible to isolate some listening performance types (see Chapter 6), it is very difficult to isolate oral production tasks that do not directly involve the interaction of aural comprehension. Only in limited contexts of speaking (monologues, speeches, or telling a story and reading aloud) can we assess oral language without the aural participation of an interlocutor.

While speaking is a productive skill that can be directly and empirically observed, those observations are invariably colored by the accuracy and effectiveness of a test-taker's listening skill, which necessarily compromises the reliability and validity of an oral production test. How do you know for certain that a speaking score is exclusively a measure of oral production without the potentially frequent clarifications of an interlocutor? This interaction of speaking and listening challenges the designer of an oral production test to tease apart, as much as possible, the factors accounted for by aural intake.

Another challenge is the design of elicitation techniques. Because most speaking is the product of creative construction of linguistic strings, the speaker makes choices of lexicon, structure, and discourse. If your goal is to have test-takers demonstrate certain spoken grammatical categories, for example, the stimulus you design must elicit those grammatical categories in ways that prohibit the test-taker from avoiding or paraphrasing and thereby dodging production of the target form.

As tasks become more and more open ended, the freedom of choice given to test-takers creates a challenge in scoring procedures. In receptive performance, the elicitation stimulus can be structured to anticipate predetermined responses and only those responses. In productive performance, the oral or written stimulus must be specific enough to elicit output within an expected range of performance such that scoring or rating procedures apply appropriately. For example, in a picture-series task, the objective of which is to elicit a story in a sequence of events, test-takers could opt for a variety of plausible ways to tell the story, all of which might be equally accurate. How can such disparate responses be evaluated? One solution is to assign not one but several scores for each response, each score representing one of several traits (pronunciation, fluency, vocabulary use, grammar, comprehensibility, etc.).

All of these issues will be addressed in this chapter as we review types of spoken language and micro- and macroskills of speaking, then outline numerous tasks for assessing speaking.

BASIC TYPES OF SPEAKING

In Chapter 6, we cited four categories of listening performance assessment tasks. A similar taxonomy emerges for oral production.

1. Imitative. At one end of a continuum of types of speaking performance is the ability to simply parrot back (**imitate**) a word or phrase or possibly a sentence. While this is a purely phonetic level of oral production, a number of prosodic, lexical, and grammatical properties of language may be included in the criterion performance. We are interested only in what is traditionally labeled "pronunciation"; no inferences are made about the test-taker's ability to understand or convey meaning or to participate in an interactive conversation. The only role of listening here is in the short-term storage of a prompt, just long enough to allow the speaker to retain the short stretch of language that must be imitated.

2. Intensive. A second type of speaking frequently employed in assessment contexts is the production of short stretches of oral language designed to demonstrate competence in a narrow band of grammatical, phrasal, lexical, or phonological relationships (such as prosodic elements—intonation, stress, rhythm, juncture). The speaker must be aware of semantic properties in order to be able to respond, but interaction with an interlocutor or test administrator is minimal at best. Examples of **intensive** assessment tasks include directed response tasks, reading aloud, sentence and dialogue completion; limited picture-cued tasks including simple sequences; and translation up to the simple sentence level.

3. Responsive. **Responsive** assessment tasks include interaction and test comprehension but at the somewhat limited level of very short conversations, standard greetings and small talk, simple requests and comments, and the like. The stimulus is almost always a spoken prompt (in order to preserve authenticity), with perhaps only one or two follow-up questions or retorts:

A. Mary: Excuse me, do you have the time?
     Doug: Yeah. Nine-fifteen.

B. T: What is the most urgent environmental problem today?
     S: I would say massive deforestation.

C. Jeff: Hey, Stef, how's it going?
     Stef: Not bad, and yourself?
     Jeff: I'm good.
     Stef: Cool. Okay, gotta go.

4. *Interactive.* The difference between responsive and interactive speaking is in the length and complexity of the interaction, which sometimes includes multiple exchanges and/or multiple participants. Interaction can take the two forms of **transactional** language, which has the purpose of exchanging specific information, or **interpersonal** exchanges, which have the purpose of maintaining social relationships. (In the three dialogues cited above, **A** and **B** were transactional, and **C** was interpersonal.) In interpersonal exchanges, oral production can become pragmatically complex with the need to speak in a casual register and use colloquial language, ellipsis, slang, humor, and other sociolinguistic conventions.

5. *Extensive (monologue).* Extensive oral production tasks include speeches, oral presentations, and story-telling, during which the opportunity for oral interaction from listeners is either highly limited (perhaps to nonverbal responses) or ruled out altogether. Language style is frequently more deliberative (planning is involved) and formal for extensive tasks, but we cannot rule out certain informal monologues such as casually delivered speech (for example, my vacation in the mountains, a recipe for outstanding pasta primavera, recounting the plot of a novel or movie).

MICRO- AND MACROSKILLS OF SPEAKING

In Chapter 6, a list of listening micro- and macroskills enumerated the various components of listening that make up criteria for assessment. A similar list of speaking skills can be drawn up for the same purpose: to serve as a taxonomy of skills from which you will select one or several that will become the objective(s) of an assessment task. The microskills refer to producing the smaller chunks of language such as phonemes, morphemes, words, collocations, and phrasal units. The macroskills imply the speaker's focus on the larger elements: fluency, discourse, function, style, cohesion, nonverbal communication, and strategic options. The micro- and macroskills total roughly 16 different objectives to assess in speaking.

Micro- and macroskills of oral production

Microskills

1. Produce differences among English phonemes and allophonic variants.
2. Produce chunks of language of different lengths.
3. Produce English stress patterns, words in stressed and unstressed positions, rhythmic structure, and intonation contours.
4. Produce reduced forms of words and phrases.
5. Use an adequate number of lexical units (words) to accomplish pragmatic purposes.
6. Produce fluent speech at different rates of delivery.

7. Monitor one's own oral production and use various strategic devices—pauses, fillers, self-corrections, backtracking—to enhance the clarity of the message.

8. Use grammatical word classes (nouns, verbs, etc.), systems (e.g., tense, agreement, pluralization), word order, patterns, rules, and elliptical forms.

9. Produce speech in natural constituents: in appropriate phrases, pause groups, breath groups, and sentence constituents.

10. Express a particular meaning in different grammatical forms.

11. Use cohesive devices in spoken discourse.

Macroskills

12. Appropriately accomplish communicative functions according to situations, participants, and goals.

13. Use appropriate styles, registers, implicature, redundancies, pragmatic conventions, conversation rules, floor-keeping and -yielding, interrupting, and other sociolinguistic features in face-to-face conversations.

14. Convey links and connections between events and communicate such relations as focal and peripheral ideas, events and feelings, new information and given information, generalization and exemplification.

15. Convey facial features, kinesics, body language, and other nonverbal cues along with verbal language.

16. Develop and use a battery of speaking strategies, such as emphasizing key words, rephrasing, providing a context for interpreting the meaning of words, appealing for help, and accurately assessing how well your interlocutor is understanding you.

As you consider designing tasks for assessing spoken language, these skills can act as a checklist of objectives. While the macroskills have the appearance of being more complex than the microskills, both contain ingredients of difficulty, depending on the stage and context of the test-taker.

There is such an array of oral production tasks that a complete treatment is almost impossible within the confines of one chapter in this book. Below is a consideration of the most common techniques with brief allusions to related tasks. As already noted in the introduction to this chapter, consider three important issues as you set out to design tasks:

1. No speaking task is capable of isolating the single skill of oral production. Concurrent involvement of the additional performance of aural comprehension, and possibly reading, is usually necessary.

2. Eliciting the specific criterion you have designated for a task can be tricky because beyond the word level, spoken language offers a number of productive options to test-takers. Make sure your elicitation prompt achieves its aims as closely as possible.

3. Because of the above two characteristics of oral production assessment, it is important to carefully specify scoring procedures for a response so that ultimately you achieve as high a reliability index as possible.

DESIGNING ASSESSMENT TASKS: IMITATIVE SPEAKING

You may be surprised to see the inclusion of simple phonological imitation in a consideration of assessment of oral production. After all, endless repeating of words, phrases, and sentences was the province of the long-since-discarded Audiolingual Method, and in an era of communicative language teaching, many believe that non-meaningful imitation of sounds is fruitless. Such opinions have faded in recent years as we discovered that an overemphasis on fluency can sometimes lead to the decline of accuracy in speech. And so we have been paying more attention to pronunciation, especially suprasegmentals, in an attempt to help learners be more comprehensible.

An occasional phonologically focused repetition task is warranted as long as repetition tasks are not allowed to occupy a dominant role in an overall oral production assessment, and as long as you artfully avoid a negative washback effect. Such tasks range from word level to sentence level, usually with each item focusing on a specific phonological criterion. In a simple repetition task, test-takers repeat the stimulus, whether it is a pair of words, a sentence, or perhaps a question (to test for intonation production).

Word repetition task

Test-takers hear:	Repeat after me:
	beat [*pause*] bit [*pause*]
	bat [*pause*] vat [*pause*] etc.
	I bought a boat yesterday.
	The glow of the candle is growing. etc.
	When did they go on vacation?
	Do you like coffee? etc.
Test-takers repeat the stimulus.	

A variation on such a task prompts test-takers with a brief written stimulus which they are to read aloud. (In the section below on intensive speaking, some tasks are described in which test-takers read aloud longer texts.) Scoring specifications must be clear in order to avoid reliability breakdowns. A common form of scoring simply indicates a two- or three-point system for each response.

Scoring scale for repetition tasks

2	acceptable pronunciation
1	comprehensible, partially correct pronunciation
0	silence, seriously incorrect pronunciation

The longer the stretch of language, the more possibility for error and therefore the more difficult it becomes to assign a point system to the text. In such a case, it may be imperative to score only the criterion of the task. For example, in the sentence "When did they go on vacation?" since the criterion is falling intonation for *wh*-questions, points should be awarded regardless of any mispronunciation.

PHONEPASS® TEST

An example of a popular test that uses imitative (as well as intensive) production tasks is PhonePass, a widely used, commercially available speaking test in many countries. Among a number of speaking tasks on the test, repetition of sentences (of 8 to 12 words) occupies a prominent role. It is remarkable that research on the PhonePass test has supported the construct validity of its repetition tasks not just for a test-taker's phonological ability but also for discourse and overall oral production ability (Townshend et al., 1998; Bernstein et al., 2000; Cascallar & Bernstein, 2000).

The PhonePass test elicits computer-assisted oral production over a telephone. Test-takers read aloud, repeat sentences, say words, and answer questions. With a downloadable test sheet as a reference, test-takers are directed to telephone a designated number and listen for directions. The test has five sections.

PhonePass® test specifications

Part A:

Test-takers read aloud selected sentences from among those printed on the test sheet. Examples:

1. Traffic is a huge problem in Southern California.
2. The endless city has no coherent mass transit system.
3. Sharing rides was going to be the solution to rush-hour traffic.
4. Most people still want to drive their own cars, though.

Part B:

Test-takers repeat sentences dictated over the phone. Examples: "Leave town on the next train."

Part C:

Test-takers answer questions with a single word or a short phrase of two or three words. Example: "Would you get water from a bottle or a newspaper?"

Part D:

Test-takers hear three word groups in random order and must link them in a correctly ordered sentence. Example: was reading/my mother/a magazine.

Part E:

Test-takers have 30 seconds to talk about their opinion about some topic that is dictated over the phone. Topics center on family, preferences, and choices.

Scores for the PhonePass test are calculated by a computerized scoring template and reported back to the test-taker within minutes. Six scores are given: an overall score between 20 and 80 and five subscores on the same scale that rate pronunciation, reading fluency, repeat accuracy, repeat fluency, and listening vocabulary.

The tasks on Parts A and B of the PhonePass test do not extend beyond the level of oral reading and imitation. Parts C and D represent intensive speaking (see the next section in this chapter). Section E is used only for experimental data-gathering and does not figure into the scoring. The scoring procedure has been validated against human scoring with extraordinarily high reliabilities and correlation statistics (.94 overall). Further, this ten-minute test correlates with the elaborate Oral Proficiency Interview (OPI, described later in this chapter) at .75, indicating a very high degree of correspondence between the machine-scored PhonePass and the human-scored OPI (Bernstein et al., 2000).

The PhonePass findings could signal an increase in the future use of repetition and read-aloud procedures for the assessment of oral production. Because a test-taker's output is completely controlled, scoring using speech-recognition technology becomes achievable and practical. As researchers uncover the constructs underlying both repetition/read-aloud tasks and oral production in all its complexities, we will have access to more comprehensive explanations of why such simple tasks appear to be reliable and valid indicators of very complex oral production proficiency. Here are some details on the PhonePass test.

PhonePass® test

Producer:	Ordinate Corporation, Menlo Park, CA
Objective:	To test oral production skills of non-native English speakers
Primary market:	Worldwide, primarily in workplace settings where employees require a comprehensible command of spoken English; secondarily in academic settings for placement and evaluation of students

Type:	Computer-assisted telephone operated, with a test sheet
Response modes:	Oral, mostly repetition tasks
Specifications:	(see above)
Time allocations:	Ten minutes
Internet access:	**www.ordinate.com**

DESIGNING ASSESSMENT TASKS: INTENSIVE SPEAKING

At the intensive level, test-takers are prompted to produce short stretches of discourse (no more than a sentence) through which they demonstrate linguistic ability at a specified level of language. Many tasks are "cued" tasks in that they lead the test-taker into a narrow band of possibilities.

Parts C and D of the PhonePass test fulfill the criteria of intensive tasks as they elicit certain expected forms of language. Antonyms like *high* and *low, happy* and *sad* are prompted so that the automated scoring mechanism anticipates only one word. The either/or task of Part D fulfills the same criterion. Intensive tasks may also be described as **limited** response tasks (Madsen, 1983), or **mechanical** tasks (Underhill, 1987), or what classroom pedagogy would label as **controlled** responses.

Directed Response Tasks

In this type of task, the test administrator elicits a particular grammatical form or a transformation of a sentence. Such tasks are clearly mechanical and not communicative, but they do require minimal processing of meaning in order to produce the correct grammatical output.

Directed response

Test-takers hear:	Tell me he went home.
	Tell me that you like rock music.
	Tell me that you aren't interested in tennis.
	Tell him to come to my office at noon.
	Remind him what time it is.

Read-Aloud Tasks

Intensive reading-aloud tasks include reading beyond the sentence level up to a paragraph or two. This technique is easily administered by selecting a passage that incorporates test specs and by recording the test-taker's output; the scoring is relatively easy because all of the test-taker's oral production is controlled. Because of the results of research on the PhonePass test, reading aloud may actually be a surprisingly strong indicator of overall oral production ability.

For many decades, foreign language programs have used reading passages to analyze oral production. Prator's (1972) *Manual of American English Pronunciation* included a "diagnostic passage" of about 150 words that students could read aloud into a tape recorder. Teachers listening to the recording would then rate students on a number of phonological factors (vowels, diphthongs, consonants, consonant clusters, stress, and intonation) by completing a two-page diagnostic checklist on which all errors or questionable items were noted. These checklists ostensibly offered direction to the teacher for emphases in the course to come.

An earlier form of the Test of Spoken English (TSE®, see below) incorporated one read-aloud passage of about 120 to 130 words with a rating scale for pronunciation and fluency. The following passage is typical:

Read-aloud stimulus, paragraph length

Despite the decrease in size—and, some would say, quality—of our cultural world, there still remain strong differences between the usual British and American writing styles. The question is, how do you get your message across? English prose conveys its most novel ideas as if they were timeless truths, while American writing exaggerates; if you believe half of what is said, that's enough. The former uses understatement; the latter, overstatement. There are also disadvantages to each characteristic approach. Readers who are used to being screamed at may not listen when someone chooses to whisper politely. At the same time, the individual who is used to a quiet manner may reject a series of loud imperatives.

The scoring scale for this passage provided a four-point scale for pronunciation and for fluency, as shown in the box below.

Test of Spoken English scoring scale (1987, p. 10)

Pronunciation:

Points:

0.0–0.4	Frequent phonemic errors and foreign stress and intonation patterns that cause the speaker to be unintelligible.
0.5–1.4	Frequent phonemic errors and foreign stress and intonation patterns that cause the speaker to be occasionally unintelligible.
1.5–2.4	Some consistent phonemic errors and foreign stress and intonation patterns, but the speaker is intelligible.
2.5–3.0	Occasional non-native pronunciation errors, but the speaker is always intelligible.

Fluency:

Points:

0.0–0.4	Speech is so halting and fragmentary or has such a non-native flow that intelligibility is virtually impossible.
0.5–1.4	Numerous non-native pauses and/or a non-native flow that interferes with intelligibility.
1.5–2.4	Some non-native pauses but with a more nearly native flow so that the pauses do not interfere with intelligibility.
2.5–3.0	Speech is smooth and effortless, closely approximating that of a native speaker.

Such a rating list does not indicate how to gauge *intelligibility*, which is mentioned in both lists. Such slippery terms remind us that oral production scoring, even with the controls that reading aloud offers, is still an inexact science.

Underhill (1987, pp. 77–78) suggested some variations on the task of simply reading a short passage:

- reading a scripted dialogue, with someone else reading the other part
- reading sentences containing minimal pairs, for example:
    Try not to heat/hit the pan too much.
    The doctor gave me a bill/pill.
- reading information from a table or chart

If reading aloud shows certain practical advantages (predictable output, practicality, reliability in scoring), there are several drawbacks to using this technique for assessing oral production. Reading aloud is somewhat inauthentic in that we seldom read anything aloud to someone else in the real world, with the exception of a parent reading to a child, occasionally sharing a written story with someone, or giving a scripted oral presentation. Also, reading aloud calls on certain specialized oral abilities that may not indicate one's pragmatic ability to communicate orally in face-to-face contexts. You should therefore employ this technique with some caution, and certainly supplement it as an assessment task with other, more communicative procedures.

Sentence/Dialogue Completion Tasks and Oral Questionnaires

Another technique for targeting intensive aspects of language requires test-takers to read dialogue in which one speaker's lines have been omitted. Test-takers are first given time to read through the dialogue to get its gist and to think about appropriate lines to fill in. Then as the tape, teacher, or test administrator produces one part orally, the test-taker responds. Here's an example.

Dialogue completion task

Test-takers read (and then hear):

In a department store:

Salesperson:	May I help you?
Customer:	_____ .
Salesperson:	Okay, what size do you wear?
Customer:	_____ .
Salesperson:	Hmmm. How about this green sweater here?
Customer:	_____ .
Salesperson:	Oh. Well, if you don't like green, what color would you like?
Customer:	_____ .
Salesperson:	How about this one?
Customer:	_____ .
Salesperson:	Great!
Customer:	_____ .
Salesperson:	It's on sale today for $39.95.
Customer:	_____ .
Salesperson:	Sure, we take Visa, MasterCard, and American Express.
Customer:	_____ .

Test-takers respond with appropriate lines.

An advantage of this technique lies in its moderate control of the output of the test-taker. While individual variations in responses are accepted, the technique taps into a learner's ability to discern expectancies in a conversation and to produce sociolinguistically correct language. One disadvantage of this technique is its reliance on literacy and an ability to transfer easily from written to spoken English. Another disadvantage is the contrived, inauthentic nature of this task: Couldn't the same criterion performance be elicited in a live interview in which an impromptu role-play technique is used?

Perhaps more useful is a whole host of shorter dialogues of two or three lines, each of which aims to elicit a specified target. In the following examples, somewhat unrelated items attempt to elicit the past tense, future tense, *yes/no* question formation, and asking for the time. Again, test-takers see the stimulus in written form.

Directed response tasks

Test-takers see:

Interviewer:	What did you do last weekend?
Test-taker:	_____ .
Interviewer:	What will you do after you graduate from this program?
Test-taker:	_____ .
Test-taker:	_____ ?
Interviewer:	I was in Japan for two weeks.
Test-taker:	_____ ?
Interviewer:	It's ten-thirty.

Test-takers respond with appropriate lines.

One could contend that performance on these items is *responsive,* rather than *intensive.* True, the discourse involves responses, but there is a degree of control here that predisposes the test-taker to respond with certain expected forms. Such arguments underscore the fine lines of distinction between and among the selected five categories.

It could also be argued that such techniques are nothing more than a written form of questions that might otherwise (and more appropriately) be part of a standard oral interview. True, but the advantage that the written form offers is to provide a little more time for the test-taker to anticipate an answer, and it begins to remove the potential ambiguity created by aural misunderstanding. It helps to unlock the almost ubiquitous link between listening and speaking performance.

Underhill (1987) describes yet another technique that is useful for controlling the test-taker's output: form-filling, or what I might rename "oral questionnaire." Here the test-taker sees a questionnaire that asks for certain categories of information (personal data, academic information, job experience, etc.) and supplies the information orally.

Picture-Cued Tasks

One of the more popular ways to elicit oral language performance at both intensive and extensive levels is a picture-cued stimulus that requires a description from the test-taker. Pictures may be very simple, designed to elicit a word or a phrase; somewhat more elaborate and "busy"; or composed of a series that tells a story or incident. Here is an example of a picture-cued elicitation of the production of a simple minimal pair.

Picture-cued elicitation of minimal pairs

> Test-takers see:
>
>
>
> Test-takers hear: [*test administrator points to each picture in succession*]
> What's this?

Grammatical categories may be cued by pictures. In the following sequences, comparatives are elicited:

Picture-cued elicitation of comparatives (Brown & Sahni, 1994, p. 135)

> Test-takers see:
>
> Test-takers hear: Use a comparative form to compare these objects.

The future tense is elicited with the following picture:

Picture-cued elicitation of future tense (Brown & Sahni, 1994, p. 145)

Test-takers see:

Test-takers hear: This family is at an airport going on their vacation.

1. [*point to the picture in general*] Where are they going for their vacation?
2. [*point to the father*] What will he do in Hawaii?
3. [*point to the mother*] What will she do there?
4. [*point to the girl*] What is she going to do there?
5. [*point to the boy*] What is he going to do in Hawaii?

Notice that a little sense of humor is injected here: the family, bundled up in their winter coats, is looking forward to leaving the wintry scene behind them! A touch of authenticity is added in that almost everyone can identify with looking forward to a vacation on a tropical island.

Assessment of oral production may be stimulated through a more elaborate picture such as the one on the next page, a party scene.

Picture-cued elicitation of nouns, negative responses, numbers, and location
(Brown & Sahni, 1994, p. 116)

Test-takers see:

Test-takers hear: **1.** [*point to the table*] What's this?

2. [*point to the end table*] What's this?

3. [*point to several chairs*] What are these?

4. [*point to the clock*] What's that?

5. [*point to both lamps*] What are those?

6. [*point to the table*] Is this a chair?

7. [*point to the lamps*] Are these clocks?

8. [*point to the woman standing up*] Is she sitting?

9. [*point to the whole picture*] How many chairs are there?

10. [*point to the whole picture*] How many women are there?

11. [*point to the TV*] Where is the TV?

12. [*point to the chair beside the lamp*] Where is this chair?

13. [*point to one person*] Describe this person.

In the first five questions, test-takers are asked to orally identify selected vocabulary items. In questions 6–13, assessment of the oral production of negatives, numbers, prepositions, and descriptions of people is elicited.

Moving into more open-ended performance, the following picture asks test-takers not only to identify certain specific information but also to elaborate with their own opinion, to accomplish a persuasive function, and to describe preferences in paintings.

Picture-cued elicitation of responses and description
(Brown & Sahni, 1994, p. 162)

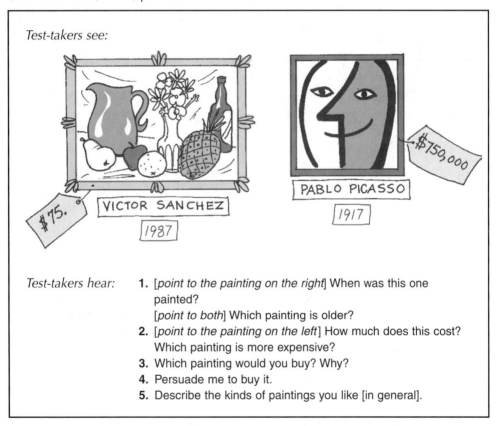

Test-takers see:

VICTOR SANCHEZ
1987
$75.

PABLO PICASSO
1917
$750,000

Test-takers hear:

1. [*point to the painting on the right*] When was this one painted?
   [*point to both*] Which painting is older?
2. [*point to the painting on the left*] How much does this cost? Which painting is more expensive?
3. Which painting would you buy? Why?
4. Persuade me to buy it.
5. Describe the kinds of paintings you like [in general].

Maps are another visual stimulus that can be used to assess the language forms needed to give directions and specify locations. In the following example, the test-taker must provide directions to different locations.

Map-cued elicitation of giving directions (Brown & Sahni, 1994, p. 169)

Test-takers see:

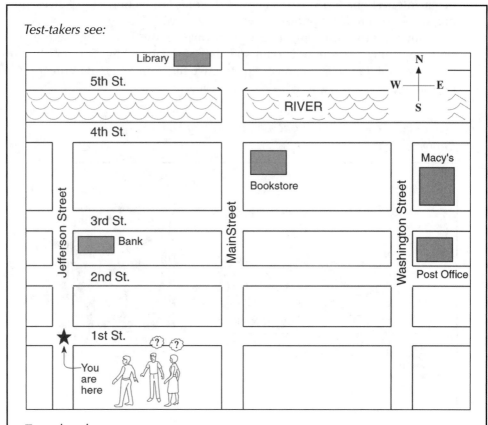

Test-takers hear:

You are at First and Jefferson Streets [*point to the spot*]. People ask you for directions to get to five different places. Listen to their questions, then give directions.

1. Please give me directions to the bank.
2. Please give me directions to Macy's Department Store.
3. How do I get to the post office?
4. Can you tell me where the bookstore is?
5. Please tell me how to get to the library.

Scoring responses on picture-cued intensive speaking tasks varies, depending on the expected performance criteria. The tasks above that asked just for one-word or simple-sentence responses can be evaluated simply as "correct" or "incorrect." The three-point rubric (2, 1, and 0) suggested earlier may apply as well, with these modifications:

Scoring scale for intensive tasks

2	comprehensible; acceptable target form
1	comprehensible; partially correct target form
0	silence, or seriously incorrect target form

Opinions about paintings, persuasive monologue, and directions on a map create a more complicated problem for scoring. More demand is placed on the test administrator to make calculated judgments, in which case a modified form of a scale such as the one suggested for evaluating interviews (below) could be used:

- grammar
- vocabulary
- comprehension
- fluency
- pronunciation
- task (accomplishing the objective of the elicited task)

Each category may be scored separately, with an additional composite score that attempts to synthesize overall performance. To attend to so many factors, you will probably need to have an audiotaped recording for multiple listening.

One moderately successful picture-cued technique involves a pairing of two test-takers. They are supplied with a set of four identical sets of numbered pictures, each minimally distinct from the others by one or two factors. One test-taker is directed by a cue card to describe *one* of the four pictures in as few words as possible. The second test-taker must then identify the picture. On the next page is an example of four pictures.

Test-takers see:

Test-taker 1 describes (for example) picture C; test-taker 2 points to the correct picture.

The task here is simple and straightforward and clearly in the intensive category as the test-taker must simply produce the relevant linguistic markers. Yet it is still the task of the test administrator to determine a correctly produced response and a correctly understood response since sources of incorrectness may not be easily pinpointed. If the pictorial stimuli are more complex than the above item, greater burdens are placed on both speaker and listener, with consequently greater difficulty in identifying which committed the error.

Translation (of Limited Stretches of Discourse)

Translation is a part of our tradition in language teaching that we tend to discount or disdain, if only because our current pedagogical stance plays down its importance. Translation methods of teaching are certainly passé in an era of direct approaches to creating communicative classrooms. But we should remember that in countries where English is not the native or prevailing language, translation is a meaningful communicative device in contexts where the English user is called on to be an interpreter. Also, translation is a well-proven communication strategy for learners of a second language.

Under certain constraints, then, it is not far-fetched to suggest translation as a device to check oral production. Instead of offering pictures or written stimuli, the test-taker is given a native language word, phrase, or sentence and is asked to translate it. Conditions may vary from expecting an instant translation of an orally elicited linguistic target to allowing more thinking time before producing a translation of somewhat longer texts, which may optionally be offered to the test-taker in written form. (Translation of extensive texts is discussed at the end of this chapter.) As an assessment procedure, the advantages of translation lie in its control of the output of the test-taker, which of course means that scoring is more easily specified.

DESIGNING ASSESSMENT TASKS: RESPONSIVE SPEAKING

Assessment of responsive tasks involves brief interactions with an interlocutor, differing from intensive tasks in the increased creativity given to the test-taker and from interactive tasks by the somewhat limited length of utterances.

Question and Answer

Question-and-answer tasks can consist of one or two questions from an interviewer, or they can make up a portion of a whole battery of questions and prompts in an oral interview. They can vary from simple questions like "What is this called in English?" to complex questions like "What are the steps governments should take, if any, to stem the rate of deforestation in tropical countries?" The first question is intensive in its purpose; it is a **display question** intended to elicit a predetermined correct response. We have already looked at some of these types of questions in the previous section. Questions at the responsive level tend to be genuine **referential questions** in which the test-taker is given more opportunity to produce meaningful language in response.

In designing such questions for test-takers, it's important to make sure that you know *why* you are asking the question. Are you simply trying to elicit strings of language output to gain a general sense of the test-taker's discourse competence? Are you combining discourse and grammatical competence in the same question? Is each question just one in a whole set of related questions? Responsive questions may take the following forms:

Questions eliciting open-ended responses

Test-takers hear:

1. What do you think about the weather today?
2. What do you like about the English language?
3. Why did you choose your academic major?
4. What kind of strategies have you used to help you learn English?
5. a. Have you ever been to the United States before?
   b. What other countries have you visited?
   c. Why did you go there? What did you like best about it?
   d. If you could go back, what would you like to do or see?
   e. What country would you like to visit next, and why?

Test-takers respond with a few sentences at most.

Notice that question #5 has five situationally linked questions that may vary slightly depending on the test-taker's response to a previous question.

Oral interaction with a test administrator often involves the latter forming all the questions. The flip side of this usual concept of question-and-answer tasks is to elicit questions from the test-taker. To assess the test-taker's ability to produce questions, prompts such as this can be used:

Elicitation of questions from the test-taker

Test-takers hear:

- Do you have any questions for me?
- Ask me about my family or job or interests.
- If you could interview the president or prime minister of your country, what would you ask that person?

Test-takers respond with questions.

A potentially tricky form of oral production assessment involves more than one test-taker with an interviewer, which is discussed later in this chapter. With two students in an interview context, both test-takers can ask questions of each other.

Giving Instructions and Directions

We are all called on in our daily routines to read instructions on how to operate an appliance, how to put a bookshelf together, or how to create a delicious clam chowder. Somewhat less frequent is the mandate to provide such instructions orally, but this speech act is still relatively common. Using such a stimulus in an assessment context provides an opportunity for the test-taker to engage in a relatively extended stretch of discourse, to be very clear and specific, and to use appropriate discourse markers and connectors. The technique is simple: the administrator poses the problem, and the test-taker responds. Scoring is based primarily on comprehensibility and secondarily on other specified grammatical or discourse categories. Here are some possibilities.

Eliciting instructions or directions

Test-takers hear:

- Describe how to make a typical dish from your country.
- What's a good recipe for making _____?
- How do you access email on a PC computer?
- How would I make a typical costume for a _____ celebration in your country?
- How do you program telephone numbers into a cell (mobile) phone?
- How do I get from _____ to _____ in your city?

Test-takers respond with appropriate instructions/directions.

Some pointers for creating such tasks: The test administrator needs to guard against test-takers knowing and preparing for such items in advance lest they simply parrot back a memorized set of sentences. An impromptu delivery of instructions is warranted here, or at most a minute or so of preparation time. Also, the choice of topics needs to be familiar enough so that you are testing not general knowledge but linguistic competence; therefore, topics beyond the content schemata of the test-taker are inadvisable. Finally, the task should require the test-taker to produce at least five or six sentences (of connected discourse) to adequately fulfill the objective.

This task can be designed to be more complex, thus placing it in the category of extensive speaking. If your objective is to keep the response short and simple, then make sure your directive does not take the test-taker down a path of complexity that he or she is not ready to face.

Paraphrasing

Another type of assessment task that can be categorized as responsive asks the test-taker to read or hear a limited number of sentences (perhaps two to five) and produce a paraphrase of the sentence. For example:

Paraphrasing a story

> *Test-takers hear:* Paraphrase the following little story in your own words.
>
> My weekend in the mountains was fabulous. The first day we backpacked into the mountains and climbed about 2,000 feet. The hike was strenuous but exhilarating. By sunset we found these beautiful alpine lakes and made camp there. The sunset was amazingly beautiful. The next two days we just kicked back and did little day hikes, some rock climbing, bird watching, swimming, and fishing. The hike out on the next day was really easy—all downhill—and the scenery was incredible.
>
> *Test-takers respond with two or three sentences.*

A more authentic context for paraphrase is aurally receiving and orally relaying a message. In the example below, the test-taker must relay information from a telephone call to an office colleague named Jeff.

Paraphrasing a phone message

> *Test-takers hear:*
>
> Please tell Jeff that I'm tied up in traffic so I'm going to be about a half hour late for the nine o'clock meeting. And ask him to bring up our question about the employee benefits plan. If he wants to check in with me on my cell phone, have him call 415-338-3095. Thanks.
>
> *Test-takers respond with two or three sentences.*

The advantages of such tasks are that they elicit short stretches of output and perhaps tap into test-takers' ability to practice the conversational art of conciseness by reducing the output/input ratio. Yet you have to question the criterion being assessed. Is it a listening task more than production? Does it test short-term memory rather than linguistic ability? And how does the teacher determine scoring of responses? If you use short paraphrasing tasks as an assessment procedure, it's important to pinpoint the objective of the task clearly. In this case, the integration of listening and speaking is probably more at stake than simple oral production alone.

TEST OF SPOKEN ENGLISH (TSE®)

Somewhere straddling responsive, interactive, and extensive speaking tasks lies another popular commercial oral production assessment, the Test of Spoken English (TSE). The TSE is a 20-minute audiotaped test of oral language ability within an academic or professional environment. TSE scores are used by many North American institutions of higher education to select international teaching assistants. The scores are also used for selecting and certifying health professionals such as physicians, nurses, pharmacists, physical therapists, and veterinarians.

The tasks on the TSE are designed to elicit oral production in various discourse categories rather than in selected phonological, grammatical, or lexical targets. The following content specifications for the TSE represent the discourse and pragmatic contexts assessed in each administration:

1. Describe something physical.
2. Narrate from presented material.
3. Summarize information of the speaker's own choice.
4. Give directions based on visual materials.
5. Give instructions.
6. Give an opinion.
7. Support an opinion.
8. Compare/contrast.
9. Hypothesize.
10. Function "interactively."
11. Define.

Using these specifications, Lazaraton and Wagner (1996) examined 15 different specific tasks in collecting background data from native and non-native speakers of English.

1. giving a personal description
2. describing a daily routine
3. suggesting a gift and supporting one's choice
4. recommending a place to visit and supporting one's choice
5. giving directions
6. describing a favorite movie and supporting one's choice
7. telling a story from pictures
8. hypothesizing about future action
9. hypothesizing about a preventative action
10. making a telephone call to the dry cleaner
11. describing an important news event
12. giving an opinion about animals in the zoo
13. defining a technical term
14. describing information in a graph and speculating about its implications
15. giving details about a trip schedule

From their findings, the researchers were able to report on the validity of the tasks, especially the match between the intended task functions and the actual output of both native and non-native speakers.

Following is a set of sample items as they appear in the TSE Manual, which is downloadable from the TOEFL® website (see reference on page 167).

Test of Spoken English sample items

Part A.

Test-takers see: A map of a town

Test-takers hear: Imagine that we are colleagues. The map below is of a neighboring town that you have suggested I visit. You will have 30 seconds to study the map. Then I'll ask you some questions about it.

1. Choose one place on the map that you think I should visit and give me some reasons why you recommend this place. (30 seconds)
2. I'd like to see a movie. Please give me directions from the bus station to the movie theater. (30 seconds)
3. One of your favorite movies is playing at the theater. Please tell me about the movie and why you like it. (60 seconds)

Part B.

Test-takers see:

A series of six pictures depicts a sequence of events. In this series, painters have just painted a park bench. Their WET PAINT sign blows away. A man approaches the bench, sits on it, and starts reading a newspaper. He quickly discovers his suit has just gotten wet paint on it and then rushes to the dry cleaner.

Test-takers hear:

Now please look at the six pictures below. I'd like you to tell me the story that the pictures show, starting with picture number 1 and going through picture number 6. Please take 1 minute to look at the pictures and think about the story. Do not begin the story until I tell you to do so.

4. Tell me the story that the picture show. (60 seconds)
5. What could the painters have done to prevent this? (30 seconds)
6. Imagine that this happens to you. After you have taken the suit to the dry cleaners, you find out that you need to wear the suit the next morning. The dry cleaning service usually takes two days. Call the dry cleaner and try to persuade them to have the suit ready later today. (45 seconds)
7. The man in the pictures is reading a newspaper. Both newspapers and television news programs can be good sources of information about current events. What do you think are the advantages and disadvantages of each of these sources? (60 seconds)

Part C.

Test-takers hear:

Now I'd like to hear your ideas about a variety of topics. Be sure to say as much as you can in responding to each question. After I ask each question, you may take a few seconds to prepare your answer, and then begin speaking when you're ready.

8. Many people enjoy visiting zoos and seeing the animals. Other people believe that animals should not be taken from their natural surroundings and put into zoos. I'd like to know what you think about this issue. (60 seconds)

9. I'm not familiar with your field of study. Select a term used frequently in your field and define it for me. (60 seconds)

Part D.

Test-takers see:

A graph showing an increase in world population over a half-century of time.

Test-takers hear:

10. This graph presents the actual and projected percentage of the world population living in cities from 1950 to 2010. Describe to me the information given in the graph. (60 seconds)

11. Now discuss what this information might mean for the future. (45 seconds)

Part E.

Test-takers see:

A printed itinerary for a one-day bus tour of Washington, D.C., on which four relatively simple pieces of information (date, departure time, etc.) have been crossed out by hand and new handwritten information added.

Test-takers hear:

12. Now please look at the information below about a trip to Washington, D.C., that has been organized for the members of the Forest City Historical Society. Imagine that you are the president of this organization. At the last meeting, you gave out a schedule for the trip, but there have been some changes. You must remind the members about the details of the trip and tell them about the changes indicated on the schedule. In your presentation, do not just read the information printed, but present it as if you were talking to a group of people. You will have one minute to plan your presentation and will be told when to begin speaking. (90 seconds)

TSE test-takers are given a holistic score ranging from 20 to 60, as described in the TSE Manual (see Table 7.1).

Table 7.1 Test of Spoken English scoring guide (1995)

TSE Rating Scale

60 **Communication almost always effective: task performed very competently; speech almost never marked by non-native characteristics**

Functions performed clearly and effectively
Appropriate response to audience/situation
Coherent, with effective use of cohesive devices
Almost always accurate pronunciation, grammar, fluency, and vocabulary

50 **Communication generally effective: task performed competently, successful use of compensatory strategies; speech sometimes marked by non-native characteristics**

Functions generally performed clearly and effectively
Generally appropriate response to audience/situation
Coherent, with some effective use of cohesive devices
Generally accurate pronunciation, grammar, fluency, and vocabulary

40 **Communication somewhat effective: task performed somewhat competently, some successful use of compensatory strategies; speech regularly marked by non-native characteristics**

Functions performed somewhat clearly and effectively
Somewhat appropriate response to audience/situation
Somewhat coherent, with some use of cohesive devices
Somewhat accurate pronunciation, grammar, fluency, and vocabulary

30 **Communication generally not effective: task generally performed poorly, ineffective use of compensatory strategies; speech very frequently marked by non-native characteristics**

Functions generally performed unclearly and ineffectively
Generally inappropriate response to audience/situation
Generally incoherent, with little use of cohesive devices
Generally inaccurate pronunciation, grammar, fluency, and vocabulary

20 **No effective communication: no evidence of ability to perform task, no effective use of compensatory strategies; speech almost always marked by non-native characteristics**

No evidence that functions were performed
Incoherent, with no use of cohesive devices
No evidence of ability to respond appropriately to audience/situation
Almost always inaccurate pronunciation, grammar, fluency, and vocabulary

Holistic scoring taxonomies such as these imply a number of abilities that comprise "effective" communication and "competent" performance of the task. The original version of the TSE (1987) specified three contributing factors to a final score on "overall comprehensibility": pronunciation, grammar, and fluency. The current scoring scale of 20 to 60 listed above incorporates task performance, function, appropriateness, and coherence as well as the form-focused factors. From reported scores, institutions are left to determine their own threshold levels of acceptability, but because scoring is holistic, they will not receive an analytic score of how each factor breaks down (see Douglas & Smith, 1997, for further information). Classroom teachers who propose to model oral production assessments after the tasks on the TSE must, in order to provide some washback effect, be more explicit in analyzing the various components of test-takers' output. Such scoring rubrics are presented in the next section.

Following is a summary of information on the TSE:

Test of Spoken English (TSE®)

Producer:	Educational Testing Service, Princeton, NJ
Objective:	To test oral production skills of non-native English speakers
Primary market:	Primarily used for screening international teaching assistants in universities in the United States; a growing secondary market is certifying health professionals in the United States
Type:	Audiotaped with written, graphic, and spoken stimuli
Response modes:	Oral tasks; connected discourse
Specifications:	(see sample items above)
Time allocation:	20 minutes
Internet access:	**http://www.toefl.org/tse/tseindx.html**

DESIGNING ASSESSMENT TASKS: INTERACTIVE SPEAKING

The final two categories of oral production assessment (interactive and extensive speaking) include tasks that involve relatively long stretches of interactive discourse (interviews, role plays, discussions, games) and tasks of equally long duration but that involve less interaction (speeches, telling longer stories, and extended explanations and translations). The obvious difference between the two sets of tasks is the degree of interaction with an interlocutor. Also, interactive tasks are what some would describe as **interpersonal,** while the final category includes more **transactional** speech events.

Interview

When "oral production assessment" is mentioned, the first thing that comes to mind is an oral interview: a test administrator and a test-taker sit down in a direct face-to-face exchange and proceed through a protocol of questions and directives. The interview, which may be tape-recorded for re-listening, is then scored on one or more parameters such as accuracy in pronunciation and/or grammar, vocabulary usage, fluency, sociolinguistic/pragmatic appropriateness, task accomplishment, and even comprehension.

Interviews can vary in length from perhaps five to forty-five minutes, depending on their purpose and context. Placement interviews, designed to get a quick spoken sample from a student in order to verify placement into a course, may need only five minutes if the interviewer is trained to evaluate the output accurately. Longer comprehensive interviews such as the OPI (see the next section) are designed to cover predetermined oral production contexts and may require the better part of an hour.

Every effective interview contains a number of mandatory stages. Two decades ago, Michael Canale (1984) proposed a framework for oral proficiency testing that has withstood the test of time. He suggested that test-takers will perform at their best if they are led through four stages:

1. Warm-up. In a minute or so of preliminary small talk, the interviewer directs mutual introductions, helps the test-taker become comfortable with the situation, apprises the test-taker of the format, and allays anxieties. No scoring of this phase takes place.

2. Level check. Through a series of preplanned questions, the interviewer stimulates the test-taker to respond using expected or predicted forms and functions. If, for example, from previous test information, grades, or other data, the test-taker has been judged to be a "Level 2" (see below) speaker, the interviewer's prompts will attempt to confirm this assumption. The responses may take very simple or very complex form, depending on the entry level of the learner. Questions are usually designed to elicit grammatical categories (such as past tense or subject–verb agreement), discourse structure (a sequence of events), vocabulary usage, and/or sociolinguistic factors (politeness conventions, formal/informal language). This stage could also give the interviewer a picture of the test-taker's extroversion, readiness to speak, and confidence, all of which may be of significant consequence in the interview's results. Linguistic target criteria are scored in this phase. If this stage is lengthy, a tape-recording of the interview is important.

3. Probe. Probe questions and prompts challenge test-takers to go to the heights of their ability, to extend beyond the limits of the interviewer's expectation through increasingly difficult questions. Probe questions may be complex in their framing and/or complex in their cognitive and linguistic demand. Through probe items, the interviewer discovers the ceiling or limitation of the test-taker's proficiency. This need not be a separate stage entirely, but might be a set of questions that are interspersed into the previous stage. At the lower levels of proficiency, probe items may simply demand a higher range of vocabulary or grammar from the test-taker than predicted. At the higher levels, probe items will typically ask the test-taker to give an opinion or a value judgment, to discuss his or her field of specialization, to recount a narrative, or to respond to questions that are worded in complex form. Responses to probe questions may be scored, or they may be ignored if the test-taker displays an inability to handle such complexity.

4. Wind-down. This final phase of the interview is simply a short period of time during which the interviewer encourages the test-taker to relax with some easy questions, sets the test-taker's mind at ease, and provides information about when and where to obtain the results of the interview. This part is not scored.

The suggested set of content specifications for an oral interview (below) may serve as sample questions that can be adapted to individual situations.

Oral interview content specifications

Warm-up:

1. Small talk

Level check:

The test-taker . . .

2. answers *wh*-questions.
3. produces a narrative without interruptions.
4. reads a passage aloud.
5. tells how to make something or do something.
6. engages in a brief, controlled, guided role play.

Probe:

The test-taker . . .

7. responds to interviewer's questions about something the test-taker doesn't know and is planning to include in an article or paper.
8. talks about his or her own field of study or profession.
9. engages in a longer, more open-ended role play (for example, simulates a difficult or embarrassing circumstance) with the interviewer.
10. gives an impromptu presentation on some aspect of test-taker's field.

Wind-down:

11. Feelings about the interview, information on results, further questions

---

Here are some possible questions, probes, and comments that fit those specifications.

Sample questions for the four stages of an oral interview

---

1. Warm-up:

How are you?
What's your name?
What country are you from? What [city, town]?
Let me tell you about this interview.

2. Level check:

How long have you been in this [country, city]?
Tell me about your family.

What is your [academic major, professional interest, job]?
How long have you been working at your [degree, job]?
Describe your home [city, town] to me.
How do you like your home [city, town]?
What are your hobbies or interests? (What do you do in your spare time?)
Why do you like your [hobby, interest]?
Have you traveled to another country beside this one and your home country?
Tell me about that country.
Compare your home [city, town] to another [city, town].
What is your favorite food?
Tell me how to [make, do] something you know well.
What will you be doing ten years from now?
I'd like you to ask me some questions.
Tell me about an exciting or interesting experience you've had.
Read the following paragraph, please. *[test-taker reads aloud]*
Pretend that you are _____ and I am a _____. *[guided role play follows]*

3. Probe:

What are your goals for learning English in this program?
Describe your [academic field, job] to me. What do you like and dislike about it?
What is your opinion of [a recent headline news event]?
Describe someone you greatly respect, and tell me why you respect that person.
If you could redo your education all over again, what would you do differently?
How do eating habits and customs reflect the culture of the people of a country?
If you were [president, prime minister] of your country, what would you like to change about your country?
What career advice would you give to your younger friends?
Imagine you are writing an article on a topic you don't know very much about. Ask me some questions about that topic.
You are in a shop that sells expensive glassware. Accidentally you knock over an expensive vase, and it breaks. What will you say to the store owner? *[Interviewer role-plays the store owner]*

4. Wind-down:

Did you feel okay about this interview?
What are your plans for [the weekend, the rest of today, the future]?
You'll get your results from this interview [tomorrow, next week].
Do you have any questions you want to ask me?
It was interesting to talk with you. Best wishes.

The success of an oral interview will depend on

- clearly specifying administrative procedures of the assessment (practicality),
- focusing the questions and probes on the purpose of the assessment (validity),
- appropriately eliciting an optimal amount and quality of oral production from the test-taker (biased for best performance), and
- creating a consistent, workable scoring system (reliability).

This last issue is the thorniest. In oral production tasks that are open-ended and that involve a significant level of interaction, the interviewer is forced to make judgments that are susceptible to some unreliability. Through experience, training, and careful attention to the linguistic criteria being assessed, the ability to make such judgments accurately will be acquired. In Table 7.2, a set of descriptions is given for scoring open-ended oral interviews. These descriptions come from an earlier version of the Oral Proficiency Interview and are useful for classroom purposes.

The test administrator's challenge is to assign a score, ranging from 1 to 5, for each of the six categories indicated above. It may look easy to do, but in reality the lines of distinction between levels is quite difficult to pinpoint. Some training or at least a good deal of interviewing experience is required to make accurate assessments of oral production in the six categories. Usually the six scores are then amalgamated into one holistic score, a process that might not be relegated to a simple mathematical average if you wish to put more weight on some categories than you do on others.

This five-point scale, once known as "FSI levels" (because they were first advocated by the Foreign Service Institute in Washington, D.C.), is still in popular use among U.S. government foreign service staff for designating proficiency in a foreign language. To complicate the scoring somewhat, the five-point holistic scoring categories have historically been subdivided into "pluses" and "minuses" as indicated in Table 7.3. To this day, even though the official nomenclature has now changed (see OPI description below), in-group conversations refer to colleagues and co-workers by their FSI level: "Oh, Bob, yeah, he's a good 3+ in Turkish—he can easily handle that assignment."

A variation on the usual one-on-one format with one interviewer and one test-taker is to place two test-takers at a time with the interviewer. An advantage of a two-on-one interview is the practicality of scheduling twice as many candidates in the same time frame, but more significant is the opportunity for student–student interaction. By deftly posing questions, problems, and role plays, the interviewer can maximize the output of the test-takers while lessening the need for his or her own output. A further benefit is the probable increase in authenticity when two test-takers can actually converse with each other. Disadvantages are equalizing the output between the two test-takers, discerning the interaction effect of unequal comprehension and production abilities, and scoring two people simultaneously.

Table 7.2. Oral proficiency scoring categories (Brown, 2001, pp. 406–407)

	Grammar	**Vocabulary**	**Comprehension**
I	Errors in grammar are frequent, but speaker can be understood by a native speaker used to dealing with foreigners attempting to speak his language.	Speaking vocabulary inadequate to express anything but the most elementary needs.	Within the scope of his very limited language experience, can understand simple questions and statements if delivered with slowed speech, repetition, or paraphrase.
II	Can usually handle elementary constructions quite accurately but does not have thorough or confident control of the grammar.	Has speaking vocabulary sufficient to express himself simply with some circumlocutions.	Can get the gist of most conversations of non-technical subjects (i.e., topics that require no specialized knowledge).
III	Control of grammar is good. Able to speak the language with sufficient structural accuracy to participate effectively in most formal and informal conversations on practical, social, and professional topics.	Able to speak the language with sufficient vocabulary to participate effectively in most formal and informal conversations on practical, social, and professional topics. Vocabulary is broad enough that he rarely has to grope for a word.	Comprehension is quite complete at a normal rate of speech.
IV	Able to use the language accurately on all levels normally pertinent to professional needs. Errors in grammar are quite rare.	Can understand and participate in any conversation within the range of his experience with a high degree of precision of vocabulary.	Can understand any conversation within the range of his experience.
V	Equivalent to that of an educated native speaker.	Speech on all levels is fully accepted by educated native speakers in all its features including breadth of vocabulary and idioms, colloquialisms, and pertinent cultural references.	Equivalent to that of an educated native speaker.

Fluency	Pronunciation	Task
(No specific fluency description. Refer to other four language areas for implied level of fluency.)	Errors in pronunciation are frequent but can be understood by a native speaker used to dealing with foreigners attempting to speak his language.	Can ask and answer questions on topics very familiar to him. Able to satisfy routine travel needs and minimum courtesy requirements. (Should be able to order a simple meal, ask for shelter or lodging, ask and give simple directions, make purchases, and tell time.)
Can handle with confidence but not with facility most social situations, including introductions and casual conversations about current events, as well as work, family, and autobiographical information.	Accent is intelligible though often quite faulty.	Able to satisfy routine social demands and work requirements; needs help in handling any complication or difficulties.
Can discuss particular interests of competence with reasonable ease. Rarely has to grope for words.	Errors never interfere with understanding and rarely disturb the native speaker. Accent may be obviously foreign.	Can participate effectively in most formal and informal conversations on practical, social, and professional topics.
Able to use the language fluently on all levels normally pertinent to professional needs. Can participate in any conversation within the range of this experience with a high degree of fluency.	Errors in pronunciation are quite rare.	Would rarely be taken for a native speaker but can respond appropriately even in unfamiliar situations. Can handle informal interpreting from and into language.
Has complete fluency in the language such that his speech is fully accepted by educated native speakers.	Equivalent to and fully accepted by educated native speakers.	Speaking proficiency equivalent to that of an educated native speaker.

Table 7.3. Subcategories of oral proficiency scores

Level	Description
0	Unable to function in the spoken language
0+	Able to satisfy immediate needs using rehearsed utterances
1	Able to satisfy minimum courtesy requirements and maintain very simple face-to-face conversations on familiar topics
1+	Can initiate and maintain predictable face-to-face conversations and satisfy limited social demands
2	Able to satisfy routine social demands and limited work requirements
2+	Able to satisfy most work requirements with language usage that is often, but not always, acceptable and effective
3	Able to speak the language with sufficient structural accuracy and vocabulary to participate effectively in most formal and informal conversations on practical, social, and professional topics
3+	Often able to use the language to satisfy professional needs in a wide range of sophisticated and demanding tasks
4	Able to use the language fluently and accurately on all levels normally pertinent to professional needs
4+	Speaking proficiency is regularly superior in all respects, usually equivalent to that of a well-educated, highly articulate native speaker
5	Speaking proficiency is functionally equivalent to that of a highly articulate, well-educated native speaker and reflects the cultural standards of the country where the language is spoken

Role Play

Role playing is a popular pedagogical activity in communicative language-teaching classes. Within constraints set forth by the guidelines, it frees students to be somewhat creative in their linguistic output. In some versions, role play allows some rehearsal time so that students can map out what they are going to say. And it has the effect of lowering anxieties as students can, even for a few moments, take on the persona of someone other than themselves.

As an assessment device, role play opens some windows of opportunity for test-takers to use discourse that might otherwise be difficult to elicit. With prompts such as "Pretend that you're a tourist asking me for directions" or "You're buying a necklace from me in a flea market, and you want to get a lower price," certain personal, strategic, and linguistic factors come into the foreground of the test-taker's oral abilities. While role play can be controlled or "guided" by the interviewer, this technique takes test-takers beyond simple intensive and responsive levels to a level of creativity and complexity that approaches real-world pragmatics. Scoring presents the usual issues in any task that elicits somewhat unpredictable responses from test-takers. The test administrator must determine the assessment objectives of the role play, then devise a scoring technique that appropriately pinpoints those objectives.

Discussions and Conversations

As formal assessment devices, discussions and conversations with and among students are difficult to specify and even more difficult to score. But as *informal* techniques to assess learners, they offer a level of authenticity and spontaneity that other assessment techniques may not provide. Discussions may be especially appropriate tasks through which to elicit and observe such abilities as

- topic nomination, maintenance, and termination;
- attention getting, interrupting, floor holding, control;
- clarifying, questioning, paraphrasing;
- comprehension signals (nodding, "uh-huh," "hmm," etc.);
- negotiating meaning;
- intonation patterns for pragmatic effect;
- kinesics, eye contact, proxemics, body language; and
- politeness, formality, and other sociolinguistic factors.

Assessing the performance of participants through scores or checklists (in which appropriate or inappropriate manifestations of any category are noted) should be carefully designed to suit the objectives of the observed discussion. Of course, discussion is an integrative task, and so it is also advisable to give some cognizance to comprehension performance in evaluating learners.

Games

Among informal assessment devices are a variety of games that directly involve language production. Consider the following types:

Assessment games

1. "Tinkertoy" game: A Tinkertoy (or Lego block) structure is built behind a screen. One or two learners are allowed to view the structure. In successive stages of construction, the learners tell "runners" (who can't observe the structure) how to re-create the structure. The runners then tell "builders" behind another screen how to build the structure. The builders may question or confirm as they proceed, but only through the two degrees of separation. Object: re-create the structure as accurately as possible.

2. Crossword puzzles are created in which the names of all members of a class are clued by obscure information about them. Each class member must ask questions of others to determine who matches the clues in the puzzle.

> **3.** Information gap grids are created such that class members must conduct mini-interviews of other classmates to fill in boxes, e.g., "born in July," "plays the violin," "has a two-year-old child," etc.
> **4.** City maps are distributed to class members. Predetermined map directions are given to one student who, with a city map in front of him or her, describes the route to a partner, who must then trace the route and get to the correct final destination.

Clearly, such tasks have wandered away from the traditional notion of an oral production test and may even be well beyond *assessments,* but if you remember the discussion of these terms in Chapter 1 of this book, you can put the tasks into perspective. As assessments, the key is to specify a set of criteria and a reasonably practical and reliable scoring method. The benefit of such an informal assessment may not be as much in a summative evaluation as in its formative nature, with washback for the students.

ORAL PROFICIENCY INTERVIEW (OPI)

The best-known oral interview format is one that has gone through a considerable metamorphosis over the last half-century, the Oral Proficiency Interview (OPI). Originally known as the Foreign Service Institute (FSI) test, the OPI is the result of a historical progression of revisions under the auspices of several agencies, including the Educational Testing Service and the American Council on Teaching Foreign Languages (ACTFL). The latter, a professional society for research on foreign language instruction and assessment, has now become the principal body for promoting the use of the OPI. The OPI is widely used across dozens of languages around the world. Only certified examiners are authorized to administer the OPI; certification workshops are available, at costs of around $700 for ACTFL members, through ACTFL at selected sites and conferences throughout the year.

Specifications for the OPI approximate those delineated above under the discussion of oral interviews in general. In a series of structured tasks, the OPI is carefully designed to elicit pronunciation, fluency and integrative ability, sociolinguistic and cultural knowledge, grammar, and vocabulary. Performance is judged by the examiner to be at one of ten possible levels on the ACTFL-designated proficiency guidelines for speaking: Superior; Advanced—high, mid, low; Intermediate—high, mid, low; Novice—high, mid, low. A summary of those levels is provided in Table 7.4.

The ACTFL Proficiency Guidelines may appear to be just another form of the "FSI levels" described earlier. Holistic evaluation is still implied, and in this case

Table 7.4. Summary highlights: ACTFL proficiency guidelines—speaking

Superior	Advanced	Intermediate	Novice
Superior-level speakers are characterized by the ability to	Advanced-level speakers are characterized by the ability to	Intermediate-level speakers are characterized by the ability to	Novice-level speakers are characterized by the ability to:
• participate fully and effectively in conversations in formal and informal settings on topics related to practical needs and areas of professional and/or scholarly interests	• participate actively in conversations in most informal and some formal settings on topics of personal and public interest	• participate in simple, direct conversations on generally predictable topics related to daily activities and personal environment	• respond to simple questions on the most common features of daily life
• provide a structured argument to explain and defend opinions and develop effective hypotheses within extended discourse	• narrate and describe in major time frames with good control of aspect	• create with the language and communicate personal meaning to sympathetic interlocutors by combining language elements in discrete sentences and strings of sentences	• convey minimal meaning to interlocutors experienced in dealing with foreigners by using isolated words, lists of words, memorized phrases, and some personalized recombinations of words and phrases
• discuss topics concretely and abstractly	• deal effectively with unanticipated complications through a variety of communicative devices	• obtain and give information by asking and answering questions	• satisfy a very limited number of immediate needs
• deal with a linguistically unfamiliar situation	• sustain communication by using, with suitable accuracy and confidence, connected discourse of paragraph length and substance	• sustain and bring to a close a number of basic, uncomplicated communicative exchanges, often in a reactive mode	
• maintain a high degree of linguistic accuracy	• satisfy the demands of work and/or school situations	• satisfy simple personal needs and social demands to survive in the target language culture	
• satisfy the linguistic demands of professional and/or scholarly life			

four levels are described. On closer scrutiny, however, they offer a markedly different set of descriptors. First, they are more reflective of a unitary definition of ability, as discussed earlier in this book (page 71). Instead of focusing on separate abilities in grammar, vocabulary, comprehension, fluency, and pronunciation, they focus more strongly on the overall task and on the discourse ability needed to accomplish the goals of the tasks. Second, for classroom assessment purposes, the six FSI categories more appropriately describe the components of oral ability than do the ACTFL holistic scores, and therefore offer better washback potential. Third, the ACTFL requirement for specialized training renders the OPI less useful for classroom adaptation. Which form of evaluation is best is an issue that is still hotly debated (Reed & Cohen, 2001).

It was noted above that for official purposes, the OPI relies on an administrative network that mandates certified examiners, who pay a significant fee to achieve examiner status. This systemic control of the OPI adds test reliability to the procedure and assures test-takers that examiners are specialists who have gone through a rigorous training course. All these safeguards discourage the appearance of "outlaw" examiners who might render unreliable scores.

On the other hand, the whole idea of an oral interview under the control of an interviewer has come under harsh criticism from a number of language-testing specialists. Valdman (1988, p. 125) summed up the complaint:

> From a Vygotskyan perspective, the OPI forces test-takers into a closed system where, because the interviewer is endowed with full social control, they are unable to negotiate a social world. For example, they cannot nominate topics for discussion, they cannot switch formality levels, they cannot display a full range of stylistic maneuver. The total control the OPI interviewers possess is reflected by the parlance of the test methodology. . . . In short, the OPI can only inform us of how learners can deal with an artificial social *imposition* rather than enabling us to predict how they would be likely to manage authentic linguistic interactions with target-language native speakers.

Bachman (1988, p. 149) also pointed out that the validity of the OPI simply cannot be demonstrated "because it confounds abilities with elicitation procedures in its design, and it provides only a single rating, which has no basis in either theory or research."

Meanwhile, a great deal of experimentation continues to be conducted to design better oral proficiency testing methods (Bailey, 1998; Young & He, 1998). With ongoing critical attention to issues of language assessment in the years to come, we may be able to solve some of the thorny problems of how best to elicit oral production in authentic contexts and to create valid and reliable scoring methods.

Here is a summary of the ACTFL OPI:

American Council of Teaching Foreign Languages (ACTFL)
Oral Proficiency Interview (OPI)

Producer:	American Council on Teaching Foreign Languages, Yonkers, NY
Objective:	To test oral production skills of speakers in 37 different foreign languages
Primary market:	Certification of speakers for government personnel and employees in the workplace; evaluation of students in language programs
Type:	Oral interview—telephoned or in person
Response modes:	Oral production in a variety of genres and tasks
Specifications:	Personalized questions geared to the test-taker's interests and experiences; a variety of communication tasks designed to gauge the test-taker's upper limits; role play
Time allocation:	30–40 minutes
Internet access:	**http://www.actfl.org/**

DESIGNING ASSESSMENTS: EXTENSIVE SPEAKING

Extensive speaking tasks involve complex, relatively lengthy stretches of discourse. They are frequently variations on monologues, usually with minimal verbal interaction.

Oral Presentations

In the academic and professional arenas, it would not be uncommon to be called on to present a report, a paper, a marketing plan, a sales idea, a design of a new product, or a method. A summary of oral assessment techniques would therefore be incomplete without some consideration of extensive speaking tasks. Once again the rules for effective assessment must be invoked: (a) specify the criterion, (b) set appropriate tasks, (c) elicit optimal output, and (d) establish practical, reliable scoring procedures. And once again scoring is the key assessment challenge.

For oral presentations, a checklist or grid is a common means of scoring or evaluation. Holistic scores are tempting to use for their apparent practicality, but they may obscure the variability of performance across several subcategories, especially the two major components of content and delivery. Following is an example of a checklist for a prepared oral presentation at the intermediate or advanced level of English.

Oral presentation checklist

Evaluation of oral presentation

Assign a number to each box according to your assessment of the various aspects of the speaker's presentation.

3	Excellent
2	Good
1	Fair
0	Poor

Content:

☐ The purpose or objective of the presentation was accomplished.
☐ The introduction was lively and got my attention.
☐ The main idea or point was clearly stated toward the beginning.
☐ The supporting points were
  • clearly expressed
  • supported well by facts, argument
☐ The conclusion restated the main idea or purpose.

Delivery:

☐ The speaker used gestures and body language well.
☐ The speaker maintained eye contact with the audience.
☐ The speaker's language was natural and fluent.
☐ The speaker's volume of speech was appropriate.
☐ The speaker's rate of speech was appropriate.
☐ The speaker's pronunciation was clear and comprehensible.
☐ The speaker's grammar was correct and didn't prevent understanding.
☐ The speaker used visual aids, handouts, etc., effectively.
☐ The speaker showed enthusiasm and interest.
☐ [*If appropriate*] The speaker responded to audience questions well.

Such a checklist is reasonably practical. Its reliability can vary if clear standards for scoring are not maintained. Its authenticity can be supported in that all of the items on the list contribute to an effective presentation. The washback effect of such a checklist will be enhanced by written comments from the teacher, a conference with the teacher, peer evaluations using the same form, and self-assessment.

Picture-Cued Story-Telling

One of the most common techniques for eliciting oral production is through visual pictures, photographs, diagrams, and charts. We have already looked at this elicitation device for intensive tasks, but at this level we consider a picture or a series of pictures as a stimulus for a longer story or description. Consider the following set of pictures:

Picture-cued story-telling task (Brown, 1999, p. 29)

Test-takers see the following six-picture sequence:

Test-takers hear or read: Tell the story that these pictures describe.

Test-takers use the pictures as a sequence of cues to tell a story.

It's always tempting to throw any picture sequence at test-takers and have them talk for a minute or so about them. But as is true of every assessment of speaking ability, the objective of eliciting narrative discourse needs to be clear. In the above example (with a little humor added!), are you testing for oral vocabulary (*girl, alarm, coffee, telephone, wet, cat,* etc.), for time relatives (*before, after, when*), for sentence connectors (*then, and then, so*), for past tense of irregular verbs (*woke, drank, rang*), and/or for fluency in general? If you are eliciting specific grammatical or discourse features, you might add to the directions something like "Tell the story that these pictures describe. *Use the past tense of verbs.*" Your criteria for scoring need to be clear about what it is you are hoping to assess. Refer back to some of the guidelines suggested under the section on oral interviews, above, or to the OPI for some general suggestions on scoring such a narrative.

Retelling a Story, News Event

In this type of task, test-takers hear or read a story or news event that they are asked to retell. This differs from the paraphrasing task discussed above (pages 161–162) in that it is a longer stretch of discourse and a different genre. The objectives in assigning such a task vary from listening comprehension of the original to production of a number of oral discourse features (communicating sequences and relationships of events, stress and emphasis patterns, "expression" in the case of a dramatic story), fluency, and interaction with the hearer. Scoring should of course meet the intended criteria.

Translation (of Extended Prose)

Translation of words, phrases, or short sentences was mentioned under the category of intensive speaking. Here, longer texts are presented for the test-taker to read in the native language and then translate into English. Those texts could come in many forms: dialogue, directions for assembly of a product, a synopsis of a story or play or movie, directions on how to find something on a map, and other genres. The advantage of translation is in the control of the content, vocabulary, and, to some extent, the grammatical and discourse features. The disadvantage is that translation of longer texts is a highly specialized skill for which some individuals obtain post-baccalaureate degrees! To judge a nonspecialist's oral language ability on such a skill may be completely invalid, especially if the test-taker has not engaged in translation at this level. Criteria for scoring should therefore take into account not only the purpose in stimulating a translation but the possibility of errors that are unrelated to oral production ability.

§   §   §   §   §

One consequence of our being articulate mammals is an extraordinarily complex system of vocal communication that has evolved over the millennia of human existence. This chapter has offered a relatively sweeping overview of some of the ways we have learned to assess our wonderful ability to produce sounds, words, and sentences, and to string them together to make meaningful texts. This chapter's limited number of assessment techniques may encourage your imagination to explore a potentially limitless number of possibilities for assessing oral production.

EXERCISES

[Note: (**I**) Individual work; (**G**) Group or pair work; (**C**) Whole-class discussion.]

1. (**G**) In the introduction to the chapter, the unique challenges of testing speaking were described (interaction effect, elicitation techniques, and scoring). In pairs, offer practical examples of one of the challenges, as assigned to your pair. Explain your examples to the class.

2. (**C**) Review the five basic types of speaking that were outlined at the beginning of the chapter. Offer examples of each and pay special attention to distinguishing between imitative and intensive, and between responsive and interactive.

3. (**G**) Look at the list of micro- and macroskills of speaking on pages 142–143. In pairs, each assigned to a different skill (or two), brainstorm some tasks that assess those skills. Present your findings to the rest of the class.

4. (**C**) In Chapter 6, eight characteristics of listening (page 122) that make listening "difficult" were listed. What makes speaking difficult? Devise a similar list that could form a set of specifications to pay special attention to in assessing speaking.

5. (**G**) Divide the five basic types of speaking among groups or pairs, one type for each. Look at the sample assessment techniques provided and evaluate them according to the five principles (practicality, reliability, validity [especially face and content], authenticity, and washback). Present your critique to the rest of the class.

6. (**G**) In the same groups as in question #5 above, with the same type of speaking, design some other item types, different from the one(s) provided here, that assess the same type of speaking performance.

7. (**I**) Visit the website listed for the PhonePass test. If you can afford it and you are a non-native speaker of English, take the test. Report back to the class on how valid, reliable, and authentic you felt the test was.

8. (**G**) Several scoring scales are offered in this chapter, ranging from simple (2–1–0) score categories to the more elaborate rubric used for the OPI. In groups, each assigned to a scoring scale, evaluate the strengths and weaknesses of each. Pay special attention to intra-rater and inter-rater reliability.

9. (**C**) If possible, role-play a formal oral interview in your class, with one student (with beginning to intermediate proficiency in a language) acting as the test-taker and another (with advanced proficiency) as the test administrator. Use the sample questions provided on pages 169–170 as a guide. This role play will require some preparation. The rest of the class will then evaluate the effectiveness of the oral interview. Finally, the test-taker and administrator can offer their perspectives on the experience.

FOR YOUR FURTHER READING

Underhill, Nic. (1987). *Testing spoken language: A handbook of oral testing techniques.* Cambridge: Cambridge University Press.

This practical manual on assessing spoken language is still a widely used collection of techniques despite the fact that it was published in 1987. The chapters are organized into types of tests, elicitation techniques, scoring systems, and a discussion of several types of validity along with reliability.

Brown, J.D. (1998). *New ways of classroom assessment.* Alexandria, VA: Teachers of English to Speakers of Other Languages.

One of the many volumes in TESOL's "New Ways" series, this one presents a collection of assessment techniques across a wide range of skill areas. The two sections on assessing oral skills offer 17 different techniques.

Celce-Murcia, Marianne, Brinton, Donna, and Goodwin, Janet. (1996). *Teaching pronunciation: A reference for teachers of English to speakers of other languages.* Cambridge: Cambridge University Press.

This broadly based pedagogical reference book on teaching pronunciation also offers numerous examples and commentaries on assessment of pronunciation (which of course goes hand in hand with teaching). Most of the references to assessment deal with informal assessment, but the book also addresses formal assessment.

CHAPTER 8

ASSESSING READING

Even as we are bombarded with an unending supply of visual and auditory media, the written word continues in its function to convey information, to amuse and entertain us, to codify our social, economic, and legal conventions, and to fulfill a host of other functions. In literate societies, most "normal" children learn to read by the age of five or six, and some even earlier. With the exception of a small number of people with learning disabilities, reading is a skill that is taken for granted.

In foreign language learning, reading is likewise a skill that teachers simply expect learners to acquire. Basic, beginning-level textbooks in a foreign language presuppose a student's reading ability if only because it's a *book* that is the medium. Most formal tests use the written word as a stimulus for test-taker response; even oral interviews may require reading performance for certain tasks. Reading, arguably the most essential skill for success in all educational contexts, remains a skill of paramount importance as we create assessments of general language ability.

Is reading so natural and normal that learners should simply be exposed to written texts with no particular instruction? Will they just absorb the skills necessary to convert their perception of a handful of letters into meaningful chunks of information? Not necessarily. For learners of English, two primary hurdles must be cleared in order to become efficient readers. First, they need to be able to master fundamental **bottom-up** strategies for processing separate letters, words, and phrases, as well as **top-down,** conceptually driven strategies for comprehension. Second, as part of that top-down approach, second language readers must develop appropriate content and formal **schemata**—background information and cultural experience—to carry out those interpretations effectively.

The assessment of reading ability does not end with the measurement of comprehension. Strategic pathways to full understanding are often important factors to include in assessing learners, especially in the case of most classroom assessments that are **formative** in nature. An inability to comprehend may thus be traced to a need to enhance a test-taker's strategies for achieving ultimate comprehension. For example, an academic technical report may be comprehensible to a student at the sentence level, but if the learner has not exercised certain strategies for noting the discourse conventions of that genre, misunderstanding may occur.

As we consider a number of different types or genres of written texts, the components of reading ability, and specific tasks that are commonly used in the assessment of reading, let's not forget the unobservable nature of reading. Like listening, one cannot see the **process** of reading, nor can one observe a specific **product** of reading. Other than observing a reader's eye movements and page turning, there is no technology that enables us to "see" sequences of graphic symbols traveling from the pages of a book into compartments of the brain (in a possible bottom-up process). Even more outlandish is the notion that one might be able to watch information from the brain make its way down onto the page (in typical top-down strategies). Further, once something is read—information from the written text is stored—no technology allows us to empirically measure exactly what is lodged in the brain. All assessment of reading must be carried out by inference.

TYPES (GENRES) OF READING

Each type or **genre** of written text has its own set of governing rules and conventions. A reader must be able to anticipate those conventions in order to process meaning efficiently. With an extraordinary number of genres present in any literate culture, the reader's ability to process texts must be very sophisticated. Consider the following abridged list of common genres, which ultimately form part of the specifications for assessments of reading ability.

Genres of reading

---

1. **Academic reading**

   general interest articles (in magazines, newspapers, etc.)
   technical reports (e.g., lab reports), professional journal articles
   reference material (dictionaries, etc.)
   textbooks, theses
   essays, papers
   test directions
   editorials and opinion writing

2. **Job-related reading**

   messages (e.g., phone messages)
   letters/emails
   memos (e.g., interoffice)
   reports (e.g., job evaluations, project reports)
   schedules, labels, signs, announcements
   forms, applications, questionnaires
   financial documents (bills, invoices, etc.)
   directories (telephone, office, etc.)
   manuals, directions

---

3. Personal reading

> newspapers and magazines
> letters, emails, greeting cards, invitations
> messages, notes, lists
> schedules (train, bus, plane, etc.)
> recipes, menus, maps, calendars
> advertisements (commercials, want ads)
> novels, short stories, jokes, drama, poetry
> financial documents (e.g., checks, tax forms, loan applications)
> forms, questionnaires, medical reports, immigration documents
> comic strips, cartoons

When we realize that this list is only the beginning, it is easy to see how overwhelming it is to learn to read in a foreign language! The genre of a text enables readers to apply certain **schemata** that will assist them in extracting appropriate meaning. If, for example, readers know that a text is a recipe, they will expect a certain arrangement of information (ingredients) and will know to search for a sequential order of directions. Efficient readers also have to know what their purpose is in reading a text, the strategies for accomplishing that purpose, and how to retain the information.

The content validity of an assessment procedure is largely established through the genre of a text. For example, if learners in a program of English for tourism have been learning how to deal with customers needing to arrange bus tours, then assessments of their ability should include guidebooks, maps, transportation schedules, calendars, and other relevant texts.

MICROSKILLS, MACROSKILLS, AND STRATEGIES FOR READING

Aside from attending to genres of text, the skills and strategies for accomplishing reading emerge as a crucial consideration in the assessment of reading ability. The micro- and macroskills below represent the spectrum of possibilities for objectives in the assessment of reading comprehension.

Micro- and macroskills for reading comprehension

Microskills

1. Discriminate among the distinctive graphemes and orthographic patterns of English.
2. Retain chunks of language of different lengths in short-term memory.
3. Process writing at an efficient rate of speed to suit the purpose.

4. Recognize a core of words, and interpret word order patterns and their significance.
5. Recognize grammatical word classes (nouns, verbs, etc.), systems (e.g., tense, agreement, pluralization), patterns, rules, and elliptical forms.
6. Recognize that a particular meaning may be expressed in different grammatical forms.
7. Recognize cohesive devices in written discourse and their role in signaling the relationship between and among clauses.

Macroskills

8. Recognize the rhetorical forms of written discourse and their significance for interpretation.
9. Recognize the communicative functions of written texts, according to form and purpose.
10. Infer context that is not explicit by using background knowledge.
11. From described events, ideas, etc., infer links and connections between events, deduce causes and effects, and detect such relations as main idea, supporting idea, new information, given information, generalization, and exemplification.
12. Distinguish between literal and implied meanings.
13. Detect culturally specific references and interpret them in a context of the appropriate cultural schemata.
14. Develop and use a battery of reading strategies, such as scanning and skimming, detecting discourse markers, guessing the meaning of words from context, and activating schemata for the interpretation of texts.

The assessment of reading can imply the assessment of a storehouse of reading strategies, as indicated in item #14. Aside from simply testing the ultimate achievement of comprehension of a written text, it may be important in some contexts to assess one or more of a storehouse of classic reading strategies. The brief taxonomy of strategies below is a list of possible assessment criteria.

Some principal strategies for reading comprehension

1. Identify your purpose in reading a text.
2. Apply spelling rules and conventions for bottom-up decoding.
3. Use lexical analysis (prefixes, roots, suffixes, etc.) to determine meaning.
4. Guess at meaning (of words, idioms, etc.) when you aren't certain.
5. Skim the text for the gist and for main ideas.
6. Scan the text for specific information (names, dates, key words).
7. Use silent reading techniques for rapid processing.

> **8.** Use marginal notes, outlines, charts, or semantic maps for understanding and retaining information.
> **9.** Distinguish between literal and implied meanings.
> **10.** Capitalize on discourse markers to process relationships.

TYPES OF READING

In the previous chapters we saw that both listening and speaking could be subdivided into at least five different types of listening and speaking performance. In the case of reading, variety of performance is derived more from the multiplicity of types of texts (the genres listed above) than from the variety of overt types of performance. Nevertheless, for considering assessment procedures, several types of reading performance are typically identified, and these will serve as organizers of various assessment tasks.

1. Perceptive. In keeping with the set of categories specified for listening comprehension, similar specifications are offered here, except with some differing terminology to capture the uniqueness of reading. Perceptive reading tasks involve attending to the *components* of larger stretches of discourse: letters, words, punctuation, and other graphemic symbols. Bottom-up processing is implied.

2. Selective. This category is largely an artifact of assessment formats. In order to ascertain one's reading recognition of lexical, grammatical, or discourse features of language within a very short stretch of language, certain typical tasks are used: picture-cued tasks, matching, true/false, multiple-choice, etc. Stimuli include sentences, brief paragraphs, and simple charts and graphs. Brief responses are intended as well. A combination of bottom-up and top-down processing may be used.

3. Interactive. Included among interactive reading types are stretches of language of several paragraphs to one page or more in which the reader must, in a psycholinguistic sense, *interact* with the text. That is, reading is a process of negotiating meaning; the reader brings to the text a set of schemata for understanding it, and intake is the product of that interaction. Typical genres that lend themselves to interactive reading are anecdotes, short narratives and descriptions, excerpts from longer texts, questionnaires, memos, announcements, directions, recipes, and the like. The focus of an interactive task is to identify relevant features (lexical, symbolic, grammatical, and discourse) within texts of moderately short length with the objective of retaining the information that is processed. Top-down processing is typical of such tasks, although some instances of bottom-up performance may be necessary.

4. Extensive. Extensive reading, as discussed in this book, applies to texts of more than a page, up to and including professional articles, essays, technical reports, short stories, and books. (It should be noted that reading research commonly refers to "extensive reading" as longer stretches of discourse, such as long articles and books that are usually read outside a classroom hour. Here that definition is massaged a little in order to encompass any text longer than a page.) The purposes of assessment usually are to tap into a learner's global understanding of a text, as opposed to asking test-takers to "zoom in" on small details. Top-down processing is assumed for most extensive tasks.

The four types of reading are demonstrated in Figure 8.1, which shows the relationships of length, focus, and processing mode among the four types.

	Length			Focus		Process	
	Short	**Medium**	**Long**	**Form**	**Meaning**	**Bottom-Up**	**Top-Down**
Perceptive	••			••		••	
Selective	•	•		••	•	•	•
Interactive		••		•	••	•	••
Extensive			••		••		••

•• strong emphasis
• moderate emphasis

Figure 8.1. Types of reading by length, focus, and process

DESIGNING ASSESSMENT TASKS: PERCEPTIVE READING

At the beginning level of reading a second language lies a set of tasks that are fundamental and basic: recognition of alphabetic symbols, capitalized and lowercase letters, punctuation, words, and grapheme–phoneme correspondences. Such tasks of perception are often referred to as **literacy** tasks, implying that the learner is in the early stages of becoming "literate." Some learners are already literate in their own native language, but in other cases the second language may be the first language that they have ever learned to read. This latter context poses cognitive and sometimes age-related issues that need to be considered carefully. Assessment of literacy is no easy assignment, and if you are interested in this particular challenging area, further reading beyond this book is advised (Harp, 1991; Farr & Tone, 1994; Genesee, 1994; Cooper, 1997). Assessment of basic reading skills may be carried out in a number of different ways.

Reading Aloud

The test-taker sees separate letters, words, and/or short sentences and reads them aloud, one by one, in the presence of an administrator. Since the assessment is of *reading* comprehension, any recognizable oral approximation of the target response is considered correct.

Written Response

The same stimuli are presented, and the test-taker's task is to reproduce the probe in writing. Because of the transfer across different skills here, evaluation of the test-taker's response must be carefully treated. If an error occurs, make sure you determine its source; what might be assumed to be a writing error, for example, may actually be a reading error, and vice versa.

Multiple-Choice

Multiple-choice responses are not only a matter of choosing one of four or five possible answers. Other formats, some of which are especially useful at the low levels of reading, include same/different, circle the answer, true/false, choose the letter, and matching. Here are some possibilities.

Minimal pair distinction

*Test-takers read:**	Circle "S" for same or "D" for different.			
1. led	let	S	D	
2. bit	bit	S	D	
3. seat	set	S	D	
4. too	to	S	D	

In the case of very low level learners, the teacher/administrator reads directions.

Grapheme recognition task

*Test-takers read:**	Circle the "odd" item, the one that doesn't "belong."	
1. piece	peace	piece
2. book	book	boot

In the case of very low level learners, the teacher/administrator reads directions.

Picture-Cued Items

Test-takers are shown a picture, such as the one on the next page, along with a written text and are given one of a number of possible tasks to perform.

Picture-cued word identification (Brown & Sahni, 1994, p. 124)

Test-takers hear: Point to the word that you read here.

cat	**clock**	**chair**

With the same picture, the test-taker might read sentences and then point to the correct part of the picture:

Picture-cued sentence identification

Test-takers hear: Point to the part of the picture that you read about here.

Test-takers see the picture and read each sentence written on a separate card.

The man is reading a book.

The cat is under the table.

Or a true/false procedure might be presented with the same picture cue:

Picture-cued true/false sentence identification

Test-takers read:

1. The pencils are under the table.   T   F
2. The cat is on the table.   T   F
3. The picture is over the couch.   T   F

Matching can be an effective method of assessing reading at this level. With objects labeled A, B, C, D, E in the picture, the test-taker reads words and writes the appropriate letter beside the word:

Picture-cued matching word identification

Test-takers read:

1. clock   _____
2. chair   _____
3. books   _____
4. cat   _____
5. table   _____

Finally, test-takers might see a word or phrase and then be directed to choose one of four pictures that is being described, thus requiring the test-taker to transfer from a verbal to a nonverbal mode. In the following item, test-takers choose the correct letter:

Multiple-choice picture-cued word identification

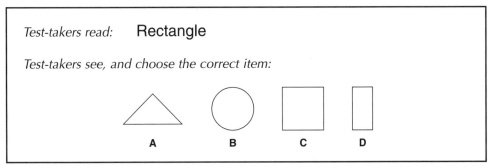

DESIGNING ASSESSMENT TASKS: SELECTIVE READING

Just above the rudimentary skill level of perception of letters and words is a category in which the test designer focuses on formal aspects of language (lexical, grammatical, and a few discourse features). This category includes what many incorrectly think of as testing "vocabulary and grammar." How many textbooks provide little tests and quizzes labeled "vocabulary and grammar" and never feature any other skill besides reading? Lexical and grammatical aspects of language are simply the forms we use to perform all four of the skills of listening, speaking, reading, and writing. (Notice that in all of these chapters on the four skills, formal features of language have become a potential focus for assessment.)

Here are some of the possible tasks you can use to assess lexical and grammatical aspects of *reading* ability.

Multiple-Choice (for Form-Focused Criteria)

By far the most popular method of testing a reading knowledge of vocabulary and grammar is the multiple-choice format, mainly for reasons of practicality: it is easy to administer and can be scored quickly. The most straightforward multiple-choice items may have little context, but might serve as a vocabulary or grammar check.

Multiple-choice vocabulary/grammar tasks

---

1. He's not married. He's _____.
   A. young
   B. single
   C. first
   D. a husband

2. If there's no doorbell, please _____ on the door.
   A. kneel
   B. type
   C. knock
   D. shout

3. The mouse is _____ the bed.
   A. under
   B. around
   C. between

4. The bank robbery occurred _____ I was in the restroom.
   A. that
   B. during
   C. while
   D. which

---

5. Yeast is an organic catalyst _____ known to prehistoric
humanity.
   A. was
   B. which was
   C. which it
   D. which

This kind of darting from one context to another to another in a test has become so commonplace that learners almost expect the disjointedness. Some improvement of these items is possible by providing some context within each item:

Contextualized multiple-choice vocabulary/grammar tasks

1. Oscar: Do you like champagne?
   Lucy: No, I can't _____ it!
   A. stand
   B. prefer
   C. hate

2. Manager: Do you like to work by yourself?
   Employee: Yes, I like to work _____.
   A. independently
   B. definitely
   C. impatiently

3. Jack: Do you have a coat like this?
   John: Yes, mine is _____ yours.
   A. so same as
   B. the same like
   C. as same as
   D. the same as

4. Boss: Where did I put the Johnson file?
   Sectretary: I think _____ is on your desk.
   A. you were the file looking at
   B. the you were looking at file
   C. the file you were looking at
   D. you were looking at the file

A better contextualized format is to offer a modified cloze test (see page 201 for a treatment of cloze testing) adjusted to fit the objectives being assessed. In the example below, a few lines of English add to overall context.

Multiple-choice cloze vocabulary/grammar task

I've lived in the United States (**21**) _____ three years. I (**22**) _____ live in Costa Rica. I (**23**) _____ speak any English. I used to (**24**) _____ homesick, but now I enjoy (**25**) _____ here. I have never (**26**) _____ back home (**27**) _____ I came to the United States, but I might (**28**) _____ to visit my family soon.

21.	A. since	**25.**	A. live
	B. for		B. to live
	C. during		C. living
22.	A. used to	**26.**	A. be
	B. use to		B. been
	C. was		C. was
23.	A. couldn't	**27.**	A. when
	B. could		B. while
	C. can		C. since
24.	A. been	**28.**	A. go
	B. be		B. will go
	C. being		C. going

The context of the story in this example may not specifically help the test-taker to respond to the items more easily, but it allows the learner to attend to one set of related sentences for eight items that assess vocabulary and grammar. Other contexts might involve some content dependencies, such that earlier sentences predict the correct response for a later item. Thus, a pair of sentences in a short narrative might read:

He showed his suitcase (**29**) _____ me, but it wasn't big (**30**) _____ to fit all his clothes. So I gave him my suitcase, which was (**31**) _____.

29. A. for
 B. from
 C. to

30. A. so
 B. too
 C. enough

31. A. larger
 B. smaller
 C. largest

To respond to item **#31** correctly, the test-taker needs to be able to comprehend the context of needing a *larger,* but not an equally grammatically correct *smaller,* suitcase. While such dependencies offer greater authenticity to an assessment, they also add the potential problem of a test-taker's missing several later items because of an earlier comprehension error.

Matching Tasks

At this selective level of reading, the test-taker's task is simply to respond correctly, which makes matching an appropriate format. The most frequently appearing criterion in matching procedures is vocabulary. Following is a typical format:

Vocabulary matching task

Write in the letter of the definition on the right that matches the word on the left.

_____ **1.** exhausted	a. unhappy
_____ **2.** disappointed	b. understanding of others
_____ **3.** enthusiastic	c. tired
_____ **4.** empathetic	d. excited

To add a communicative quality to matching, the first numbered list is sometimes a set of sentences with blanks in them, with a list of words to choose from:

Selected response fill-in vocabulary task

---

1. At the end of the long race, the runners were totally _____.
2. My parents were _____ with my bad performance on the final exam.
3. Everyone in the office was _____ about the new salary raises.
4. The _____ listening of the counselor made Christina feel well understood.

Choose from among the following:
   disappointed
   empathetic
   exhausted
   enthusiastic

Alderson (2000, p. 218) suggested matching procedures at an even more sophisticated level, where test-takers have to discern pragmatic interpretations of certain signs or labels such as "Freshly made sandwiches" and "Use before 10/23/02." Matches for those two are "We sell food" and "This is too old," which are selected from a number of other options.

Matching tasks have the advantage of offering an alternative to traditional multiple-choice or fill-in-the-blank formats and are sometimes easier to construct than multiple-choice items, as long as the test designer has chosen the matches carefully. Some disadvantages do come with this framework, however. They can become more of a puzzle-solving process than a genuine test of comprehension as test-takers struggle with the search for a match, possibly among 10 or 20 different items. Like other tasks in this section, they also are contrived exercises that are endemic to academia that will seldom be found in the real world.

Editing Tasks

Editing for grammatical or rhetorical errors is a widely used test method for assessing linguistic competence in reading. The TOEFL® and many other tests employ this technique with the argument that it not only focuses on grammar but also introduces a simulation of the authentic task of editing, or discerning errors in written passages. Its authenticity may be supported if you consider proof-reading as a real-world skill that is being tested. Here is a typical set of examples of editing.

Multiple-choice grammar editing task (Phillips, 2001, p. 219)

Test-takers read: Choose the letter of the underlined word that is not correct.

1. The <u>abrasively</u> action of the wind <u>wears</u> away <u>softer</u> <u>layers</u> of rock.
       A   B   C   D

2. There are two <u>way</u> of <u>making</u> a gas <u>condense</u>: cooling it or <u>putting</u> it under
                      A   B   C   D

   pressure.

3. Researchers have <u>discovered</u> that the <u>application</u> of bright light can sometimes
                          A   B

   be <u>uses</u> to <u>overcome</u> jet lag.
       C   D

The above examples, with their disparate subject-matter content, are not as authentic as asking test-takers to edit a whole essay (see discussion below, pages 207–208). Of course, if learners have never practiced error detection tasks, the task itself is of some difficulty. Nevertheless, error detection has been shown to be positively correlated with both listening comprehension and reading comprehension results on the TOEFL, at r = .58 and .76, respectively (*TOEFL Score User Guide,* 2001). Despite some authenticity quibbles, this task maintains a construct validity that justifies its use.

Picture-Cued Tasks

In the previous section we looked at picture-cued tasks for perceptive recognition of symbols and words. Pictures and photographs may be equally well utilized for examining ability at the selective level. Several types of picture-cued methods are commonly used.

1. Test-takers read a sentence or passage and choose one of four pictures that is being described. The sentence (or sentences) at this level is more complex. A computer-based example follows:

Multiple-choice picture-cued response (Phillips, 2001, p. 276)

Test-takers read a three-paragraph passage, one sentence of which is:

During at least three quarters of the year, the Arctic is frozen.

Click on the chart that shows the relative amount of time each year that water is available to plants in the Arctic.

Test-takers see the following four pictures:

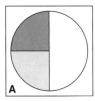 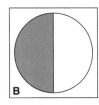 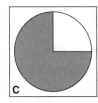 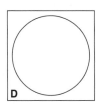

2. Test-takers read a series of sentences or definitions, each describing a labeled part of a picture or diagram. Their task is to identify each labeled item. In the following diagram, test-takers do not necessarily know each term, but by reading the definition they are able to make an identification. For example:

Diagram-labeling task

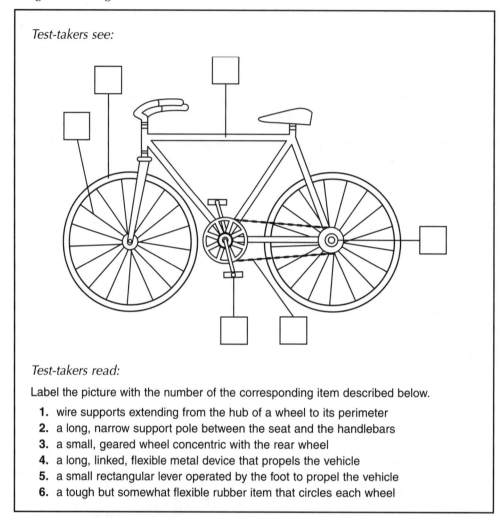

Test-takers see:

Test-takers read:

Label the picture with the number of the corresponding item described below.

1. wire supports extending from the hub of a wheel to its perimeter
2. a long, narrow support pole between the seat and the handlebars
3. a small, geared wheel concentric with the rear wheel
4. a long, linked, flexible metal device that propels the vehicle
5. a small rectangular lever operated by the foot to propel the vehicle
6. a tough but somewhat flexible rubber item that circles each wheel

The essential difference between the picture-cued tasks here and those that were outlined in the previous section is the complexity of the language.

Gap-Filling Tasks

Many of the multiple-choice tasks described above can be converted into gap-filling, or "fill-in-the-blank," items in which the test-taker's response is to write a word or phrase. An extension of simple gap-filling tasks is to create sentence completion items where test-takers read part of a sentence and then complete it by writing a phrase.

Sentence completion tasks

Oscar:	Doctor, what should I do if I get sick?
Doctor:	It is best to stay home and _____.
	If you have a fever, _____.
	You should drink as much _____.
	The worst thing you can do is _____.
	You should also _____.

The obvious disadvantage of this type of task is its questionable assessment of reading ability. The task requires both reading and writing performance, thereby rendering it of low validity in isolating reading as the sole criterion. Another drawback is scoring the variety of creative responses that are likely to appear. You will have to make a number of judgment calls on what comprises a correct response. In a test of reading comprehension only, you must accept as correct any responses that demonstrate comprehension of the first part of the sentence. This alone indicates that such tasks are better categorized as integrative procedures.

DESIGNING ASSESSMENT TASKS: INTERACTIVE READING

Tasks at this level, like selective tasks, have a combination of form-focused and meaning-focused objectives but with more emphasis on meaning. Interactive tasks may therefore imply a little more focus on top-down processing than on bottom-up. Texts are a little longer, from a paragraph to as much as a page or so in the case of ordinary prose. Charts, graphs, and other graphics may be somewhat complex in their format.

Cloze Tasks

One of the most popular types of reading assessment task is the **cloze** procedure. The word *cloze* was coined by educational psychologists to capture the Gestalt psychological concept of "closure," that is, the ability to fill in gaps in an incomplete image (visual, auditory, or cognitive) and supply (from background schemata) omitted details.

In written language, a sentence with a word left out should have enough context that a reader can close that gap with a calculated guess, using linguistic expectancies (formal schemata), background experience (content schemata), and some strategic competence. Based on this assumption, cloze tests were developed for native language readers and defended as an appropriate gauge of reading ability. Some research (Oller, 1973, 1976, 1979) on second language acquisition vigorously defends cloze testing as an integrative measure not only of reading ability but also of other language abilities. It was argued that the ability to make coherent guesses in cloze gaps also taps into the ability to listen, speak, and write. With the decline of zeal for the search for the ideal integrative test in recent years, cloze testing has returned to a more appropriate status as one of a number of assessment procedures available for testing reading ability.

Cloze tests are usually a minimum of two paragraphs in length in order to account for discourse expectancies. They can be constructed relatively easily as long as the specifications for choosing deletions and for scoring are clearly defined. Typically every seventh word (plus or minus two) is deleted (known as **fixed-ratio deletion**), but many cloze test designers instead use a **rational deletion** procedure of choosing deletions according to the grammatical or discourse functions of the words. Rational deletion also allows the designer to avoid deleting words that would be difficult to predict from the context. For example, in the sentence "Everyone in the crowd enjoyed the gorgeous sunset," the seventh word is *gorgeous,* but learners could easily substitute other appropriate adjectives. Traditionally, cloze passages have between 30 and 50 blanks to fill, but a passage with as few as half a dozen blanks can legitimately be labeled a cloze test.

Two approaches to the scoring of cloze tests are commonly used. The **exact word** method gives credit to test-takers only if they insert the exact word that was originally deleted. The second method, **appropriate word** scoring, credits the test-taker for supplying any word that is grammatically correct and that makes good sense in the context. In the sentence above about the "gorgeous sunset," the test-takers would get credit for supplying *beautiful, amazing,* and *spectacular.* The choice between the two methods of scoring is one of practicality/reliability vs. face validity. In the exact word approach, scoring can be done quickly (especially if the procedure uses a multiple-choice technique) and reliably. The second approach takes more time because the teacher must determine whether each response is indeed appropriate, but students will perceive the test as being fairer: they won't get "marked off" for appropriate, grammatically correct responses.

The following excerpts from a longer essay illustrate the difference between rational and fixed-ratio deletion, and between exact word and appropriate word scoring.

Cloze procedure, fixed-ratio deletion (every seventh word)

The recognition that one's feelings of (**1**) _____ and unhappiness can coexist much like (**2**) _____ and hate in a close relationship (**3**) _____ offer valuable clues on how to (**4**) _____ a happier life. It suggests, for (**5**) _____, that changing or avoiding things that (**6**) _____ you miserable may well make you (**7**) _____ miserable but probably no happier.

Cloze procedure, rational deletion (prepositions and conjunctions)

The recognition that one's feelings (**1**) _____ happiness (**2**) _____ unhappiness can coexist much like love and hate (**3**) _____ a close relationship may offer valuable clues (**4**) _____ how to lead a happier life. It suggests, (**5**) _____ example, that changing (**6**) _____ avoiding things that make you miserable may well make you less miserable (**7**) _____ probably no happier.

In both versions there are seven deletions, but the second version allows the test designer to tap into prediction of prepositions and conjunctions in particular. And the second version provides more washback as students focus on targeted grammatical features.

Both of the scoring methods named above could present problems, with the first version presenting a little more ambiguity. Possible responses might include:

Fixed-ratio version, blank   **#3:** *may, might, could, can*
                           #4: *lead, live, have, seek*
                           #5: *example, instance*

Rational deletion version, blank   **#4:** *on, about*
                                #6: *or, and*
                                #7: *but, and*

Arranging a cloze test in a multiple-choice format allows even more rapid scoring: hand scoring with an answer key or hole-punched grid, or computer scoring using scannable answer sheets. Multiple-choice cloze tests must of course adhere to all the other guidelines for effective multiple-choice items that were covered in Chapter 4, especially the choice of appropriate distractors; therefore they can take much longer to construct—possibly too long to pay off in a classroom setting.

Some variations on standard cloze testing have appeared over the years; two of the better known are the C-test and the cloze-elide procedure. In the **C-test** (Klein-Braley & Raatz, 1984; Klein-Braley, 1985; Dörnyei & Katona, 1992), the second half (according to the number of letters) of every other word is obliterated and the test-taker must restore each word. While Klein-Braley and others vouched for its validity and reliability, many consider this technique to be "even more irritating to complete than cloze tests" (Alderson, 2000, p. 225). Look at the following example and judge for yourself:

C-test procedure

> The recognition th_ _ one's feel_ _ _ _ of happ_ _ _ _ _ and unhap_ _ _ _ _ _ can
> coe_ _ _ _ much li_ _ love a_ _ hate i_ a cl_ _ _ relati_ _ _ _ _ _ may of_ _ _
> valuable cl_ _ _ on h_ _ to le_ _ a hap_ _ _ _ life. I_ suggests, f_ _ example, th_ _
> changing o_ avoiding thi_ _ _ that ma_ _ you mise_ _ _ _ _ may we_ _ make y_ _
> less mise_ _ _ _ _ but prob_ _ _ _ no hap_ _ _ _.

The second variation, the **cloze-elide** procedure, inserts words into a text that don't belong. The test-taker's task is to detect and cross out the "intrusive" words. Look at the same familiar passage:

Cloze-elide procedure

> The recognition that one's now feelings of happiness and unhappiness can under coexist much like love and hate in a close then relationship may offer valuable clues on how to lead a happier with life. It suggests, for example, that changing or avoiding my things that make you miserable may well make you less miserable ever but probably no happier.

Critics of this procedure (Davies, 1975) claimed that the cloze-elide procedure is actually a test of reading speed and not of proofreading skill, as its proponents asserted. Two disadvantages are nevertheless immediately apparent: (1) Neither the words to insert nor the frequency of insertion appears to have any rationale. (2) Fast and efficient readers are not adept at detecting the intrusive words. Good readers naturally weed out such potential interruptions.

Impromptu Reading Plus Comprehension Questions

If cloze testing is the most-researched procedure for assessing reading, the traditional "Read a passage and answer some questions" technique is undoubtedly the oldest and the most common. Virtually every proficiency test uses the format, and one would rarely consider assessing reading without some component of the assessment involving impromptu reading and responding to questions.

In Chapter 4, in the discussion on proficiency testing, we looked at a typical reading comprehension passage and a set of questions from the TOEFL. Here's another such passage.

Reading comprehension passage (Phillips, 2001, pp. 421–422)

Questions 1–10

The Hollywood sign in the hills that line the northern border of Los Angeles is a famous landmark recognized the world over. The white-painted, 50-foot-high, sheet metal letters can be seen from great distances across the Los Angeles basin.

Line
(5)
The sign was not constructed, as one might suppose, by the movie business as a means of celebrating the importance of Hollywood to this industry; instead, it was first constructed in 1923 as a means of advertising homes for sale in a 500-acre housing subdivision in a part of Los Angeles called "Hollywoodland." The sign that was constructed at the time, of course, said "Hollywoodland." Over the years, people began referring to the area by the shortened version "Hollywood," and after the sign and its site were donated to the city in 1945, the last four letters were removed.

(10)
The sign suffered from years of disrepair, and in 1973 it needed to be completely replaced, at a cost of $27,700 per letter. Various celebrities were instrumental in helping to raise needed funds. Rock star Alice Cooper, for example, bought an O in memory of Groucho Marx, and Hugh Hefner of *Playboy* fame held a benefit party to raise the money for the Y. The construction of the new sign was finally completed in 1978.

1. What is the topic of this passage?
   (A) A famous sign
   (B) A famous city
   (C) World landmarks
   (D) Hollywood versus Hollywoodland

2. The expression "the world over" in line 2 could best be replaced by
   (A) in the northern parts of the world
   (B) on top of the world
   (C) in the entire world
   (D) in the skies

3. It can be inferred from the passage that most people think that the Hollywood sign was first constructed by
   (A) an advertising company
   (B) the movie industry
   (C) a construction company
   (D) the city of Los Angeles

4. The pronoun "it" in line 5 refers to
   (A) the sign
   (B) the movie business
   (C) the importance of Hollywood
   (D) this industry

5. According to the passage, the Hollywood sign was first built in
   (A) 1923
   (B) 1949
   (C) 1973
   (D) 1978

6. Which of the following is NOT mentioned about Hollywoodland?
   (A) It used to be the name of an area of Los Angeles.

   (B) It was formerly the name on the sign in the hills.
   (C) There were houses for sale there.
   (D) It was the most expensive area of Los Angeles.

7. The passage indicates that the sign suffered because
   (A) people damaged it
   (B) it was not fixed
   (C) the weather was bad
   (D) it was poorly constructed

8. It can be inferred from the passage that the Hollywood sign was how old when it was necessary to replace it completely?
   (A) Ten years old
   (B) Twenty-six years old
   (C) Fifty years old
   (D) Fifty-five years old

9. The word "replaced" in line 10 is closest in meaning to which of the following?
   (A) Moved to a new location
   (B) Destroyed
   (C) Found again
   (D) Exchanged for a newer one

10. According to the passage, how did celebrities help with the new sign?
    (A) They played instruments.
    (B) They raised the sign.
    (C) They helped get the money.
    (D) They took part in work parties to build the sign.

Notice that this set of questions, based on a 250-word passage, covers the comprehension of these features:

- main idea (topic)
- expressions/idioms/phrases in context
- inference (implied detail)
- grammatical features
- detail (scanning for a specifically stated detail)
- excluding facts not written (unstated details)
- supporting idea(s)
- vocabulary in context

These specifications, and the questions that exemplify them, are *not* just a string of "straight" comprehension questions that follow the thread of the passage. The questions represent a sample of the test specifications for TOEFL reading passages, which are derived from research on a variety of abilities good readers exhibit. Notice that many of them are consistent with strategies of effective reading: skimming for main idea, scanning for details, guessing word meanings from context, inferencing, using discourse markers, etc. To construct your own assessments that involve short reading passages followed by questions, you can begin with TOEFL-like specs as a basis. Your focus in your own classroom will determine which of these—and possibly other specifications—you will include in your assessment procedure, how you will frame questions, and how much weight you will give each item in scoring.

The technology of computer-based reading comprehension tests of this kind enables some additional types of items. Items such as the following are typical:

Computer-based TOEFL® reading comprehension item

- Click on the word in paragraph 1 that means "subsequent work."
- Look at the word *they* in paragraph 2. Click on the word that *they* refers to.
- The following sentence could be added to paragraph 2:

    Instead, he used the pseudonym Mrs. Silence Dogood.

    Where would it best fit into the paragraph? Click on the square ☐ to add the sentence to the paragraph.

- Click on the drawing that most closely resembles the prehistoric coelacanth.
  [*Four drawings are depicted on the screen.*]

Short-Answer Tasks

Multiple-choice items are difficult to construct and validate, and classroom teachers rarely have time in their busy schedules to design such a test. A popular alternative to multiple-choice questions following reading passages is the age-old short-answer format. A reading passage is presented, and the test-taker reads questions that must be answered in a sentence or two. Questions might cover the same specifications indicated above for the TOEFL reading, but be worded in question form. For example, in a passage on the future of airline travel, the following questions might appear:

Open-ended reading comprehension questions

---

1. What do you think the main idea of this passage is?
2. What would you infer from the passage about the future of air travel?
3. In line 6 the word *sensation* is used. From the context, what do you think this word means?
4. What two ideas did the writer suggest for increasing airline business?
5. Why do you think the airlines have recently experienced a decline?

Do not take lightly the design of questions. It can be difficult to make sure that they reach their intended criterion. You will also need to develop consistent specifications for acceptable student responses and be prepared to take the time necessary to accomplish their evaluation. But these rather predictable disadvantages may be outweighed by the face validity of offering students a chance to construct their own answers, and by the washback effect of potential follow-up discussion.

Editing (Longer Texts)

The previous section of this chapter (on selective reading) described editing tasks, but there the discussion was limited to a list of unrelated sentences, each presented with an error to be detected by the test-taker. The same technique has been applied successfully to longer passages of 200 to 300 words. Several advantages are gained in the longer format.

First, *authenticity* is increased. The likelihood that students in English classrooms will read connected prose of a page or two is greater than the likelihood of their encountering the contrived format of unconnected sentences. Second, the task *simulates proofreading* one's own essay, where it is imperative to find and correct errors. And third, if the test is connected to a specific curriculum (such as placement into one of several writing courses), the test designer can draw up specifications for a number of grammatical and rhetorical *categories that match the content* of the courses. Content validity is thereby supported, and along with it the face validity of a task in which students are willing to invest.

Imao's (2001) test introduced one error in each numbered sentence. Test-takers followed the same procedure for marking errors as described in the previous section. Instructions to the student included a sample of the kind of connected prose that test-takers would encounter:

Contextualized grammar editing tasks (Imao, 2001)

(**1**) <u>Ever</u> since supermarkets first <u>appeared</u>, they have been <u>take</u> over <u>the</u> world.
    A   B   C   D

(**2**) <u>Supermarkets</u> have changed people's life <u>styles</u>, yet <u>and</u> at the same time,
      A   B   C

changes in people's life <u>styles</u> have encouraged the opening of supermarkets. (**3**) As
                      D

a <u>result this</u>, many small <u>stores</u> have been <u>forced</u> out <u>of</u> business. (**4**) <u>Moreover</u>, some
   A   B   C   D   B

small stores <u>will</u> be able to survive <u>this</u> unfavorable <u>situation</u>.
          A   C   D

This can all be achieved in a multiple-choice format with computer scannable scoring for a rapid return of results. Moreover, not only does an overall score provide a holistic assessment, but for the placement purposes that Imao's research addressed, teachers were able to be given a diagnostic chart of each student's results within all of the specified categories of the test. For a total of 32 to 56 items in his editing test, Imao (2001, p. 185) was able to offer teachers a computer-generated breakdown of performance in the following categories:

> Sentence structure
> Verb tense
> Noun/article features
> Modal auxiliaries
> Verb complements
> Noun clauses
> Adverb clauses
> Conditionals
> Logical connectors
> Adjective clauses (including relative clauses)
> Passives

These categories were selected for inclusion from a survey of instructors' syllabuses in writing courses and proofreading workshops. This is an excellent example of the washback effect of a relatively large-scale, standardized multiple-choice test. While one would not want to use such data as absolutely predictive of students' future work, they can provide guidelines to a teacher on areas of potential focus as the writing course unfolds.

Scanning

Scanning is a strategy used by all readers to find relevant information in a text. Assessment of scanning is carried out by presenting test-takers with a text (prose or something in a chart or graph format) and requiring rapid identification of relevant bits of information. Possible stimuli include

- a one- to two-page news article,
- an essay,
- a chapter in a textbook,
- a technical report,
- a table or chart depicting some research findings,
- a menu, and
- an application form.

Among the variety of scanning objectives (for each of the genres named above), the test-taker must locate

- a date, name, or place in an article;
- the setting for a narrative or story;
- the principal divisions of a chapter;
- the principal research finding in a technical report;
- a result reported in a specified cell in a table;
- the cost of an item on a menu; and
- specified data needed to fill out an application.

Scoring of such scanning tasks is amenable to specificity if the initial directions are specific ("How much does the dark chocolate torte cost?"). Since one of the purposes of scanning is to *quickly* identify important elements, timing may also be calculated into a scoring procedure.

Ordering Tasks

Students always enjoy the activity of receiving little strips of paper, each with a sentence on it, and assembling them into a story, sometimes called the "strip story" technique. Variations on this can serve as an assessment of overall global understanding of a story and of the cohesive devices that signal the order of events or ideas. Alderson et al. (1995, p. 53) warn, however, against assuming that there is only one logical order. They presented these sentences for forming a little story.

Sentence-ordering task

Put the following sentences in the correct order:

A   it was called "The Last Waltz"
B   the street was in total darkness
C   because it was one he and Richard had learnt at school
D   Peter looked outside
E   he recognised the tune
F   and it seemed deserted
G   he thought he heard someone whistling

"D" was the first sentence, and test-takers were asked to order the sentences. It turned out that two orders were acceptable (DGECABF and DBFGECA), creating difficulties in assigning scores and leading the authors to discourage the use of this technique as an assessment device. But if you are willing to place this procedure in the category of informal and/or formative assessment, you might consider the technique useful. Different acceptable sentence orders become an instructive point for subsequent discussion in class, and you thereby offer washback into students' understanding of how to connect sentences and ideas in a story or essay.

Information Transfer: Reading Charts, Maps, Graphs, Diagrams

Every educated person must be able to comprehend charts, maps, graphs, calendars, diagrams, and the like. Converting such nonverbal input into comprehensible intake requires not only an understanding of the graphic and verbal conventions of the medium but also a linguistic ability to interpret that information to someone else. Reading a map implies understanding the conventions of map graphics, but it is often accompanied by telling someone where to turn, how far to go, etc. Scanning a menu requires an ability to understand the structure of most menus as well as the capacity to give an order when the time comes. Interpreting the numbers on a stock market report involves the interaction of understanding the numbers and of conveying that understanding to others.

All of these media presuppose the reader's appropriate schemata for interpreting them and often are accompanied by oral or written discourse in order to convey, clarify, question, argue, and debate, among other linguistic functions. Virtually every language curriculum, from rock-bottom beginning levels to high-advanced, utilizes this nonverbal, visual/symbolic dimension. It is therefore imperative that assessment procedures include measures of comprehension of nonverbal media.

To comprehend information in this medium (hereafter referred to simply as "graphics"), learners must be able to

- comprehend specific conventions of the various types of graphics;
- comprehend labels, headings, numbers, and symbols;
- comprehend the possible relationships among elements of the graphic; and
- make inferences that are not presented overtly.

The act of comprehending graphics includes the linguistic performance of oral or written interpretations, comments, questions, etc. This implies a process of **information transfer** from one skill to another: in this case, from reading verbal and/or nonverbal information to speaking/writing. Assessment of these abilities covers a broad spectrum of tasks. Here is a start of the many possibilities.

Tasks for assessing interpretation of graphic information

---

1. Read a graphic; answer simple, direct information questions. For example:

   map: "Where is the post office?"
   family tree: "Who is Tony's great grandmother?"
   statistical table: "What does $p < .05$ mean?"
   diagram of a steam engine: "Label the following parts."

2. Read a graphic; describe or elaborate on information.

   map: "Compare the distance between San Francisco and Sacramento to the distance between San Francisco and Monterey."
   store advertisements: "Who has the better deal on grapes, Safeway or Albertsons?"
   menu: "What comes with the grilled salmon entrée?"

3. Read a graphic; infer/predict information.

   stock market report: "Based on past performance, how do you think Macrotech Industries will do in the future?"
   directions for assembling a bookshelf: "How long do you think it will take to put this thing together?"

4. Read a passage; choose the correct graphic for it.

   article about the size of the ozone hole in the Antarctic: "Which chart represents the size of the ozone hole?"
   passage about the history of bicycles: "Click on the drawing that shows a penny-farthing bicycle."

5. Read a passage with an accompanying graphic; interpret both.

   article about hunger and population, with a bar graph: "Which countries have the most hungry people and why?"
   article on number of automobiles produced and their price over a 10-year period, with a table: "What is the best generalization you can make about production and the cost of automobiles?"

---

6. Read a passage; create or use a graphic to illustrate.

> directions from the bank to the post office: "On the map provided, trace the route from the bank to the post office."
>
> article about deforestation and carbon dioxide levels: "Make a bar graph to illustrate the information in the article."
>
> story including members of a family: "Draw Jeff and Christina's family tree."
>
> description of a class schedule: "Fill in Mary's weekly class schedule."

All these tasks involve retrieving information from either written or graphic media and transferring that information to productive performance. It is sometimes too easy to simply conclude that *reading* must involve only 26 alphabetic letters, with spaces and punctuation, thus omitting a huge number of resources that we consult every day.

DESIGNING ASSESSMENT TASKS: EXTENSIVE READING

Extensive reading involves somewhat longer texts than we have been dealing with up to this point. Journal articles, technical reports, longer essays, short stories, and books fall into this category. The reason for placing such reading into a separate category is that reading of this type of discourse almost always involves a focus on meaning using mostly top-down processing, with only occasional use of a targeted bottom-up strategy. Also, because of the extent of such reading, formal assessment is unlikely to be contained within the time constraints of a typical formal testing framework, which presents a unique challenge for assessment purposes.

Another complication in assessing extensive reading is that the expected response from the reader is likely to involve as much written (or sometimes oral) performance as reading. For example, in asking test-takers to respond to an article or story, one could argue that a greater emphasis is placed on writing than on reading. This is no reason to sweep extensive reading assessment under the rug; teachers should not shrink from the assessment of this highly sophisticated skill.

Before examining a few tasks that have proved to be useful in assessing extensive reading, it is essential to note that a number of the tasks described in previous categories can apply here. Among them are

- impromptu reading plus comprehension questions,
- short-answer tasks,
- editing,
- scanning,
- ordering,
- information transfer, and
- interpretation (discussed under graphics).

In addition to those applications are tasks that are unique to extensive reading: skimming, summarizing, responding to reading, and note-taking.

Skimming Tasks

Skimming is the process of rapid coverage of reading matter to determine its gist or main idea. It is a prediction strategy used to give a reader a sense of the topic and purpose of a text, the organization of the text, the perspective or point of view of the writer, its ease or difficulty, and/or its usefulness to the reader. Of course skimming can apply to texts of less than one page, so it would be wise not to confine this type of task just to extensive texts.

Assessment of skimming strategies is usually straightforward: the test-taker skims a text and answers questions such as the following:

Skimming tasks

What is the main idea of this text?
What is the author's purpose in writing the text?
What kind of writing is this [newspaper article, manual, novel, etc.]?
What type of writing is this [expository, technical, narrative, etc.]?
How easy or difficult do you think this text will be?
What do you think you will learn from the text?
How useful will the text be for your [profession, academic needs, interests]?

Responses are oral or written, depending on the context. Most assessments in the domain of skimming are informal and formative: they are grist for an imminent discussion, a more careful reading to follow, or an in-class discussion, and therefore their washback potential is good. Insofar as the subject matter and tasks are useful to a student's goals, authenticity is preserved. Scoring is less of an issue than providing appropriate feedback to students on their strategies of prediction.

Summarizing and Responding

One of the most common means of assessing extensive reading is to ask the test-taker to write a summary of the text. The task that is given to students can be very simply worded:

Directions for summarizing

Write a summary of the text. Your summary should be about one paragraph in length (100–150 words) and should include your understanding of the main idea and supporting ideas.

Evaluating summaries is difficult: Do you give test-takers a certain number of points for targeting the main idea and its supporting ideas? Do you use a full/partial/no-credit point system? Do you give a holistic score? Imao (2001) used four criteria for the evaluation of a summary:

Criteria for assessing a summary (Imao, 2001, p. 184)

> 1. Expresses accurately the main idea and supporting ideas.
> 2. Is written in the student's own words; occasional vocabulary from the original text is acceptable.
> 3. Is logically organized.
> 4. Displays facility in the use of language to clearly express ideas in the text.

As you can readily see, a strict adherence to the criterion of assessing reading, and reading only, implies consideration of only the first factor; the other three pertain to writing performance. The first criterion is nevertheless a crucial factor; otherwise the reader-writer could pass all three of the other criteria with virtually no understanding of the text itself. Evaluation of the reading comprehension criterion will of necessity remain somewhat subjective because the teacher will need to determine degrees of fulfillment of the objective (see below for more about scoring this task).

Of further interest in assessing extensive reading is the technique of asking a student to **respond** to a text. The two tasks should not be confused with each other: summarizing requires a synopsis or overview of the text, while responding asks the reader to provide his or her own opinion on the text as a whole or on some statement or issue within it. Responding may be prompted by such directions as this:

Directions for responding to reading

> In the article "Poisoning the Air We Breathe," the author suggests that a global dependence on fossil fuels will eventually make air in large cities toxic. Write an essay in which you agree or disagree with the author's thesis. Support your opinion with information from the article and from your own experience.

One criterion for a good response here is the extent to which the test-taker accurately reflects the content of the article and some of the arguments therein. Scoring is also difficult here because of the subjectivity of determining an accurate reflection of the article itself. For the reading component of this task, as well as the summary task described above, a holistic scoring system may be feasible:

Holistic scoring scale for summarizing and responding to reading

3	Demonstrates clear, unambiguous comprehension of the main and supporting ideas.
2	Demonstrates comprehension of the main idea but lacks comprehension of some supporting ideas.
1	Demonstrates only a partial comprehension of the main and supporting ideas.
0	Demonstrates no comprehension of the main and supporting ideas.

The teacher or test administrator must still determine shades of gray between the point categories, but the descriptions help to bridge the gap between an empirically determined evaluation (which is impossible) and wild, impressionistic guesses.

An attempt has been made here to underscore the *reading* component of summarizing and responding to reading, but it is crucial to consider the interactive relationship between reading and writing that is highlighted in these two tasks. As you direct students to engage in such integrative performance, it is advisable not to treat them as tasks for assessing reading alone.

Note-Taking and Outlining

Finally, a reader's comprehension of extensive texts may be assessed through an evaluation of a process of note-taking and/or outlining. Because of the difficulty of controlling the conditions and time frame for both these techniques, they rest firmly in the category of informal assessment. Their utility is in the strategic training that learners gain in retaining information through marginal notes that highlight key information or organizational outlines that put supporting ideas into a visually manageable framework. A teacher, perhaps in one-on-one conferences with students, can use student notes/outlines as indicators of the presence or absence of effective reading strategies, and thereby point the learners in positive directions.

§   §   §   §   §

In his introduction to Alderson's (2000, p. xx) book on assessing reading, Lyle Bachman observed: "Reading, through which we can access worlds of ideas and feelings, as well as the knowledge of the ages and visions of the future, is at once the most extensively researched and the most enigmatic of the so-called language skills." It's the almost mysterious "psycholinguistic guessing game" (Goodman, 1970) of reading that poses the enigma. We still have much to learn about how people learn to read, and especially about how the brain accesses, stores, and recalls visually represented language. This chapter has illustrated a number of possibilities for assessment of reading across the continuum of skills, from basic letter/word recognition to the retention of meaning extracted from vast quantities of linguistic symbols. I hope it will spur you to go beyond the confines of these suggestions and create your own methods of assessing reading.

EXERCISES

[Note: (**I**) Individual work; (**G**) Group or pair work; (**C**) Whole-class discussion.]

1. (**C**) Genres of reading are listed at the beginning of the chapter. Add other examples to each of the three categories. Among the listed examples and your additions, be specific in citing what makes certain genres more difficult than others. Select a few of the more difficult genres and discuss what you would assess (criteria) and how you would assess (some possible assessment techniques) them.
2. (**G**) Look at the list of micro- and macroskills of reading on pages 187–188. In pairs, each assigned to a different skill (or two), brainstorm some tasks that assess those skills. Present your findings to the rest of the class.
3. (**C**) Critique Figure 8.1 on page 190. Do you agree with the categorizations of length, focus, and process for each of the four types of reading?
4. (**C**) Review the four basic types of reading that were outlined at the beginning of the chapter. Offer examples of each and pay special attention to distinguishing between perceptive and selective, and between interactive and extensive.
5. (**C**) In Chapter 6, eight characteristics of listening were listed (page 122) that make listening "difficult." What makes *reading* difficult? Devise a similar list that could form a set of specifications to pay special attention to in assessing reading.
6. (**G**) Divide the four basic types of reading among groups or pairs, one type for each. Look at the sample assessment techniques provided and evaluate them according the five principles (practicality, reliability, validity [especially face and content], authenticity, and washback). Present your critique to the rest of the class.
7. (**G**) In the same groups as #6 above with the same type of reading, design some item types, different from the one(s) provided here, that assess the same type of reading performance.
8. (**G**) In the same groups as #6 above with the same type of reading, identify which of the 10 strategies for reading comprehension (pages 188–189) are essential in order to perform the assessment task. Present those findings, possibly in a tabular format, to the rest of the class.
9. (**C**) In the concluding paragraph of this chapter, reference was made to the "enigmatic" nature of reading as a "psycholinguistic guessing game." Why is reading enigmatic? Why is it a "guessing game"? And what does that say about the prospects of assessing reading?

FOR YOUR FURTHER READING

Alderson, J. Charles. (2000). *Assessing reading.* Cambridge: Cambridge University Press.

This volume in the Cambridge Language Assessment Series provides a comprehensive overview of the history and current state of the art of assessing reading. With an authoritative backdrop of research underlying the construct validation of techniques for the assessment of reading comprehension, a host of testing techniques are surveyed and evaluated.

Read, John. (2000). *Assessing vocabulary.* Cambridge: Cambridge University Press.

Another in the same Cambridge series, this book addresses issues in assessing vocabulary. Do not be misled by its placement in this chapter: vocabulary can be assessed through performance in *all four* skills, not just reading. A good portion of this book centers on vocabulary knowledge for reading performance, however, and therefore is recommended here. Background research and practical techniques are explored.

Nuttall, Christine. (1996). *Teaching reading skills in a foreign language.* Second Edition. Oxford: Heinemann.

This broadly based pedagogical reference book on teaching reading also offers numerous examples and commentaries on assessment of reading (which of course goes hand in hand with teaching). Most of the references to assessment deal with informal assessment, but the book also addresses formal assessment.

CHAPTER 9

ASSESSING WRITING

Not many centuries ago, writing was a skill that was the exclusive domain of scribes and scholars in educational or religious institutions. Almost every aspect of everyday life for "common" people was carried out orally. Business transactions, records, legal documents, political and military agreements—all were written by specialists whose vocation it was to render language into the written word. Today, the ability to write has become an indispensable skill in our global literate community. Writing skill, at least at rudimentary levels, is a necessary condition for achieving employment in many walks of life and is simply taken for granted in literate cultures.

In the field of second language teaching, only a half-century ago experts were saying that writing was primarily a convention for recording speech and for reinforcing grammatical and lexical features of language. Now we understand the uniqueness of writing as a skill with its own features and conventions. We also fully understand the difficulty of learning to write "well" in any language, even in our own native language. Every educated child in developed countries learns the rudiments of writing in his or her native language, but very few learn to express themselves clearly with logical, well-developed organization that accomplishes an intended purpose. And yet we expect second language learners to write coherent essays with artfully chosen rhetorical and discourse devices!

With such a monumental goal, the job of teaching writing has occupied the attention of papers, articles, dissertations, books, and even separate professional journals exclusively devoted to writing in a second language. I refer specifically to the *Journal of Second Language Writing*; consult the website **http://icdweb.cc. purdue.edu/~silvat/jslw/** for information. (For further information on issues and practical techniques in teaching writing, refer to *TBP,* Chapter 19.)

It follows logically that the assessment of writing is no simple task. As you consider assessing students' writing ability, as usual you need to be clear about your objective or criterion. What is it you want to test: handwriting ability? correct spelling? writing sentences that are grammatically correct? paragraph construction? logical development of a main idea? All of these, and more, are possible objectives. And each objective can be assessed through a variety of tasks, which we will examine in this chapter.

Before looking at specific tasks, we must scrutinize the different genres of written language (so that context and purpose are clear), types of writing (so that stages of the development of writing ability are accounted for), and micro- and macroskills of writing (so that objectives can be pinpointed precisely).

GENRES OF WRITTEN LANGUAGE

Chapter 8's discussion of assessment of reading listed more than 50 written language genres. The same classification scheme is reformulated here to include the most common genres that a second language *writer* might produce, within and beyond the requirements of a curriculum. Even though this list is slightly shorter, you should be aware of the surprising multiplicity of options of written genres that second language learners need to acquire.

Genres of writing

---

1. Academic writing

  papers and general subject reports
  essays, compositions
  academically focused journals
  short-answer test responses
  technical reports (e.g., lab reports)
  theses, dissertations

2. Job-related writing

  messages (e.g., phone messages)
  letters/emails
  memos (e.g., interoffice)
  reports (e.g., job evaluations, project reports)
  schedules, labels, signs
  advertisements, announcements
  manuals

3. Personal writing

  letters, emails, greeting cards, invitations
  messages, notes
  calendar entries, shopping lists, reminders
  financial documents (e.g., checks, tax forms, loan applications)
  forms, questionnaires, medical reports, immigration documents
  diaries, personal journals
  fiction (e.g., short stories, poetry)

TYPES OF WRITING PERFORMANCE

Four categories of written performance that capture the range of written production are considered here. Each category resembles the categories defined for the other three skills, but these categories, as always, reflect the uniqueness of the skill area.

1. Imitative. To produce written language, the learner must attain skills in the fundamental, basic tasks of writing letters, words, punctuation, and very brief sentences. This category includes the ability to spell correctly and to perceive phoneme–grapheme correspondences in the English spelling system. It is a level at which learners are trying to master the mechanics of writing. At this stage, form is the primary if not exclusive focus, while context and meaning are of secondary concern.

2. Intensive (controlled). Beyond the fundamentals of imitative writing are skills in producing appropriate vocabulary within a context, collocations and idioms, and correct grammatical features up to the length of a sentence. Meaning and context are of some importance in determining correctness and appropriateness, but most assessment tasks are more concerned with a focus on form, and are rather strictly controlled by the test design.

3. Responsive. Here, assessment tasks require learners to perform at a limited discourse level, connecting sentences into a paragraph and creating a logically connected sequence of two or three paragraphs. Tasks respond to pedagogical directives, lists of criteria, outlines, and other guidelines. Genres of writing include brief narratives and descriptions, short reports, lab reports, summaries, brief responses to reading, and interpretations of charts or graphs. Under specified conditions, the writer begins to exercise some freedom of choice among alternative forms of expression of ideas. The writer has mastered the fundamentals of sentence-level grammar and is more focused on the discourse conventions that will achieve the objectives of the written text. Form-focused attention is mostly at the discourse level, with a strong emphasis on context and meaning.

4. Extensive. Extensive writing implies successful management of all the processes and strategies of writing for all purposes, up to the length of an essay, a term paper, a major research project report, or even a thesis. Writers focus on achieving a purpose, organizing and developing ideas logically, using details to support or illustrate ideas, demonstrating syntactic and lexical variety, and in many cases, engaging in the **process** of multiple drafts to achieve a final product. Focus on grammatical form is limited to occasional editing or proofreading of a draft.

MICRO- AND MACROSKILLS OF WRITING

We turn once again to a taxonomy of micro- and macroskills that will assist you in defining the ultimate criterion of an assessment procedure. The earlier microskills apply more appropriately to imitative and intensive types of writing task, while the macroskills are essential for the successful mastery of responsive and extensive writing.

Micro- and macroskills of writing

Microskills

1. Produce graphemes and orthographic patterns of English.
2. Produce writing at an efficient rate of speed to suit the purpose.
3. Produce an acceptable core of words and use appropriate word order patterns.
4. Use acceptable grammatical systems (e.g., tense, agreement, pluralization), patterns, and rules.
5. Express a particular meaning in different grammatical forms.
6. Use cohesive devices in written discourse.

Macroskills

7. Use the rhetorical forms and conventions of written discourse.
8. Appropriately accomplish the communicative functions of written texts according to form and purpose.
9. Convey links and connections between events, and communicate such relations as main idea, supporting idea, new information, given information, generalization, and exemplification.
10. Distinguish between literal and implied meanings when writing.
11. Correctly convey culturally specific references in the context of the written text.
12. Develop and use a battery of writing strategies, such as accurately assessing the audience's interpretation, using prewriting devices, writing with fluency in the first drafts, using paraphrases and synonyms, soliciting peer and instructor feedback, and using feedback for revising and editing.

DESIGNING ASSESSMENT TASKS: IMITATIVE WRITING

With the recent worldwide emphasis on teaching English at young ages, it is tempting to assume that every English learner knows how to handwrite the Roman alphabet. Such is not the case. Many beginning-level English learners, from young children to older adults, need basic training in and assessment of imitative writing: the rudiments of forming letters, words, and simple sentences. We examine this level of writing first.

Tasks in [Hand] Writing Letters, Words, and Punctuation

First, a comment should be made on the increasing use of personal and laptop computers and handheld instruments for creating written symbols. Handwriting has the potential of becoming a lost art as even very young children are more and more likely to use a keyboard to produce writing. Making the shapes of letters and other symbols is now more a question of learning typing skills than of training the muscles of the hands to use a pen or pencil. Nevertheless, for all practical purposes, handwriting remains a skill of paramount importance within the larger domain of language assessment.

A limited variety of types of tasks are commonly used to assess a person's ability to produce written letters and symbols. A few of the more common types are described here.

1. *Copying.* There is nothing innovative or modern about directing a test-taker to copy letters or words. The test-taker will see something like the following:

Handwriting letters, words, and punctuation marks

The test-taker reads: Copy the following words in the spaces given:

bit	bet	bat	but	Oh?	Oh!
___	___	___	___	___	___

bin	din	gin	pin	Hello, John.
___	___	___	___	_____

---

2. *Listening cloze selection tasks.* These tasks combine dictation with a written script that has a relatively frequent deletion ratio (every fourth or fifth word, perhaps). The test sheet provides a list of missing words from which the test-taker must select. The purpose at this stage is not to test spelling but to give practice in writing. To increase the difficulty, the list of words can be deleted, but then spelling might become an obstacle. Probes look like this:

Listening cloze selection task

Test-takers hear:
Write the missing word in each blank. Below the story is a list of words to choose from.

Have you ever visited San Francisco? It is a very nice city. It is cool in the summer and warm in the winter. I like the cable cars and bridges.

Test-takers see:

Have _____ ever visited San Francisco? It _____ a very nice _____. It is _____ in _____ summer and _____ in the winter. I _____ the cable cars _____ bridges.

is	you	cool	city
like	and	warm	the

---

3. Picture-cued tasks. Familiar pictures are displayed, and test-takers are told to write the word that the picture represents. Assuming no ambiguity in identifying the picture (cat, hat, chair, table, etc.), no reliance is made on aural comprehension for successful completion of the task.

4. Form completion tasks. A variation on pictures is the use of a simple form (registration, application, etc.) that asks for name, address, phone number, and other data. Assuming, of course, that prior classroom instruction has focused on filling out such forms, this task becomes an appropriate assessment of simple tasks such as writing one's name and address.

5. Converting numbers and abbreviations to words. Some tests have a section on which numbers are written—for example, hours of the day, dates, or schedules—and test-takers are directed to write out the numbers. This task can serve as a reasonably reliable method to stimulate handwritten English. It lacks authenticity, however, in that people rarely write out such numbers (except in writing checks), and it is more of a reading task (recognizing numbers) than a writing task. If you plan to use such a method, be sure to specify exactly what the criterion is, and then proceed with some caution. Converting abbreviations to words is more authentic: we actually do have occasions to write out days of the week, months, and words like *street, boulevard, telephone,* and *April* (months of course are often abbreviated with numbers). Test tasks may take this form:

Writing numbers and abbreviations

Test-takers hear: Fill in the blanks with words.

Test-takers see:

9:00 _____   5:45 _____

Tues. _____   5/3 _____

726 S. Main St. _____

Spelling Tasks and Detecting Phoneme–Grapheme Correspondences

A number of task types are in popular use to assess the ability to spell words correctly and to process phoneme–grapheme correspondences.

1. Spelling tests. In a traditional, old-fashioned spelling test, the teacher dictates a simple list of words, one word at a time, followed by the word in a sentence, repeated again, with a pause for test-takers to write the word. Scoring emphasizes correct spelling. You can help to control for listening errors by choosing words that the students have encountered before—words that they have spoken or heard in their class.

2. Picture-cued tasks. Pictures are displayed with the objective of focusing on familiar words whose spelling may be unpredictable. Items are chosen according to the objectives of the assessment, but this format is an opportunity to present some challenging words and word pairs: *boot/book, read/reed, bit/bite,* etc.

3. Multiple-choice techniques. Presenting words and phrases in the form of a multiple-choice task risks crossing over into the domain of assessing reading, but if the items have a follow-up writing component, they can serve as formative reinforcement of spelling conventions. They might be more challenging with the addition of homonyms (see item #**3** below). Here are some examples.

Multiple-choice reading-writing spelling tasks

Test-takers read:

Choose the word with the correct spelling to fit the sentence, then write the word in the space provided.

1. He washed his hands with _____.
   A. soap
   B. sope
   C. sop
   D. soup

2. I tried to stop the car, but the _____ didn't work.
   A. braicks
   B. brecks
   C. brakes
   D. bracks

3. The doorbell rang, but when I went to the door, no one was _____.
   A. their
   B. there
   C. they're
   D. thair

---

4. Matching phonetic symbols. If students have become familiar with the phonetic alphabet, they could be shown phonetic symbols and asked to write the correctly spelled word alphabetically. This works best with letters that do not have one-to-one correspondence with the phonetic symbol (e.g., /æ/ and **a**). In the sample below, the answers, which of course do not appear on the test sheet, are included in brackets for your reference.

Converting phonetic symbols

Test-takers read:

In each of the following words, a letter or combination of letters has been written in a phonetic symbol. Write the word using the regular alphabet.

1. tea /tʃ/ er   _____   [teacher]

2. d /e/   _____   [day]

3. /ð/ is   _____   [this]

4. n /ɑu/   _____   [now]

5. l /ɑɪ/ /k/   _____   [like]

6. c /æ/ t   _____   [cat]

Such a task risks confusing students who don't recognize the phonetic alphabet or use it in their daily routine. Opinion is mixed on the value of using phonetic symbols at the literacy level. Some claim it helps students to perceive the relationship between phonemes and graphemes. Others caution against using yet another system of symbols when the alphabet already poses a challenge, especially for adults for whom English is the only language they have learned to read or write.

DESIGNING ASSESSMENT TASKS: INTENSIVE (CONTROLLED) WRITING

This next level of writing is what second language teacher training manuals have for decades called **controlled** writing. It may also be thought of as form-focused writing, grammar writing, or simply guided writing. A good deal of writing at this level is **display** writing as opposed to **real** writing: students produce language to display their competence in grammar, vocabulary, or sentence formation, and not necessarily to convey meaning for an authentic purpose. The traditional grammar/vocabulary test has plenty of display writing in it, since the response mode demonstrates only the test-taker's ability to combine or use words correctly. No new information is passed on from one person to the other.

Dictation and Dicto-Comp

In Chapter 6, dictation was described as an assessment of the integration of listening and writing, but it was clear that the primary skill being assessed is listening. Because of its response mode, however, it deserves a second mention in this chapter. Dictation is simply the rendition in writing of what one hears aurally, so it could be classified as an *imitative* type of writing, especially since a proportion of the test-taker's performance centers on correct spelling. Also, because the test-taker must listen to stretches of discourse and in the process insert punctuation, dictation of a paragraph or more can arguably be classified as a controlled or intensive form of writing. (For a further explanation on administering a dictation, consult Chapter 6, pages 131–132.)

A form of controlled writing related to dictation is a **dicto-comp**. Here, a paragraph is read at normal speed, usually two or three times; then the teacher asks students to rewrite the paragraph from the best of their recollection. In one of several variations of the dicto-comp technique, the teacher, after reading the passage, distributes a handout with key words from the paragraph, in sequence, as cues for the students. In either case, the dicto-comp is genuinely classified as an intensive, if not a responsive, writing task. Test-takers must internalize the content of the passage, remember a few phrases and lexical items as key words, then recreate the story in their own words.

Grammatical Transformation Tasks

In the heyday of structural paradigms of language teaching with slot-filler techniques and slot substitution drills, the practice of making grammatical transformations—orally or in writing—was very popular. To this day, language teachers have also used this technique as an assessment task, ostensibly to measure grammatical competence. Numerous versions of the task are possible:

- Change the tenses in a paragraph.
- Change full forms of verbs to reduced forms (contractions).
- Change statements to *yes/no* or *wh*-questions.
- Change questions into statements.
- Combine two sentences into one using a relative pronoun.
- Change direct speech to indirect speech.
- Change from active to passive voice.

The list of possibilities is almost endless. The tasks are virtually devoid of any meaningful value. Sometimes test designers attempt to add authenticity by providing a context ("Today Doug is doing all these things. Tomorrow he will do the same things again. Write about what Doug will do tomorrow by using the future tense."), but this is just a backdrop for a written substitution task. On the positive side, grammatical transformation tasks are easy to administer and are therefore practical, quite high in scorer reliability, and arguably tap into a knowledge of grammatical *forms* that will be performed through writing. If you are only interested in a person's ability to produce the forms, then such tasks may prove to be justifiable.

Picture-Cued Tasks

A variety of picture-cued controlled tasks have been used in English classrooms around the world. The main advantage in this technique is in detaching the almost ubiquitous reading and writing connection and offering instead a nonverbal means to stimulate written responses.

1. *Short sentences.* A drawing of some simple action is shown; the test-taker writes a brief sentence.

Picture-cued sentence writing (Brown, 1999, p. 40)

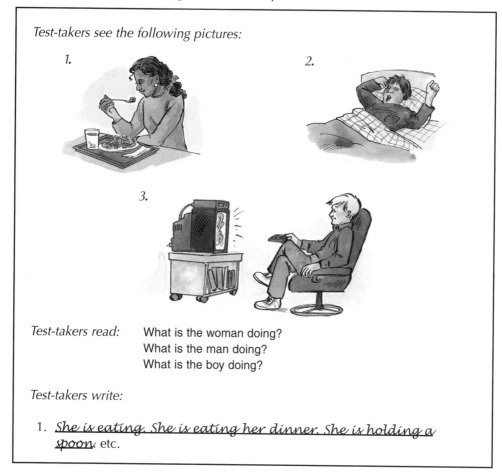

Test-takers see the following pictures:

1.

2.

3.

Test-takers read: What is the woman doing?
What is the man doing?
What is the boy doing?

Test-takers write:

1. *She is eating. She is eating her dinner. She is holding a spoon.* etc.

2. *Picture description.* A somewhat more complex picture may be presented showing, say, a person reading on a couch, a cat under a table, books and pencils on the table, chairs around the table, a lamp next to the couch, and a picture on the wall over the couch (see Chapter 8, page 192). Test-takers are asked to describe the picture using four of the following prepositions: *on, over, under, next to, around.* As long as the prepositions are used appropriately, the criterion is considered to be met.

3. *Picture sequence description.* A sequence of three to six pictures depicting a story line can provide a suitable stimulus for written production. The pictures must be simple and unambiguous because an open-ended task at the selective level would give test-takers too many options. If writing the correct grammatical form of a verb is the only criterion, then some test items might include the simple form of the verb below the picture. The time sequence in the following task is intended to give writers some cues.

Picture-cued story sequence (Brown, 1999, p. 43)

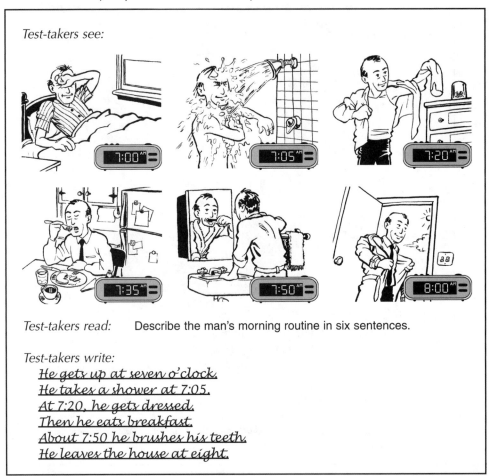

Test-takers see:

Test-takers read: Describe the man's morning routine in six sentences.

Test-takers write:
    He gets up at seven o'clock.
    He takes a shower at 7:05.
    At 7:20, he gets dressed.
    Then he eats breakfast.
    About 7:50 he brushes his teeth.
    He leaves the house at eight.

While these kinds of tasks are designed to be controlled, even at this very simple level, a few different correct responses can be made for each item in the sequence. If your criteria in this task are both lexical and grammatical choice, then you need to design a rating scale to account for variations between completely right and completely wrong in both categories.

Scoring scale for controlled writing

2	Grammatically and lexically correct.
1	Either grammar or vocabulary is incorrect, but not both.
0	Both grammar and vocabulary are incorrect.

The following are some test-takers' responses to the first picture:

> He gets up at 7.
> He get up at 7.
> He is getting up at 7.
> He wakes seven o'clock.
> The man is arise at seven.
> He sleeps at seven o'clock.
> Sleeps on morning.

How would you rate each response? With the scoring scale above, the first response is a "2," the next five responses are a "1," and the last earns a zero.

Vocabulary Assessment Tasks

Most vocabulary study is carried out through reading. A number of assessments of reading recognition of vocabulary were discussed in the previous chapter: multiple-choice techniques, matching, picture-cued identification, cloze techniques, guessing the meaning of a word in context, etc. The major techniques used to assess vocabulary are (a) defining and (b) using a word in a sentence. The latter is the more authentic, but even that task is constrained by a contrived situation in which the test-taker, usually in a matter of seconds, has to come up with an appropriate sentence, which may or may not indicate that the test-taker "knows" the word.

Read (2000) suggested several types of items for assessment of basic knowledge of the meaning of a word, collocational possibilities, and derived morphological forms. His example centered on the word *interpret*, as follows:

Vocabulary writing tasks (Read, 2000, p. 179)

Test-takers read:

1. Write two sentences, A and B. In each sentence, use the two words given.

A. *interpret, experiment* _____.

B. *interpret, language* _____.

2. Write three words that can fit in the blank.

To interpret a(n) _____

    i. _____

    ii. _____

    iii. _____

3. Write the correct ending for the word in each of the following sentences:

Someone who interprets is an interpret _____.

Something that can be interpreted is interpret _____.

Someone who interprets gives an interpret _____.

Vocabulary assessment is clearly form-focused in the above tasks, but the procedures are creatively linked by means of the target word, its collocations, and its morphological variants. At the responsive and extensive levels, where learners are called upon to create coherent paragraphs, performance obviously becomes more authentic, and lexical choice is one of several possible components of the evaluation of extensive writing.

Ordering Tasks

One task at the sentence level may appeal to those who are fond of word games and puzzles: ordering (or reordering) a scrambled set of words into a correct sentence. Here is the way the item format appears.

Reordering words in a sentence

Test-takers read:
Put the words below into the correct order to make a sentence:

   1. cold / winter / is / weather / the / in / the

   2. studying / what / you / are

   3. next / clock / the / the / is / picture / to

Test-takers write:

   1. *The weather is cold in the winter.*

   2. *What are you studying?*

   3. *The clock is next to the picture.*

While this somewhat inauthentic task generates writing performance and may be said to tap into grammatical word-ordering rules, it presents a challenge to test-takers whose learning styles do not dispose them to logical-mathematical problem solving. If sentences are kept very simple (such as #2) with perhaps no more than four or five words, if only one possible sentence can emerge, and if students have practiced the technique in class, then some justification emerges. But once again, as in so many writing techniques, this task involves as much, if not more, reading performance as writing.

Short-Answer and Sentence Completion Tasks

Some types of short-answer tasks were discussed in Chapter 8 because of the heavy participation of reading performance in their completion. Such items range from very simple and predictable to somewhat more elaborate responses. Look at the range of possibilities.

Limited response writing tasks

Test-takers see:

1. Alicia: Who's that?
   Tony: _____ Gina.
   Alicia: Where's she from?
   Tony: _____ Italy.

2. Jennifer: _____?
   Kathy: I'm studying English.

3. Restate the following sentences in your own words, using the underlined word.
   You may need to change the meaning of the sentence a little.
   3a. I never miss a day of school.   <u>always</u>
   3b. I'm pretty healthy most of the time.   <u>seldom</u>
   3c. I play tennis twice a week.   <u>sometimes</u>

4. You are in the kitchen helping your roommate cook. You need to ask questions
   about quantities. Ask a question using *how much* (#4a) and a question using
   how many (#4b), using nouns like *sugar, pounds, flour, onions, eggs, cups.*
   4a. _____.
   4b. _____.

5. Look at the schedule of Roberto's week. Write two sentences describing what
   Roberto does, using the words *before* (#5a) and *after* (#5b).
   5a. _____.
   5b. _____.

6. Write three sentences describing your preferences: #6a: a big, expensive car or a
   small, cheap car; #6b: a house in the country or an apartment in the city; #6c:
   money or good health.
   6a. _____.
   6b. _____.
   6c. _____.

The reading-writing connection is apparent in the first three item types but has less
of an effect in the last three, where reading is necessary in order to understand the
directions but is not crucial in creating sentences. Scoring on a 2-1-0 scale (as
described above) may be the most appropriate way to avoid self-arguing about the
appropriateness of a response.

ISSUES IN ASSESSING RESPONSIVE AND EXTENSIVE WRITING

Responsive writing creates the opportunity for test-takers to offer an array of possible creative responses within a pedagogical or assessment framework: test-takers
are "responding" to a prompt or assignment. Freed from the strict control of intensive

writing, learners can exercise a number of options in choosing vocabulary, grammar, and discourse, but with some constraints and conditions. Criteria now begin to include the discourse and rhetorical conventions of paragraph structure and of connecting two or three such paragraphs in texts of limited length. The learner is responsible for accomplishing a purpose in writing, for developing a sequence of connected ideas, and for empathizing with an audience.

The genres of text that are typically addressed here are

- short reports (with structured formats and conventions);
- responses to the reading of an article or story;
- summaries of articles or stories;
- brief narratives or descriptions; and
- interpretations of graphs, tables, and charts.

It is here that writers become involved in the art (and science) of *composing,* or real writing, as opposed to display writing.

Extensive, or "free," writing, which is amalgamated into our discussion here, takes all the principles and guidelines of responsive writing and puts them into practice in longer texts such as full-length essays, term papers, project reports, and theses and dissertations. In extensive writing, however, the writer has been given even more freedom to choose: topics, length, style, and perhaps even conventions of formatting are less constrained than in the typical responsive writing exercise. At this stage, all the rules of effective writing come into play, and the second language writer is expected to meet all the standards applied to native language writers.

Both responsive and extensive writing tasks are the subject of some classic, widely debated assessment issues that take on a distinctly different flavor from those at the lower-end production of writing.

1. *Authenticity.* Authenticity is a trait that is given special attention: if test-takers are being asked to perform a task, its face and content validity need to be assured in order to bring out the best in the writer. A good deal of writing performance in academic contexts is constrained by the pedagogical necessities of establishing the basic building blocks of writing; we have looked at assessment techniques that address those foundations. But once those fundamentals are in place, the would-be writer is ready to fly out of the protective nest of the writing classroom and assume his or her own voice. Offering that freedom to learners requires the setting of authentic real-world contexts in which to write. The teacher becomes less of an instructor and more of a coach or facilitator. Assessment therefore is typically formative, not summative, and positive washback is more important than practicality and reliability.

2. *Scoring.* Scoring is the thorniest issue at these final two stages of writing. With so many options available to a learner, each evaluation by a test administrator needs to be finely attuned not just to how the writer strings words together (the *form*) but also to what the writer is saying (the *function* of the text). The quality of writing (its impact and effectiveness) becomes as important, if not more important, than all the nuts and bolts that hold it together. How are you to score such creative production, some of which is more artistic than scientific? A discussion of different scoring options will continue below, followed by a reminder that responding and editing are nonscoring options that yield washback to the writer.

3. Time. Yet another assessment issue surrounds the unique nature of writing: it is the only skill in which the language producer is not necessarily constrained by *time,* which implies the freedom to process multiple drafts before the text becomes a finished product. Like a sculptor creating an image, the writer can take an initial rough conception of a text and continue to refine it until it is deemed presentable to the public eye. Virtually all *real* writing of prose texts presupposes an extended time period for it to reach its final form, and therefore the revising and editing processes are implied. Responsive writing, along with the next category of extensive writing, often relies on this essential drafting process for its ultimate success.

How do you assess writing ability within the confines of traditional, formal assessment procedures that are almost always, by logistical necessity, *timed?* We have a whole testing industry that has based large-scale assessment of writing on the premise that the **timed impromptu** format is a valid method of assessing writing ability. Is this an authentic format? Can a language learner—or a native speaker, for that matter—adequately perform writing tasks within the confines of a brief timed period of composition? Is that hastily written product an appropriate reflection of what that same test-taker might produce after several drafts of the same work? Does this format favor fast writers at the expense of slower but possibly equally good or better writers? Alderson (2002) and Weigle (2002) both cited this as one of the most pressing unresolved issues in the assessment of writing today. We will return to this question below.

Because of the complexity of assessing responsive and extensive writing, the discussion that ensues will now have a different look from the one used in the previous three chapters. Four major topics will be addressed: (1) a few fundamental task types at the lower (responsive) end of the continuum of writing at this level; (2) a description and analysis of the *Test of Written English*® as a typical timed impromptu test of writing; (3) a survey of methods of scoring and evaluating writing production; and (4) a discussion of the assessment qualities of editing and responding to a series of writing drafts.

DESIGNING ASSESSMENT TASKS: RESPONSIVE AND EXTENSIVE WRITING

In this section we consider both responsive and extensive writing tasks. They will be regarded here as a continuum of possibilities ranging from lower-end tasks whose complexity exceeds those in the previous category of intensive or controlled writing, through more open-ended tasks such as writing short reports, essays, summaries, and responses, up to texts of several pages or more.

Paraphrasing

One of the more difficult concepts for second language learners to grasp is paraphrasing. The initial step in teaching paraphrasing is to ensure that learners understand the importance of paraphrasing: to say something in one's own words, to avoid plagiarizing, to offer some variety in expression. With those possible motivations and purposes in mind, the test designer needs to elicit a paraphrase of a sentence or paragraph, usually not more.

Scoring of the test-taker's response is a judgment call in which the criterion of conveying the same or similar message is primary, with secondary evaluations of discourse, grammar, and vocabulary. Other components of analytic or holistic scales (see discussion below, page 242) might be considered as criteria for an evaluation. Paraphrasing is more often a part of informal and formative assessment than of formal, summative assessment, and therefore student responses should be viewed as opportunities for teachers and students to gain positive washback on the art of paraphrasing.

Guided Question and Answer

Another lower-order task in this type of writing, which has the pedagogical benefit of guiding a learner without dictating the form of the output, is a guided question-and-answer format in which the test administrator poses a series of questions that essentially serve as an outline of the emergent written text. In the writing of a narrative that the teacher has already covered in a class discussion, the following kinds of questions might be posed to stimulate a sequence of sentences.

Guided writing stimuli

---

1. Where did this story take place? [setting]
2. Who were the people in the story? [characters]
3. What happened first? and then? and then? [sequence of events]
4. Why did _____ do _____? [reasons, causes]
5. What did _____ think about _____? [opinion]
6. What happened at the end? [climax]
7. What is the moral of this story? [evaluation]

Guided writing texts, which may be as long as two or three paragraphs, may be scored on either an analytic or a holistic scale (discussed below). Guided writing prompts like these are less likely to appear on a formal test and more likely to serve as a way to prompt initial drafts of writing. This first draft can then undergo the editing and revising stages discussed in the next section of this chapter.

A variation on using guided questions is to prompt the test-taker to write from an outline. The outline may be self-created from earlier reading and/or discussion, or, which is less desirable, be provided by the teacher or test administrator. The outline helps to guide the learner through a presumably logical development of ideas that have been given some forethought. Assessment of the resulting text follows the same criteria listed below (#**3** in the next section, paragraph construction tasks).

Paragraph Construction Tasks

The participation of reading performance is inevitable in writing effective paragraphs. To a great extent, writing is the art of emulating what one reads. You read an effective paragraph; you analyze the ingredients of its success; you emulate it. Assessment of paragraph development takes on a number of different forms:

1. Topic sentence writing. There is no cardinal rule that says every paragraph must have a topic sentence, but the stating of a topic through the lead sentence (or a subsequent one) has remained as a tried-and-true technique for teaching the concept of a paragraph. Assessment thereof consists of

- specifying the writing of a topic sentence,
- scoring points for its presence or absence, and
- scoring and/or commenting on its effectiveness in stating the topic.

2. Topic development within a paragraph. Because paragraphs are intended to provide a reader with "clusters" of meaningful, connected thoughts or ideas, another stage of assessment is development of an idea within a paragraph. Four criteria are commonly applied to assess the quality of a paragraph:

- the clarity of expression of ideas
- the logic of the sequence and connections
- the cohesiveness or unity of the paragraph
- the overall effectiveness or impact of the paragraph as a whole

3. Development of main and supporting ideas across paragraphs. As writers string two or more paragraphs together in a longer text (and as we move up the continuum from responsive to extensive writing), the writer attempts to articulate a thesis or **main idea** with clearly stated **supporting ideas**. These elements can be considered in evaluating a multi-paragraph essay:

- addressing the topic, main idea, or principal purpose
- organizing and developing supporting ideas
- using appropriate details to undergird supporting ideas
- showing facility and fluency in the use of language
- demonstrating syntactic variety

Strategic Options

Developing main and supporting ideas is the goal for the writer attempting to create an effective text, whether a short one- to two-paragraph one or an extensive one of several pages. A number of strategies are commonly taught to second language writers to accomplish their purposes. Aside from strategies of freewriting, outlining, drafting, and revising, writers need to be aware of the task that has been demanded and to focus on the genre of writing and the expectations of that genre.

1. Attending to task. In responsive writing, the context is seldom completely open-ended: a task has been defined by the teacher or test administrator, and the writer must fulfill the criterion of the task. Even in extensive writing of longer texts, a set of directives has been stated by the teacher or is implied by the conventions of the genre. Four types of tasks are commonly addressed in academic writing courses: compare/contrast, problem/solution, pros/cons, and cause/effect. Depending on the genre of the text, one or more of these task types will be needed to achieve the writer's purpose. If students are asked, for example, to "agree or disagree with the author's statement," a likely strategy would be to cite pros and cons and then take a stand. A task that asks students to argue for one among several political candidates in an election might be an ideal compare-and-contrast context, with an appeal to problems present in the constituency and the relative value of candidates' solutions. Assessment of the fulfillment of such tasks could be formative and informal (comments in marginal notes, feedback in a conference in an editing/revising stage), but the product might also be assigned a holistic or analytic score.

2. Attending to genre. The genres of writing that were listed at the beginning of this chapter provide some sense of the many varieties of text that may be produced by a second language learner in a writing curriculum. Another way of looking at the strategic options open to a writer is the extent to which both the constraints and the opportunities of the genre are exploited. Assessment of any writing necessitates attention to the conventions of the genre in question. Assessment of the more common genres may include the following criteria, along with chosen factors from the list in item #**3** (main and supporting ideas) above:

Reports (Lab Reports, Project Summaries, Article/Book Reports, etc.)
- conform to a conventional format (for this case, field)
- convey the purpose, goal, or main idea
- organize details logically and sequentially
- state conclusions or findings
- use appropriate vocabulary and jargon for the specific case

Summaries of Readings/Lectures/Videos
- effectively capture the main and supporting ideas of the original
- maintain objectivity in reporting
- use writer's own words for the most part

- use quotations effectively when appropriate
- omit irrelevant or marginal details
- conform to an expected length

Responses to Readings/Lectures/Videos
- accurately reflect the message or meaning of the original
- appropriately select supporting ideas to respond to
- express the writer's own opinion
- defend or support that opinion effectively
- conform to an expected length

Narration, Description, Persuasion/Argument, and Exposition
- follow expected conventions for each type of writing
- convey purpose, goal, or main idea
- use effective writing strategies
- demonstrate syntactic variety and rhetorical fluency

Interpreting Statistical, Graphic, or Tabular Data
- provides an effective global, overall description of the data
- organizes the details in clear, logical language
- accurately conveys details
- appropriately articulates relationships among elements of the data
- conveys specialized or complex data comprehensibly to a lay reader
- interprets beyond the data when appropriate

Library Research Paper
- states purpose or goal of the research
- includes appropriate citations and references in correct format
- accurately represents others' research findings
- injects writer's own interpretation, when appropriate, and justifies it
- includes suggestions for further research
- sums up findings in a conclusion

TEST OF WRITTEN ENGLISH (TWE®)

One of a number of internationally available standardized tests of writing ability is the *Test of Written English* (*TWE*). Established in 1986, the TWE has gained a reputation as a well-respected measure of written English, and a number of research articles support its validity (Frase et al., 1999; Hale et al., 1996; Longford, 1996; Myford et al., 1996). In 1998, a computer-delivered version of the TWE was incorporated into the standard computer-based TOEFL and simply labeled as the "writing" section of the TOEFL. The TWE is still offered as a separate test especially where only the paper-based TOEFL is available. Correlations between the TWE and TOEFL scores (before TWE became a standard part of TOEFL) were consistently high, ranging from .57 to

.69 over 10 test administrations from 1993 to 1995. Data on the TWE are provided at the end of this section.

The TWE is in the category of a **timed impromptu** test in that test-takers are under a 30-minute time limit and are not able to prepare ahead of time for the topic that will appear. Topics are prepared by a panel of experts following specifications for topics that represent commonly used discourse and thought patterns at the university level. Here are some sample topics published on the TWE website.

Sample TWE® topics

---

1. Some people say that the best preparation for life is learning to work with others and be cooperative. Others take the opposite view and say that learning to be competitive is the best preparation. Discuss these positions, using concrete examples of both. Tell which one you agree with and explain why.
2. Some people believe that automobiles are useful and necessary. Others believe that automobiles cause problems that affect our health and well-being. Which position do you support? Give specific reasons for your answer.
3. Do you agree or disagree with the following statement?

   Teachers should make learning enjoyable and fun for their students.

   Use reasons and specific examples to support your opinion.

Test preparation manuals such as Deborah Phillips's *Longman Introductory Course for the TOEFL Test* (2001) advise TWE test-takers to follow six steps to maximize success on the test:

1. Carefully identify the topic.
2. Plan your supporting ideas.
3. In the introductory paragraph, restate the topic and state the organizational plan of the essay.
4. Write effective supporting paragraphs (show transitions, include a topic sentence, specify details).
5. Restate your position and summarize in the concluding paragraph.
6. Edit sentence structure and rhetorical expression.

The scoring guide for the TWE (see Table 9.1) follows a widely accepted set of specifications for a holistic evaluation of an essay (see below for more discussion of holistic scoring). Each point on the scoring system is defined by a set of statements that address topic, organization and development, supporting ideas, facility (fluency, naturalness, appropriateness) in writing, and grammatical and lexical correctness and choice.

Table 9.1. Test of Written English Scoring Guide

6 **Demonstrates clear competence in writing on both the rhetorical and syntactic levels, though it may have occasional errors.**

A paper in this category
- effectively addresses the writing task.
- is well organized and well developed.
- uses clearly appropriate details to support a thesis or illustrate ideas.
- displays consistent facility in the use of language.
- demonstrates syntactic variety and appropriate word choice.

5 **Demonstrates competence in writing on both the rhetorical and syntactic levels, though it will probably have occasional errors.**

A paper in this category
- may address some parts of the task more effectively than others.
- is generally well organized and developed.
- uses details to support a thesis or illustrate an idea.
- displays facility in the use of language.
- demonstrates some syntactic variety and range of vocabulary.

4 **Demonstrates minimal competence in writing on both the rhetorical and syntactic levels.**

A paper in this category
- addresses the writing topic adequately but may slight parts of the task.
- is adequately organized and developed.
- uses some details to support a thesis or illustrate an idea.
- demonstrates adequate but possibly inconsistent facility with syntax and usage.
- may contain some errors that occasionally obscure meaning.

3 **Demonstrates some developing competence in writing, but it remains flawed on either the rhetorical or syntactic level, or both.**

A paper in this category may reveal one or more of the following weaknesses:
- inadequate organization or development
- inappropriate or insufficient details to support or illustrate generalizations
- a noticeably inappropriate choice of words or word forms
- an accumulation of errors in sentence structure and/or usage.

2 **Suggests incompetence in writing.**

A paper in this category is seriously flawed by one or more of the following weaknesses:
- serious disorganization or underdevelopment
- little or no detail, or irrelevant specifics
- serious and frequent errors in sentence structure or usage
- serious problems with focus.

1 **Demonstrates incompetence in writing.**

A paper in this category
- may be incoherent.
- may be undeveloped.
- may contain severe and persistent writing errors.

0 A paper is rated 0 if it contains no response, merely copies the topic, is off-topic, is written in a foreign language, or consists only of keystroke characters.

Each essay is scored by two trained readers working independently. The final score assigned is the mean of the two independent ratings. The test-taker can achieve a score ranging from 1 to 6 with possible half-points (e.g., 4.5, 5.5) in between. In the case of a discrepancy of more than one point, a third reader resolves the difference. Discrepancy rates are extremely low, usually ranging from 1 to 2 percent per reading.

It is important to put tests like the TWE in perspective. Timed impromptu tests have obvious limitations if you are looking for an authentic sample of performance in a real-world context. How many times in real-world situations (other than in academic writing classes!) will you be asked to write an essay in 30 minutes? Probably never, but the TWE and other standardized timed tests are not intended to mirror the real world. Instead, they are intended to elicit a sample of writing performance that will be *indicative* of a person's writing ability in the real world. TWE designers sought to validate a feasible timed task that would be manageable within their constraints and at the same time offer useful information about the test-taker.

How does the Educational Testing Service justify the TWE as such an indicator? Research by Hale et al. (1996) showed that the prompts used in the TWE approximate writing tasks assigned in 162 graduate and undergraduate courses across several disciplines in eight universities. Another study (Golub-Smith et al., 1993) ascertained the reliabilities across several types of prompts (e.g., compare/contrast vs. chart-graph interpretation). Both Myford et al. (1996) and Longford (1996) studied the reliabilities of judges' ratings. The question of whether a mere 30-minute time period is sufficient to elicit a sufficient sample of a test-taker's writing was addressed by Hale (1992). Henning and Cascallar (1992) conducted a large-scale study to assess the extent to which TWE performance taps into the communicative competence of the test-taker. The upshot of this research—which is updated regularly—is that the TWE (which adheres to a high standard of excellence in standardized testing) is, within acceptable standard error ranges, a remarkably accurate indicator of writing ability.

The flip side of this controversial coin reminds us that standardized tests are indicators, not fail-safe, infallible measures of competence. Even though we might need TWE scores for the *administrative* purposes of admissions or placement, we should not rely on such tests for *instructional* purposes (see Cohen, 1994). No one would suggest that such 30-minute writing tests offer constructive feedback to the student, nor do they provide the kind of formative assessment that a process approach to writing brings. Tests like the TWE are administrative necessities in a world where hundreds or thousands of applicants must be evaluated by some means short of calculating their performance across years of instruction in academic writing.

The convenience of the TWE should not lull administrators into believing that TWEs and TOEFLs and the like are the only measures that should be applied to students. It behooves admissions and placement officers worldwide to offer secondary measures of writing ability to those test-takers who

a. are on the threshold of a minimum score,
b. may be disabled by highly time-constrained or anxiety-producing situations,
c. could be culturally disadvantaged by a topic or situation, and/or
d. (in the case of computer-based writing) have had few opportunities to compose on a computer.

While timed impromptu tests suffer from a lack of authenticity and put test-takers into an artificially time-constrained context, they nevertheless offer interesting, relevant information for an important but narrow range of administrative purposes. The classroom offers a much wider set of options for creating real-world writing purposes and contexts. The classroom becomes the locus of extended hard work and effort for building the skills necessary to create written production. The classroom provides a setting for writers, in a process of multiple drafts and revisions, to create a final, publicly acceptable product. And the classroom is a place where learners can take all the small steps, at their own pace, toward becoming proficient writers. For your reference, following is some information on the TWE:

Test of Written English (TWE®)

Producer:	Educational Testing Service (ETS), Princeton, NJ
Objective:	To test written expression
Primary market:	Almost exclusively U.S. universities and colleges for admission purposes
Type:	Computer-based, with the TOEFL. A traditional paper-based (PB) version is also available separately.
Response modes:	Written essay
Specifications:	(see above, in this section)
Time allocation:	30 minutes
Internet access:	**http://www.toefl.org/educator/edabttwe.html**

SCORING METHODS FOR RESPONSIVE AND EXTENSIVE WRITING

At responsive and extensive levels of writing, three major approaches to scoring writing performance are commonly used by test designers: holistic, primary trait, and analytical. In the first method, a single score is assigned to an essay, which represents a reader's general overall assessment. Primary trait scoring is a variation of the holistic method in that the achievement of the primary purpose, or trait, of an essay is the only factor rated. Analytical scoring breaks a test-taker's written text down into a number of subcategories (organization, grammar, etc.) and gives a separate rating for each.

Holistic Scoring

The TWE scoring scale above is a prime example of **holistic** scoring. In Chapter 7, a rubric for scoring oral production holistically was presented. Each point on a holistic scale is given a systematic set of descriptors, and the reader-evaluator matches an overall impression with the descriptors to arrive at a score. Descriptors usually (but not always) follow a prescribed pattern. For example, the first descriptor across all score categories may address the quality of task achievement, the second may deal with organization, the third with grammatical or rhetorical considerations, and so on. Scoring, however, is truly holistic in that those subsets are not quantitatively added up to yield a score.

Advantages of holistic scoring include

- fast evaluation,
- relatively high inter-rater reliability,
- the fact that scores represent "standards" that are easily interpreted by lay persons,
- the fact that scores tend to emphasize the writer's strengths (Cohen, 1994, p. 315), and
- applicability to writing across many different disciplines.

Its disadvantages must also be weighed into a decision on whether to use holistic scoring:

- One score masks differences across the subskills within each score.
- No diagnostic information is available (no washback potential).
- The scale may not apply equally well to all genres of writing.
- Raters need to be extensively trained to use the scale accurately.

In general, teachers and test designers lean toward holistic scoring only when it is expedient for administrative purposes. As long as trained evaluators are in place, differentiation across six levels may be quite adequate for admission into an institution or placement into courses. For classroom instructional purposes, holistic scores provide very little information. In most classroom settings where a teacher wishes to adapt a curriculum to the needs of a particular group of students, much more differentiated information across subskills is desirable than is provided by holistic scoring.

Primary Trait Scoring

A second method of scoring, **primary trait,** focuses on "how well students can write within a narrowly defined range of discourse" (Weigle, 2002, p. 110). This type of scoring emphasizes the task at hand and assigns a score based on the effectiveness of the text's achieving that one goal. For example, if the purpose or function of an essay is to *persuade* the reader to do something, the score for the writing would rise or fall on the accomplishment of that function. If a learner is asked to exploit the imaginative function of language by expressing personal feelings, then the response would be evaluated on that feature alone.

For rating the primary trait of the text, Lloyd-Jones (1977) suggested a four-point scale ranging from zero (no response or fragmented response) to 4 (the purpose is unequivocally accomplished in a convincing fashion). It almost goes without saying that organization, supporting details, fluency, syntactic variety, and other features will implicitly be evaluated in the process of offering a primary trait score. But the advantage of this method is that it allows both writer and evaluator to focus on function. In summary, a primary trait score would assess

- the accuracy of the account of the original (summary),
- the clarity of the steps of the procedure and the final result (lab report),
- the description of the main features of the graph (graph description), and
- the expression of the writer's opinion (response to an article).

Analytic Scoring

For classroom instruction, holistic scoring provides little washback into the writer's further stages of learning. Primary trait scoring focuses on the principal function of the text and therefore offers some feedback potential, but no washback for any of the aspects of the written production that enhance the ultimate accomplishment of the purpose. Classroom evaluation of learning is best served through **analytic scoring,** in which as many as six major elements of writing are scored, thus enabling learners to home in on weaknesses and to capitalize on strengths.

Analytic scoring may be more appropriately called analytic *assessment* in order to capture its closer association with classroom language instruction than with formal testing. Brown and Bailey (1984) designed an analytical scoring scale that specified five major categories and a description of five different levels in each category, ranging from "unacceptable" to "excellent" (see Table 9.2).

At first glance, Brown and Bailey's scale may look similar to the TWE® holistic scale discussed earlier: for each scoring category there is a description that encompasses several subsets. A closer inspection, however, reveals much more detail in the analytic method. Instead of just six descriptions, there are 25, each subdivided into a number of contributing factors.

The order in which the five categories (organization, logical development of ideas, grammar, punctuation/spelling/mechanics, and style and quality of expression) are listed may bias the evaluator toward the greater importance of organization and logical development as opposed to punctuation and style. But the mathematical assignment of the 100-point scale gives equal weight (a maximum of 20 points) to each of the five major categories. Not all writing and assessment specialists agree. You might, for example, consider the analytical scoring profile suggested by Jacobs et al. (1981), in which five slightly different categories were given the point values shown on page 246.

Table 9.2. Analytic scale for rating composition tasks (Brown & Bailey, 1984, pp. 39–41)

	20–18 Excellent to Good	17–15 Good to Adequate	14–12 Adequate to Fair	11–6 Unacceptable–not college-level work	5–1 Unacceptable–not college-level work
I. Organization: Introduction, Body, and Conclusion	Appropriate title, effective introductory paragraph, topic is stated, leads to body; transitional expressions used; arrangement of material shows plan (could be outlined by reader); supporting evidence given for generalizations; conclusion logical and complete	Adequate title, introduction, and conclusion; body of essay is acceptable, but some evidence may be lacking, some ideas aren't fully developed; sequence is logical but transitional expressions may be absent or misused	Mediocre or scant introduction or conclusion; problems with the order of ideas in body; the generalizations may not be fully supported by the evidence given; problems of organization interfere	Shaky or minimally recognizable introduction; organization can barely be seen; severe problems with ordering of ideas; lack of supporting evidence; conclusion weak or illogical; inadequate effort at organization	Absence of introduction or conclusion; no apparent organization of body; severe lack of supporting evidence; writer has not made any effort to organize the composition (could not be outlined by reader)
II. Logical development of ideas: Content	Essay addresses the assigned topic; the ideas are concrete and thoroughly developed; no extraneous material; essay reflects thought	Essay addresses the issues but misses some points; ideas could be more fully developed; some extraneous material is present	Development of ideas not complete or essay is somewhat off the topic; paragraphs aren't divided exactly right	Ideas incomplete; essay does not reflect careful thinking or was hurriedly written; inadequate effort in area of content	Essay is completely inadequate and does not reflect college-level work; no apparent effort to consider the topic carefully

III. Grammar	Native-like fluency in English grammar; correct use of relative clauses, prepositions, modals, articles, verb forms, and tense sequencing; no fragments or run-on sentences	Advanced proficiency in English grammar; some grammar problems don't influence communication, although the reader is aware of them; no fragments or run-on sentences	Ideas are getting through to the reader, but grammar problems are apparent and have a negative effect on communication; run-on sentences or fragments present	Numerous serious grammar problems interfere with communication of the writer's ideas; grammar review of some areas clearly needed; difficult to read sentences	Severe grammar problems interfere greatly with the message; reader can't understand what the writer was trying to say; unintelligible sentence structure
IV. Punctuation, spelling, and mechanics	Correct use of English writing conventions: left and right margins, all needed capitals, paragraphs indented, punctuation and spelling; very neat	Some problems with writing conventions or punctuation; occasional spelling errors; left margin correct; paper is neat and legible	Uses general writing conventions but has errors; spelling problems distract reader; punctuation errors interfere with ideas	Serious problems with format of paper; parts of essay not legible; errors in sentence punctuation and final punctuation; unacceptable to educated readers	Complete disregard for English writing conventions; paper illegible; obvious capitals missing, no margins, severe spelling problems
V. Style and quality of expression	Precise vocabulary usage; use of parallel structures; concise; register good	Attempts variety; good vocabulary; not wordy; register OK; style fairly concise	Some vocabulary misused; lacks awareness of register; may be too wordy	Poor expression of ideas; problems in vocabulary; lacks variety of structure	Inappropriate use of vocabulary; no concept of register or sentence variety

Content	30
Organization	20
Vocabulary	20
Syntax	25
Mechanics	5
Total	**100**

As your curricular goals and students' needs vary, your own analytical scoring of essays may be appropriately tailored. Level of proficiency can make a significant difference in emphasis: at the intermediate level, for example, you might give more emphasis to syntax and mechanics, while advanced levels of writing may call for a strong push toward organization and development. Genre can also dictate variations in scoring. Would a summary of an article require the same relative emphases as a narrative essay? Most likely not. Certain types of writing, such as lab reports or inter-pretations of statistical data, may even need additional—or at least redefined—cate-gories in order to capture the essential components of good writing within those genres.

Analytic scoring of compositions offers writers a little more washback than a single holistic or primary trait score. Scores in five or six major elements will help to call the writers' attention to areas of needed improvement. Practicality is lowered in that more time is required for teachers to attend to details within each of the cat-egories in order to render a final score or grade, but ultimately students receive more information about their writing. Numerical scores alone, however, are still not sufficient for enabling students to become proficient writers, as we shall see in the next section.

BEYOND SCORING: RESPONDING TO EXTENSIVE WRITING

Formal testing carries with it the burden of designing a practical and reliable instru-ment that assesses its intended criterion accurately. To accomplish that mission, designers of writing tests are charged with the task of providing as "objective" a scoring procedure as possible, and one that in many cases can be easily interpreted by agents beyond the learner. Holistic, primary trait, and analytic scoring all satisfy those ends. Yet beyond mathematically calculated scores lies a rich domain of assess-ment in which a developing writer is coached from stage to stage in a process of building a storehouse of writing skills. Here in the classroom, in the tutored rela-tionship of teacher and student, and in the community of peer learners, most of the hard work of assessing writing is carried out. Such assessment is informal, formative, and replete with washback.

Most writing specialists agree that the best way to teach writing is a hands-on approach that stimulates student output and then generates a series of self-assessments, peer editing and revision, and teacher response and conferencing (Raimes, 1991, 1998; Reid, 1993; Seow, 2002). It is not an approach that relies on a massive dose of lecturing about good writing, nor on memorizing a bunch of rules about rhetorical organization, nor on sending students home with an assignment to turn in a paper the next day. People become good writers by writing and seeking the facilitative input of others to refine their skills.

Assessment takes on a crucial role in such an approach. Learning how to become a good writer places the student in an almost constant stage of assessment. To give the student the maximum benefit of assessment, it is important to consider (a) *earlier* stages (from freewriting to the first draft or two) and (b) *later* stages (revising and finalizing) of producing a written text. A further factor in assessing writing is the involvement of self, peers, and teacher at appropriate steps in the process. (For further guidelines on the process of teaching writing, see *TBP*, Chapter 19.)

Assessing Initial Stages of the Process of Composing

Following are some guidelines for assessing the initial stages (the first draft or two) of a written composition. These guidelines are generic for self, peer, and teacher responding. Each assessor will need to modify the list according to the level of the learner, the context, and the purpose in responding.

Assessment of initial stages in composing

1. Focus your efforts primarily on meaning, main idea, and organization.
2. Comment on the introductory paragraph.
3. Make general comments about the clarity of the main idea and logic or appropriateness of the organization.
4. As a rule of thumb, ignore minor (local) grammatical and lexical errors.
5. Indicate what appear to be major (global) errors (e.g., by underlining the text in question), but allow the writer to make corrections.
6. Do not rewrite questionable, ungrammatical, or awkward sentences; rather, probe with a question about meaning.
7. Comment on features that appear to be irrelevant to the topic.

The teacher-assessor's role is as a guide, a facilitator, and an ally; therefore, assessment at this stage of writing needs to be as positive as possible to encourage the writer. An early focus on overall structure and meaning will enable writers to clarify their purpose and plan and will set a framework for the writers' later refinement of the lexical and grammatical issues.

Assessing Later Stages of the Process of Composing

Once the writer has determined and clarified his or her purpose and plan, and has completed at least one or perhaps two drafts, the focus shifts toward "fine tuning" the expression with a view toward a final revision. Editing and responding assume an appropriately different character now, with these guidelines:

Assessment of later stages in composing

---

1. Comment on the specific clarity and strength of all main ideas and supporting ideas, and on argument and logic.
2. Call attention to minor ("local") grammatical and mechanical (spelling, punctuation) errors, but direct the writer to self-correct.
3. Comment on any further word choices and expressions that may not be awkward but are not as clear or direct as they could be.
4. Point out any problems with cohesive devices within and across paragraphs.
5. If appropriate, comment on documentation, citation of sources, evidence, and other support.
6. Comment on the adequacy and strength of the conclusion.

Through all these stages it is assumed that peers and teacher are both responding to the writer through conferencing in person, electronic communication, or, at the very least, an exchange of papers. The impromptu timed tests and the methods of scoring discussed earlier may appear to be only distantly related to such an individualized process of creating a written text, but are they, in reality? All those developmental stages may be the preparation that learners need both to function in creative real-world writing tasks and to successfully demonstrate their competence on a timed impromptu test. And those holistic scores are after all generalizations of the various components of effective writing. If the hard work of successfully progressing through a semester or two of a challenging course in academic writing ultimately means that writers are ready to function in their real-world contexts, *and* to get a 5 or 6 on the TWE, then all the effort was worthwhile.

§   §   §   §   §

This chapter completes the cycle of considering the assessment of all of the four skills of listening, speaking, reading, and writing. As you contemplate using some of the assessment techniques that have been suggested, I think you can now fully appreciate two significant overarching guidelines for designing an effective assessment procedure:

1. It is virtually impossible to isolate any one of the four skills without the involvement of at least one other mode of performance. Don't underestimate the power of the integration of skills in assessments designed to target a single skill area.

2. The variety of assessment techniques and item types and tasks is virtually infinite in that there is always some possibility for creating a unique variation. Explore those alternatives, but with some caution lest your overzealous urge to be innovative distract you from a central focus on achieving the intended purpose and rendering an appropriate evaluation of performance.

EXERCISES

[Note: **(I)** Individual work; **(G)** Group or pair work; **(C)** Whole-class discussion.]

1. **(C)** Genres of reading were listed at the beginning of Chapter 8, and genres of writing in this chapter, a shorter list. Why is the list for writing shorter? Add other examples to each of the three categories. Among the listed examples and new ones you come up with, be specific in citing what makes some genres more difficult than others. Select a few of the more difficult genres and discuss what you would assess (criteria) and how you would assess (some possible assessment techniques) them.

2. **(C)** Review the four basic types of writing that were outlined at the beginning of the chapter. Offer examples of each and pay special attention to distinguishing between imitative and intensive, and between responsive and extensive.

3. **(G)** Look at the list of micro- and macroskills of writing on page 221. In pairs, each assigned to a different skill (or two), brainstorm some tasks that assess those skills. Present your findings to the rest of the class.

4. **(C)** In Chapter 6, eight characteristics of listening were listed (page 122) that make listening "difficult." What makes writing difficult? Devise a similar list, which could form a set of specifications to pay special attention to in assessing writing.

5. **(G)** Divide the four basic types of writing among groups or pairs, one type for each. Look at the sample assessment techniques provided and evaluate them according to the five principles (practicality, reliability, validity [especially face and content], authenticity, and washback). Present your critique to the rest of the class.

6. **(G)** In the same groups as #5 above with the same type of writing, design some other item types, different from the one(s) provided here, that assess the same type of writing performance.

7. **(I/C)** Visit the TOEFL website and click on the description of the Test of Written English to familiarize yourself further with the TWE. Then, do the following: (a) Look at the TWE holistic scoring guide (page 239) and evaluate its rater reliability. (b) Discuss the validity of a timed impromptu test such as this for admission to an English-speaking university.

8. **(C)** Review the advantages and disadvantages of the three kinds of scoring presented in this chapter: holistic, primary trait, and analytic. Construct a chart that shows how different contexts (types of test, objectives of a curriculum, proficiency levels, etc.) may benefit from each kind of scoring.

FOR YOUR FURTHER READING

Weigle, Sara Cushing. (2002). *Assessing writing.* Cambridge: Cambridge University Press.

This volume in the Cambridge Language Assessment Series provides a comprehensive overview of the history and current state of the art of assessing writing. With an authoritative backdrop of research underlying the construct validation of techniques for the assessment of written production, a host of actual testing techniques are surveyed and evaluated.

Raimes, Ann. (1998). Teaching writing. *Annual Review of Applied Linguistics, 18,* pp. 142–167.

In this survey article, one of the leading researchers in the field of second language writing pedagogy offers a description of recent research in teaching writing with special attention to journal writing, integrating writing with other skills, peer collaboration, responding to writing, and a note on the role of technology in teaching writing. Assessment of writing is addressed in a pedagogical context.

CHAPTER **10**

BEYOND TESTS:

ALTERNATIVES IN

ASSESSMENT

In the public eye, tests have acquired an aura of infallibility in our culture of mass producing everything, including the education of school children. Everyone wants a test for everything, especially if the test is cheap, quickly administered, and scored instantaneously. But we saw in Chapter 4 that while the standardized test industry has become a powerful juggernaut of influence on decisions about people's lives, it also has come under severe criticism from the public (Kohn, 2000). A more balanced viewpoint is offered by Bailey (1998, p. 204): "One of the disturbing things about tests is the extent to which many people accept the results uncritically, while others believe that all testing is invidious. But tests are simply measurement tools: It is the use to which we put their results that can be appropriate or inappropriate."

It is clear by now that tests are one of a number of possible types of assessment. In Chapter 1, an important distinction was made between testing and assessing. Tests are formal procedures, usually administered within strict time limitations, to sample the performance of a test-taker in a specified domain. Assessment connotes a much broader concept in that most of the time when teachers are teaching, they are also assessing. Assessment includes all occasions from informal impromptu observations and comments up to and including tests.

Early in the decade of the 1990s, in a culture of rebellion against the notion that all people and all skills could be measured by traditional tests, a novel concept emerged that began to be labeled "alternative" assessment. As teachers and students were becoming aware of the shortcomings of standardized tests, "an alternative to standardized testing and all the problems found with such testing" (Huerta-Macías, 1995, p. 8) was proposed. That proposal was to assemble additional measures of students—portfolios, journals, observations, self-assessments, peer-assessments, and the like—in an effort to triangulate data about students. For some, such alternatives held "ethical potential" (Lynch, 2001, p. 228) in their promotion of fairness and the balance of power relationships in the classroom.

Why, then, should we even refer to the notion of "alternative" when assessment already encompasses such a range of possibilities? This was the question to which Brown and Hudson (1998) responded in a *TESOL Quarterly* article. They noted that to speak of *alternative* assessments is counterproductive because the term implies something new and different that may be "exempt from the requirements of responsible test construction" (p. 657). So they proposed to refer to "alternatives" in assessment instead. Their term is a perfect fit within a model that considers tests as a subset of assessment. Throughout this book, you have been reminded that all tests are assessments but, more important, that not all assessments are tests.

The defining characteristics of the various alternatives in assessment that have been commonly used across the profession were aptly summed up by Brown and Hudson (1998, pp. 654–655). Alternatives in assessments

1. require students to perform, create, produce, or do something;
2. use real-world contexts or simulations;
3. are nonintrusive in that they extend the day-to-day classroom activities;
4. allow students to be assessed on what they normally do in class every day;
5. use tasks that represent meaningful instructional activities;
6. focus on processes as well as products;
7. tap into higher-level thinking and problem-solving skills;
8. provide information about both the strengths and weaknesses of students;
9. are multiculturally sensitive when properly administered;
10. ensure that people, not machines, do the scoring, using human judgment;
11. encourage open disclosure of standards and rating criteria; and
12. call upon teachers to perform new instructional and assessment roles.

THE DILEMMA OF MAXIMIZING BOTH PRACTICALITY AND WASHBACK

The principal purpose of this chapter is to examine some of the alternatives in assessment that are markedly different from formal tests. Tests, especially large-scale standardized tests, tend to be one-shot performances that are timed, multiple-choice, decontextualized, norm-referenced, and that foster extrinsic motivation. On the other hand, tasks like portfolios, journals, and self-assessment are

- open-ended in their time orientation and format,
- contextualized to a curriculum,
- referenced to the criteria (objectives) of that curriculum, and
- likely to build intrinsic motivation.

One way of looking at this contrast poses a challenge to you as a teacher and test designer. Formal standardized tests are almost by definition highly practical, reliable instruments. They are designed to minimize time and money on the part of test designer and test-taker, and to be painstakingly accurate in their scoring. Alternatives such as portfolios, or conferencing with students on drafts of written work, or observations of learners over time all require considerable time and effort on the part of the teacher and the student. Even more time must be spent if the teacher hopes to offer a reliable evaluation within students across time, as well as across students (taking care not to favor one student or group of students). But the alternative techniques also offer markedly greater washback, are superior formative measures, and, because of their authenticity, usually carry greater face validity.

This relationship can be depicted in a hypothetical graph that shows practicality/reliability on one axis and washback/authenticity on the other, as shown in Figure 10.1. Notice the implied negative correlation: as a technique increases in its washback and authenticity, its practicality and reliability tend to be lower. Conversely, the greater the practicality and reliability, the less likely you are to achieve beneficial washback and authenticity. I have placed three types of assessment on the regression line to illustrate.

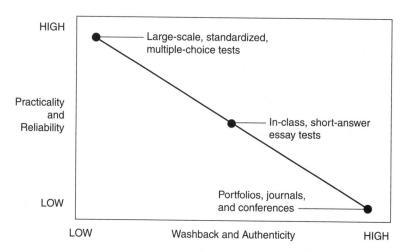

Figure 10.1. Relationship of practicality/reliability to washback/authenticity

The figure appears to imply the inevitability of the relationship: large-scale multiple-choice tests cannot offer much washback or authenticity, nor can portfolios and such alternatives achieve much practicality or reliability. This need not be the case! The challenge that faces conscientious teachers and assessors in our profession is to change the directionality of the line: to "flatten" that downward slope to some degree, or perhaps to push the various assessments on the chart leftward and upward. Surely we should not sit idly by, accepting the presumably inescapable conclusion that all standardized tests will be devoid of washback and authenticity. With some creativity and effort, we can transform otherwise inauthentic and negative-washback-producing tests into more pedagogically fulfilling learning experiences. A number of approaches to accomplishing this end are possible, many of which have already been implicitly presented in this book:

- building as much authenticity as possible into multiple-choice task types and items
- designing classroom tests that have both objective-scoring sections and open-ended response sections, varying the performance tasks
- turning multiple-choice test results into diagnostic feedback on areas of needed improvement
- maximizing the preparation period before a test to elicit performance relevant to the ultimate criteria of the test
- teaching test-taking strategies
- helping students to see beyond the test: don't "teach to the test"
- triangulating information on a student before making a final assessment of competence.

The flip side of this challenge is to understand that the alternatives in assessment are not doomed to be impractical and unreliable. As we look at alternatives in assessment in this chapter, we must remember Brown and Hudson's (1998) admonition to scrutinize the practicality, reliability, and validity of those alternatives at the same time that we celebrate their face validity, washback potential, and authenticity. It is easy to fly out of the cage of traditional testing rubrics, but it is tempting in doing so to flap our wings aimlessly and to accept virtually any classroom activity as a viable alternative. Assessments proposed to serve as triangulating measures of competence imply a responsibility to be rigorous in determining objectives, response modes, and criteria for evaluation and interpretation.

PERFORMANCE-BASED ASSESSMENT

Before proceeding to a direct consideration of types of alternatives in assessment, a word about **performance-based** assessment is in order. There has been a great deal of press in recent years about performance-based assessment, sometimes merely called performance assessment (Shohamy, 1995; Norris et al., 1998). Is this different from what is being called "alternative assessment"?

The push toward more performance-based assessment is part of the same general educational reform movement that has raised strong objections to using standardized test scores as the only measures of student competencies (see, for example, Valdez Pierce & O'Malley, 1992; Shepard & Bliem, 1993). The argument, as you can guess, was that standardized tests do not elicit actual performance on the part of test-takers. If a child were asked, for example, to write a description of earth as seen from space, to work cooperatively with peers to design a three-dimensional model of the solar system, to explain the project to the rest of the class, and to take notes on a videotape about space travel, traditional standardized testing would be involved in none of those performances. Performance-based assessment, however, *would* require the performance of the above-named actions, or samples thereof, which would be systematically evaluated through direct observation by a teacher and/or possibly by self and peers.

Performance-based assessment implies productive, observable skills, such as speaking and writing, of content-valid tasks. Such performance usually, but not always, brings with it an air of authenticity—real-world tasks that students have had time to develop. It often implies an integration of language skills, perhaps all four skills in the case of project work. Because the tasks that students perform are consistent with course goals and curriculum, students and teachers are likely to be more motivated to perform them, as opposed to a set of multiple-choice questions about facts and figures regarding the solar system.

O'Malley and Valdez Pierce (1996) considered performance-based assessment to be a subset of authentic assessment. In other words, not all authentic assessment is performance-based. One could infer that reading, listening, and thinking have many authentic manifestations, but since they are not directly observable in and of themselves, they are not performance-based. According to O'Malley and Valdez Pierce (p. 5), the following are characteristics of performance assessment:

1. Students make a *constructed response.*
2. They engage in *higher-order thinking,* with *open-ended* tasks.
3. Tasks are *meaningful, engaging, and authentic.*
4. Tasks call for the *integration of language skills.*
5. Both *process and product* are assessed.
6. *Depth* of a student's mastery is emphasized over breadth.

Performance-based assessment needs to be approached with caution. It is tempting for teachers to assume that if a student is doing something, then the process has fulfilled its own goal and the evaluator needs only to make a mark in the grade book that says "accomplished" next to a particular competency. In reality, performances as assessment procedures need to be treated with the same rigor as traditional tests. This implies that teachers should

- state the overall goal of the performance,
- specify the objectives (criteria) of the performance in detail,
- prepare students for performance in stepwise progressions,
- use a reliable evaluation form, checklist, or rating sheet,
- treat performances as opportunities for giving feedback and provide that feedback systematically, and
- if possible, utilize self- and peer-assessments judiciously.

To sum up, performance assessment is not completely synonymous with the concept of alternative assessment. Rather, it is best understood as one of the primary traits of the many available alternatives to assessment.

PORTFOLIOS

One of the most popular alternatives in assessment, especially within a framework of communicative language teaching, is portfolio development. According to Genesee and Upshur (1996), a portfolio is "a purposeful collection of students' work that demonstrates ... their efforts, progress, and achievements in given areas" (p. 99). Portfolios include materials such as

- essays and compositions in draft and final forms;
- reports, project outlines;
- poetry and creative prose;
- artwork, photos, newspaper or magazine clippings;
- audio and/or video recordings of presentations, demonstrations, etc.;
- journals, diaries, and other personal reflections;
- tests, test scores, and written homework exercises;
- notes on lectures; and
- self- and peer-assessments—comments, evaluations, and checklists.

Until recently, portfolios were thought to be applicable only to younger children who assemble a portfolio of artwork and written work for presentation to a teacher and/or a parent. Now learners of all ages and in all fields of study are benefiting from the tangible, hands-on nature of portfolio development.

Gottlieb (1995) suggested a developmental scheme for considering the nature and purpose of portfolios, using the acronym CRADLE to designate six possible attributes of a portfolio:

> Collecting
> Reflecting
> Assessing
> Documenting
> Linking
> Evaluating

As Collections, portfolios are an expression of students' lives and identities. The appropriate freedom of students to choose what to include should be respected, but at the same time the purposes of the portfolio need to be clearly specified. Reflective practice through journals and self-assessment checklists is an important ingredient of a successful portfolio. Teacher and student both need to take the role of Assessment seriously as they evaluate quality and development over time. We need to recognize that a portfolio is an important Document in demonstrating student achievement, and not just an insignificant adjunct to tests and grades and other more traditional evaluation. A portfolio can serve as an important Link between student and teacher, parent, community, and peers; it is a tangible product, created with pride, that identifies a student's uniqueness. Finally, Evaluation of portfolios requires a time-consuming but fulfilling process of generating accountability.

The advantages of engaging students in portfolio development have been extolled in a number of sources (Genesee & Upshur, 1996; O'Malley & Valdez Pierce, 1996; Brown & Hudson, 1998; Weigle, 2002). A synthesis of those characteristics gives us a number of potential benefits. Portfolios

- foster intrinsic motivation, responsibility, and ownership,
- promote student-teacher interaction with the teacher as facilitator,
- individualize learning and celebrate the uniqueness of each student,
- provide tangible evidence of a student's work,
- facilitate critical thinking, self-assessment, and revision processes,
- offer opportunities for collaborative work with peers, and
- permit assessment of multiple dimensions of language learning.

At the same time, care must be taken lest portfolios become a haphazard pile of "junk" the purpose of which is a mystery to both teacher and student. Portfolios can fail if objectives are not clear, if guidelines are not given to students, if systematic periodic review and feedback are not present, and so on. Sometimes the thought of asking students to develop a portfolio is a daunting challenge, especially for new teachers and for those who have never created a portfolio on their own. Successful portfolio development will depend on following a number of steps and guidelines.

1. State objectives clearly. Pick one or more of the CRADLE attributes named above and specify them as objectives of developing a portfolio. Show how those purposes are connected to, integrated with, and/or a reinforcement of your already stated curricular goals. A portfolio attains maximum authenticity and washback when it is an integral part of a curriculum, not just an optional box of materials. Show students how their portfolios will include materials from the course they are taking and how that collection will enhance curricular goals.

2. Give guidelines on what materials to include. Once the objectives have been determined, name the types of work that should be included. There is some disagreement among "experts" about how much negotiation should take place between student and teacher over those materials. Hamp-Lyons and Condon (2000) suggested advantages for student control of portfolio contents, but teacher guidance will keep students on target with curricular objectives. It is helpful to give clear directions on how to get started since many students will never have compiled a portfolio and may be mystified about what to do. A sample portfolio from a previous student can help to stimulate some thoughts on what to include.

3. Communicate assessment criteria to students. This is both the most important aspect of portfolio development and the most complex. Two sources—self-assessment and teacher assessment—must be incorporated in order for students to receive the maximum benefit. Self-assessment should be as clear and simple as possible. O'Malley and Valdez Pierce (1996) suggested the following half-page self-evaluation of a writing sample (with spaces for students to write) for elementary school English language students.

Portfolio self-assessment questions (O'Malley & Valdez Pierce, 1996, p. 42)

1. Look at your writing sample.
   a. What does the sample show that you can do?
   b. Write about what you did well.
2. Think about realistic goals. Write one thing you need to do better. Be specific.

Genesee and Upshur (1996) recommended using a questionnaire format for self-assessment, with questions like the following for a project:

Portfolio project self-assessment questionnaire

1. What makes this a good or interesting project?
2. What is the most interesting part of the project?
3. What was the most difficult part of the project?
4. What did you learn from the project?
5. What skills did you practice when doing this project?
6. What resources did you use to complete this project?
7. What is the best part of the project? Why?
8. How would you make the project better?

The teacher's assessment might mirror self-assessments, with similar questions designed to highlight the *formative* nature of the assessment. Conferences are important checkpoints for both student and teacher. In the case of requested written responses from students, help your students to process your feedback and show them how to respond to your responses. Above all, maintain reliability in assessing portfolios so that all students receive equal attention and are assessed by the same criteria.

An option that works for some contexts is to include peer-assessment or small group conferences to comment on one another's portfolios. Where the classroom community is relatively closely knit and supportive and where students are willing to expose themselves by revealing their portfolios, valuable feedback can be achieved from peer reviews. Such sessions should have clear objectives lest they erode into aimless chatter. Checklists and questions may serve to preclude such an eventuality.

4. *Designate time within the curriculum for portfolio development.* If students feel rushed to gather materials and reflect on them, the effectiveness of the portfolio process is diminished. Make sure that students have time set aside for portfolio work (including in-class time) and that your own opportunities for conferencing are not compromised.

5. *Establish periodic schedules for review and conferencing.* By doing so, you will prevent students from throwing everything together at the end of a term.

6. *Designate an accessible place to keep portfolios.* It is inconvenient for students to carry collections of papers and artwork. If you have a self-contained classroom or a place in a reading room or library to keep the materials, that may provide a good option. At the university level, designating a storage place on the campus may involve impossible logistics. In that case, encourage students to create their own accessible location and to bring to class only the materials they need.

7. *Provide positive washback-giving final assessments.* When a portfolio has been completed and the end of a term has arrived, a final summation is in order. Should portfolios be graded? be awarded specific numerical scores? Opinion is divided; every advantage is balanced by a disadvantage. For example, numerical scores serve as convenient data to compare performance across students, courses, and districts. For portfolios containing written work, Wolcott (1998) recommended a holistic scoring scale ranging from 1 to 6 based on such qualities as inclusion of out-of-class work, error-free work, depth of content, creativity, organization, writing style, and "engagement" of the student. Such scores are perhaps best viewed as numerical equivalents of letter grades.

One could argue that it is inappropriate to reduce the personalized and creative process of compiling a portfolio to a number or letter grade and that it is more appropriate to offer a qualitative evaluation for a work that is so open-ended. Such evaluations might include a final appraisal of the work by the student, with questions such as those listed above for self-assessment of a project, and a narrative evaluation of perceived strengths and weakness by the teacher. Those final evaluations should emphasize strengths but also point the way toward future learning challenges.

It is clear that portfolios get a relatively low practicality rating because of the time it takes for teachers to respond and conference with their students. Nevertheless, following the guidelines suggested above for specifying the criteria for evaluating portfolios can raise the reliability to a respectable level, and without question the washback effect, the authenticity, and the face validity of portfolios remain exceedingly high.

In the above discussion, I have tried to subject portfolios to the same specifications that apply to more formal tests: it should be made clear what the *objectives* are, what *tasks* are expected of the student, and how the learner's product will be *evaluated*. Strict attention to these demands is warranted for successful portfolio development to take place.

JOURNALS

Fifty years ago, journals had no place in the second language classroom. When language production was believed to be best taught under controlled conditions, the concept of "free" writing was confined almost exclusively to producing essays on assigned topics. Today, journals occupy a prominent role in a pedagogical model that stresses the importance of self-reflection in the process of students taking control of their own destiny.

A journal is a log (or "account") of one's thoughts, feelings, reactions, assessments, ideas, or progress toward goals, usually written with little attention to structure, form, or correctness. Learners can articulate their thoughts without the threat of those thoughts being judged later (usually by the teacher). Sometimes journals are rambling sets of verbiage that represent a stream of consciousness with no particular point, purpose, or audience. Fortunately, models of journal use in educational practice have sought to tighten up this style of journal in order to give them some focus (Staton et al., 1987). The result is the emergence of a number of overlapping categories or purposes in journal writing, such as the following:

- language-learning logs
- grammar journals
- responses to readings
- strategies-based learning logs
- self-assessment reflections
- diaries of attitudes, feelings, and other affective factors
- acculturation logs

Most classroom-oriented journals are what have now come to be known as **dialogue journals**. They imply an interaction between a reader (the teacher) and the student through dialogues or responses. For the best results, those responses should be dispersed across a course at regular intervals, perhaps weekly or biweekly. One of the principal objectives in a student's dialogue journal is to carry on a conversation with the teacher. Through dialogue journals, teachers can become better acquainted with their students, in terms of both their learning progress and their affective states, and thus become better equipped to meet students' individual needs.

The following journal entry from an advanced student from China, and the teacher's response, is an illustration of the kind of dialogue that can take place.

Dialogue journal sample

Journal entry by Ming Ling, China:

Yesterday at about eight o'clock I was sitting in front of my table holding a fork and eating tasteless noodles which I usually really like to eat but I lost my taste yesterday because I didn't feel well. I had a headache and a fever. My head seemed to be broken. I sometimes felt cold, sometimes hot. I didn't feel comfortable standing up and I didn't feel comfortable sitting down. I hated everything around me. It seemed to me that I got a great pressure from the atmosphere and I could not breath. I was so sleepy since I had taken some medicine which functioned as an antibiotic.

The room was so quiet. I was there by myself and felt very solitary. This dinner reminded me of my mother. Whenever I was sick in China, my mother always took care of me and cooked rice gruel, which has to cook more than three hours and is very delicious, I think. I would be better very soon under the care of my mother. But yesterday, I had to cook by myself even though I was sick, The more I thought, the less I wanted to eat, Half an hour passed. The noodles were cold, but I was still sitting there and thinking about my mother. Finally I threw out the noodles and went to bed.

Teacher's response:

This is a powerful piece of writing because you really communicate what you were feeling. You used vivid details, like "eating tasteless noodles," "my head seemed to be broken" and "rice gruel, which has to cook more than three hours and is very delicious." These make it easy for the reader to picture exactly what you were going through. The other strong point about this piece is that you bring the reader full circle by beginning and ending with "the noodles."

Being alone when you are sick is difficult. Now, I know why you were so quiet in class.

If you want to do another entry related to this one, you could have a dialogue with your "sick" self. What would your "healthy" self say to the "sick" self? Is there some advice that could be exchanged about how to prevent illness or how to take care of yourself better when you do get sick? Start the dialogue with your "sick" self speaking first.

With the widespread availability of Internet communications, journals and other student-teacher dialogues have taken on a new dimension. With such innovations as "collaboratories" (where students in a class are regularly carrying on email discussions with each other and the teacher), on-line education, and distance learning, journals—out of several genres of possible writing—have gained additional prominence.

Journals obviously serve important pedagogical purposes: practice in the mechanics of writing, using writing as a "thinking" process, individualization, and communication with the teacher. At the same time, the assessment qualities of journal writing have assumed an important role in the teaching-learning process. Because most journals are—or should be—a dialogue between student and teacher, they afford a unique opportunity for a teacher to offer various kinds of feedback.

On the other side of the issue, it is argued that journals are too free a form to be assessed accurately. With so much potential variability, it is difficult to set up criteria for evaluation. For some English language learners, the concept of free and unfettered writing is anathema. Certain critics have expressed ethical concerns: students may be asked to reveal an inner self, which is virtually unheard of in their own culture. Without a doubt, the assessing of journal entries through responding is not an exact science.

It is important to turn the advantages and potential drawbacks of journals into positive general steps and guidelines for using journals as assessment instruments. The following steps are not coincidentally parallel to those cited above for portfolio development:

1. Sensitively introduce students to the concept of journal writing. For many students, especially those from educational systems that play down the notion of teacher–student dialogue and collaboration, journal writing will be difficult at first. University-level students, who have passed through a dozen years of product writing, will have particular difficulty with the concept of writing without fear of a teacher's scrutinizing every grammatical or spelling error. With modeling, assurance, and purpose, however, students can make a remarkable transition into the potentially liberating process of journal writing. Students who are shown examples of journal entries and are given specific topics and schedules for writing will become comfortable with the process.

2. State the objective(s) of the journal. Integrate journal writing into the objectives of the curriculum in some way, especially if journal entries become topics of class discussion. The list of types of journals at the beginning of this section may coincide with the following examples of some purposes of journals:

<u>Language-learning logs.</u> In English language teaching, learning logs have the advantage of sensitizing students to the importance of setting their own goals and then self-monitoring their achievement. McNamara (1998) suggested restricting the number of skills, strategies, or language categories that students comment on; otherwise students can become overwhelmed with the process. A weekly schedule of a limited number of strategies usually accomplishes the purpose of keeping students on task.

<u>Grammar journals.</u> Some journals are focused only on grammar acquisition. These types of journals are especially appropriate for courses and workshops that focus on grammar. "Error logs" can be instructive processes of consciousness raising for students: their successes in noticing and treating errors spur them to maintain the process of awareness of error.

<u>Responses to readings.</u> Journals may have the specified purpose of simple responses to readings (and/or to other material such as lectures, presentations, films, and videos). Entries may serve as precursors to freewrites and help learners to sort out thoughts and opinions on paper. Teacher responses aid in the further development of those ideas.

Strategies-based learning logs. Closely allied to language-learning logs are specialized journals that focus only on strategies that learners are seeking to become aware of and to use in their acquisition process. In H. D. Brown's (2002) *Strategies for Success: A Practical Guide to Learning English,* a systematic strategies-based journal-writing approach is taken where, in each of 12 chapters, learners become aware of a strategy, use it in their language performance, and reflect on that process in a journal.

Self-assessment reflections. Journals can be a stimulus for self-assessment in a more open-ended way than through using checklists and questionnaires. With the possibility of a few stimulus questions, students' journals can extend beyond the scope of simple one-word or one-sentence responses.

Diaries of attitudes, feelings, and other affective factors. The affective states of learners are an important element of self-understanding. Teachers can thereby become better equipped to effectively facilitate learners' individual journeys toward their goals.

Acculturation logs. A variation on the above affectively based journals is one that focuses exclusively on the sometimes difficult and painful process of acculturation in a non-native country. Because culture and language are so strongly linked, awareness of the symptoms of acculturation stages can provide keys to eventual language success.

3. Give guidelines on what kinds of topics to include. Once the purpose or type of journal is clear, students will benefit from models or suggestions on what kinds of topics to incorporate into their journals.

4. Carefully specify the criteria for assessing or grading journals. Students need to understand the freewriting involved in journals, but at the same time, they need to know assessment criteria. Once you have clarified that journals will *not* be evaluated for grammatical correctness and rhetorical conventions, state how they *will* be evaluated. Usually the purpose of the journal will dictate the major assessment criterion. *Effort* as exhibited in the thoroughness of students' entries will no doubt be important. Also, the extent to which entries reflect the *processing of course content* might be considered. Maintain reliability by adhering conscientiously to the criteria that you have set up.

5. Provide optimal feedback in your responses. McNamara (1998, p. 39) recommended three different kinds of feedback to journals:

1. cheerleading feedback, in which you celebrate successes with the students or encourage them to persevere through difficulties,
2. instructional feedback, in which you suggest strategies or materials, suggest ways to fine-tune strategy use, or instruct students in their writing, and
3. reality-check feedback, in which you help the students set more realistic expectations for their language abilities.

The ultimate purpose of responding to student journal entries is well captured in McNamara's threefold classification of feedback. Responding to journals is a very personalized matter, but closely attending to the objectives for writing the journal and its specific directions for an entry will focus those responses appropriately.

Peer responses to journals may be appropriate if journal comments are relatively "cognitive," as opposed to very personal. Personal comments could make students feel threatened by other pairs of eyes on their inner thoughts and feelings.

6. *Designate appropriate time frames and schedules for review.* Journals, like portfolios, need to be esteemed by students as integral parts of a course. Therefore, it is essential to budget enough time within a curriculum for both writing journals and for your written responses. Set schedules for submitting journal entries periodically; return them in short order.

7. *Provide formative, washback-giving final comments.* Journals, perhaps even more than portfolios, are the most formative of all the alternatives in assessment. They are day-by-day (or at least weekly) chronicles of progress whose purpose is to provide a thread of continuous assessment and reassessment, to recognize mid-stream direction changes, and/or to refocus on goals. Should you reduce a final assessment of such a procedure to a grade or a score? Some say yes, some say no (Peyton & Reed, 1990), but it appears to be in keeping with the formative nature of journals *not* to do so. Credit might be given for the process of actually writing the journal, and possibly a distinction might be made among high, moderate, and low effort and/or quality. But to accomplish the goal of positive washback, narrative summary comments and suggestions are clearly in order.

In sum, how do journals score on principles of assessment? Practicality remains relatively low, although the appropriation of electronic communication increases practicality by offering teachers and students convenient, rapid (and legible!) means of responding. Reliability can be maintained by the journal entries adhering to stated purposes and objectives, but because of individual variations in writing and the accompanying variety of responses, reliability may reach only a moderate level. Content and face validity are very high if the journal entries are closely interwoven with curriculum goals (which in turn reflect real-world needs). In the category of washback, the potential in dialogue journals is off the charts!

CONFERENCES AND INTERVIEWS

For a number of years, conferences have been a routine part of language classrooms, especially of courses in writing. In Chapter 9, reference was made to conferencing as a standard part of the process approach to teaching writing, in which the teacher, in a conversation about a draft, facilitates the improvement of the written work. Such interaction has the advantage of one-on-one interaction between teacher and student, and the teacher's being able to direct feedback toward a student's specific needs.

Conferences are not limited to drafts of written work. Including portfolios and journals discussed above, the list of possible functions and subject matter for conferencing is substantial:

- commenting on drafts of essays and reports
- reviewing portfolios
- responding to journals
- advising on a student's plan for an oral presentation
- assessing a proposal for a project
- giving feedback on the results of performance on a test
- clarifying understanding of a reading
- exploring strategies-based options for enhancement or compensation
- focusing on aspects of oral production
- checking a student's self-assessment of a performance
- setting personal goals for the near future
- assessing general progress in a course

Conferences must assume that the teacher plays the role of a facilitator and guide, not of an administrator, of a formal assessment. In this intrinsically motivating atmosphere, students need to understand that the teacher is an ally who is encouraging self-reflection and improvement. So that the student will be as candid as possible in self-assessing, the teacher should not consider a conference as something to be scored or graded. Conferences are by nature formative, not summative, and their primary purpose is to offer positive washback.

Genesee and Upshur (1996, p. 110) offered a number of generic kinds of questions that may be useful to pose in a conference:

- What did you like about this work?
- What do you think you did well?
- How does it show improvement from previous work? Can you show me the improvement?
- Are there things about this work you do not like? Are there things you would like to improve?
- Did you have any difficulties with this piece of work? If so, where, and what did you do [will you do] to overcome them?
- What strategies did you use to figure out the meaning of words you could not understand?
- What did you do when you did not know a word that you wanted to write?

Discussions of alternatives in assessment usually encompass one specialized kind of conference: an **interview**. This term is intended to denote a context in which a teacher interviews a student for a designated assessment purpose. (We are not talking about a student conducting an interview of others in order to gather information on a topic.) Interviews may have one or more of several possible goals, in which the teacher

- assesses the student's oral production,
- ascertains a student's needs before designing a course or curriculum,

- seeks to discover a student's learning styles and preferences,
- asks a student to assess his or her own performance, and
- requests an evaluation of a course.

One overriding principle of effective interviewing centers on the nature of the questions that will be asked. It is easy for teachers to assume that interviews are just informal conversations and that they need little or no preparation. To maintain the all-important reliability factor, interview questions should be constructed carefully to elicit as focused a response as possible. When interviewing for oral production assessment, for example, a highly specialized set of probes is necessary to accomplish predetermined objectives. (Look back at Chapter 7, where oral interviews were discussed.)

Because interviews have multiple objectives, as noted above, it is difficult to generalize principles for conducting them, but the following guidelines may help to frame the questions efficiently:

1. Offer an initial atmosphere of warmth and anxiety-lowering (warm-up).
2. Begin with relatively simple questions.
3. Continue with level-check and probe questions, but adapt to the interviewee as needed.
4. Frame questions simply and directly.
5. Focus on only one factor for each question. Do not combine several objectives in the same question.
6. Be prepared to repeat or reframe questions that are not understood.
7. Wind down with friendly and reassuring closing comments.

How do conferences and interviews score in terms of principles of assessment? Their practicality, as is true for many of the alternatives to assessment, is low because they are time-consuming. Reliability will vary between conferences and interviews. In the case of conferences, it may not be important to have rater reliability because the whole purpose is to offer individualized attention, which will vary greatly from student to student. For interviews, a relatively high level of reliability should be maintained with careful attention to objectives and procedures. Face validity for both can be maintained at a high level due to their individualized nature. As long as the subject matter of the conference/interview is clearly focused on the course and course objectives, content validity should also be upheld. Washback potential and authenticity are high for conferences, but possibly only moderate for interviews unless the results of the interview are clearly folded into subsequent learning.

OBSERVATIONS

All teachers, whether they are aware of it or not, observe their students in the classroom almost constantly. Virtually every question, every response, and almost every nonverbal behavior is, at some level of perception, noticed. All those intuitive perceptions are stored as little bits and pieces of information about students that can form a composite impression of a student's ability. Without ever administering a test or a quiz, teachers know a lot about their students. In fact, experienced teachers are so good at this almost subliminal process of assessment that their estimates of a student's competence are often highly correlated with actual independently administered test scores. (See Acton, 1979, for an example.)

How do all these chunks of information become stored in a teacher's brain cells? Usually not through rating sheets and checklists and carefully completed observation charts. Still, teachers' intuitions about students' performance are not infallible, and certainly both the reliability and face validity of their feedback to students can be increased with the help of empirical means of observing their language performance. The value of systematic observation of students has been extolled for decades (Flanders, 1970; Moskowitz, 1971; Spada & Frölich, 1995), and its utilization greatly enhances a teacher's intuitive impressions by offering tangible corroboration of conclusions. Occasionally, intuitive information is disconfirmed by observation data.

We will not be concerned in this section with the kind of observation that rates a formal presentation or any other prepared, prearranged performance in which the student is fully aware of some evaluative measure being applied, and in which the teacher scores or comments on the performance. We *are* talking about observation as a systematic, planned procedure for real-time, almost surreptitious recording of student verbal and nonverbal behavior. One of the objectives of such observation is to assess students without their awareness (and possible consequent anxiety) of the observation so that the naturalness of their linguistic performance is maximized.

What kinds of student performance can be usefully observed? Consider the following possibilities:

Potential observation foci

- sentence-level oral production skills (see microskills, Chapter 7)
  —pronunciation of target sounds, intonation, etc.
  —grammatical features (verb tenses, question formation, etc.)
- discourse-level skills (conversation rules, turn-taking, and other macroskills)
- interaction with classmates (cooperation, frequency of oral production)
- reactions to particular students, optimal productive pairs and groups, which "zones" of the classroom are more vocal, etc.
- frequency of student-initiated responses (whole class, group work)
- quality of teacher-elicited responses
- latencies, pauses, silent periods (number of seconds, minutes, etc.)
- length of utterances
- evidence of listening comprehension (questions, clarifications, attention-giving verbal and nonverbal behavior)

- affective states (apparent self-esteem, extroversion, anxiety, motivation, etc.)
- evidence of attention-span issues, learning style preferences, etc.
- students' verbal or nonverbal response to materials, types of activities, teaching styles
- use of strategic options in comprehension or production (use of communication strategies, avoidance, etc.)
- culturally specific linguistic and nonverbal factors (kinesics; proxemics; use of humor, slang, metaphor, etc.)

The list could be even more specific to suit the characteristics of students, the focus of a lesson or module, the objectives of a curriculum, and other factors. The list might expand, as well, to include other possible observed performance. In order to carry out classroom observation, it is of course important to take the following steps:

1. Determine the specific objectives of the observation.
2. Decide how many students will be observed at one time.
3. Set up the logistics for making unnoticed observations.
4. Design a system for recording observed performances.
5. Do not overestimate the number of different elements you can observe at one time—keep them very limited.
6. Plan how many observations you will make.
7. Determine specifically how you will use the results.

Designing a system for observing is no simple task. Recording your observations can take the form of anecdotal records, checklists, or rating scales. Anecdotal records should be as specific as possible in focusing on the objective of the observation, but they are so varied in form that to suggest formats here would be counterproductive. Their very purpose is more note-taking than record-keeping. The key is to devise a system that maintains the principle of reliability as closely as possible.

Checklists are a viable alternative for recording observation results. Some checklists of student classroom performance, such as the COLT observation scheme devised by Spada and Fröhlich (1995), are elaborate grids referring to such variables as

- whole-class, group, and individual participation,
- content of the topic,
- linguistic competence (form, function, discourse, sociolinguistic),
- materials being used, and
- skill (listening, speaking, reading, writing),

with subcategories for each variable. The observer identifies an activity or episode, as well as the starting time for each, and checks appropriate boxes along the grid.

Completing such a form in real time may present some difficulty with so many factors to attend to at once.

Checklists can also be quite simple, which is a better option for focusing on only a few factors within real time. On one occasion I assigned teachers the task of noting occurrences of student errors in third-person singular, plural, and *-ing* morphemes across a period. of six weeks. Their records needed to specify only the number of occurrences of each and whether each occurrence of the error was ignored, treated by the teacher, or self-corrected. Believe it or not, this was not an easy task! Simply noticing errors is hard enough, but making entries on even a very simple checklist required careful attention. The checklist looked like this:

Observation checklist, student errors

	Grammatical Feature		
	Third person singular	**Plural/s/**	***-ing* progressive**
Ignored	|||	||	||||
Treated by the teacher					
Self-corrected					||

Each of the 30-odd checklists that were eventually completed represented a two-hour class period and was filled in with "ticks" to show the occurrences and the follow-up in the appropriate cell.

Rating scales have also been suggested for recording observations. One type of rating scale asks teachers to indicate the frequency of occurrence of target performance on a separate frequency scale (always = 5; never = 1). Another is a holistic assessment scale, like the TWE scale described in the previous chapter or the OPI scale discussed in Chapter 7, that requires an overall assessment within a number of categories (for example, vocabulary usage, grammatical correctness, fluency). Rating scales may be appropriate for recording observations after the fact—on the same day but after class, for example. Specific quantities of occurrences may be difficult to record while teaching a lesson and managing a classroom, but immediate subsequent evaluations can include some data on observations that would otherwise fade from memory in a day or so.

If you scrutinize observations under the microscope of principles of assessment, you will probably find moderate practicality and reliability in this type of procedure, especially if the objectives are kept very simple. Face validity and content validity are likely to get high marks since observations are likely to be integrated into the ongoing process of a course. Washback is only moderate if you do little follow-up on observing. Some observations for research purposes may yield no washback whatever if the researcher simply disappears with the information and never communicates anything back to the student. But a subsequent conference with a student can then yield very high washback as the student is made aware of empirical data on targeted performance. Authenticity is high because, if an observation goes relatively unnoticed by the student, then there is little likelihood of contrived contexts or playacting.

SELF- AND PEER-ASSESSMENTS

A conventional view of language assessment might consider the notion of self- and peer-assessment as an absurd reversal of politically correct power relationships. After all, how could learners who are still in the process of acquisition, especially the early processes, be capable of rendering an accurate assessment of their own performance? Nevertheless, a closer look at the acquisition of any skill reveals the importance, if not the necessity, of self-assessment and the benefit of peer-assessment. What successful learner has not developed the ability to monitor his or her own performance and to use the data gathered for adjustments and corrections? Most successful learners extend the learning process well beyond the classroom and the presence of a teacher or tutor, autonomously mastering the art of self-assessment. Where peers are available to render assessments, the advantage of such additional input is obvious.

Self-assessment derives its theoretical justification from a number of well-established principles of second language acquisition. The principle of **autonomy** stands out as one of the primary foundation stones of successful learning. The ability to set one's own goals both within and beyond the structure of a classroom curriculum, to pursue them without the presence of an external prod, and to independently monitor that pursuit are all keys to success. Developing **intrinsic motivation** that comes from a self-propelled desire to excel is at the top of the list of successful acquisition of any set of skills.

Peer-assessment appeals to similar principles, the most obvious of which is **cooperative learning**. Many people go through a whole regimen of education from kindergarten up through a graduate degree and never come to appreciate the value of collaboration in learning—the benefit of a community of learners capable of teaching each other something. Peer-assessment is simply one arm of a plethora of tasks and procedures within the domain of learner-centered and collaborative education.

Researchers (such as Brown & Hudson, 1998) agree that the above theoretical underpinnings of self- and peer-assessment offer certain benefits: direct involvement of students in their own destiny, the encouragement of autonomy, and increased motivation because of their self-involvement. Of course, some noteworthy drawbacks must also be taken into account. Subjectivity is a primary obstacle to overcome. Students may be either too harsh on themselves or too self-flattering, or they may not have the necessary tools to make an accurate assessment. Also, especially in the case of direct assessments of performance (see below), they may not be able to discern their own errors. In contrast, Bailey (1998) conducted a study in which learners showed moderately high correlations (between .58 and .64) between self-rated oral production ability and scores on the OPI, which suggests that in the assessment of general competence, learners' self-assessments may be more accurate than one might suppose.

Types of Self- and Peer-Assessment

It is important to distinguish among several different types of self- and peer-assessment and to apply them accordingly. I have borrowed from widely accepted classifications of strategic options to create five categories of self- and peer-assessment: (1) direct assessment of performance, (2) indirect assessment of performance, (3) metacognitive assessment, (4) assessment of socioaffective factors, and (5) student self-generated tests.

1. Assessment of [a specific] performance. In this category, a student typically monitors him- or herself—in either oral or written production—and renders some kind of evaluation of performance. The evaluation takes place immediately or very soon after the performance. Thus, having made an oral presentation, the student (or a peer) fills out a checklist that rates performance on a defined scale. Or perhaps the student views a video-recorded lecture and completes a self-corrected comprehension quiz. A journal may serve as a tool for such self-assessment. Peer editing is an excellent example of direct assessment of a specific performance.

Today, the availability of media opens up a number of possibilities for self- and peer-assessment beyond the classroom. Internet sites such as Dave's ESL Café (**http://www.eslcafe.com/**) offer many self-correcting quizzes and tests. On this and other similar sites, a learner may access a grammar or vocabulary quiz on the Internet and then self-score the result, which may be followed by comparing with a partner. Television and film media also offer convenient resources for self- and peer-assessment. Gardner (1996) recommended that students in non-English-speaking countries access bilingual news, films, and television programs and then self-assess their comprehension ability. He also noted that video versions of movies with subtitles can be viewed first without the subtitles, then with them, as another form of self- and/or peer-assessment.

2. Indirect assessment of [general] competence. Indirect self- or peer-assessment targets larger slices of time with a view to rendering an evaluation of general ability, as opposed to one specific, relatively time-constrained performance. The distinction between direct and indirect assessments is the classic competence–performance distinction. Self- and peer-assessments of performance are limited in time and focus to a relatively short performance. Assessments of competence may encompass a lesson over several days, a module, or even a whole term of course work, and the objective is to ignore minor, nonrepeating performance flaws and thus to evaluate general ability. A list of attributes can offer a scaled rating, from "strongly agree" to "strongly disagree," on such items as these:

Indirect self-assessment rating scale

I demonstrate active listening in class.	5 4 3 2 1
I volunteer my comments in small-group work.	5 4 3 2 1
When I don't know a word, I guess from context.	5 4 3 2 1
My pronunciation is very clear.	5 4 3 2 1
I make very few mistakes in verb tenses.	5 4 3 2 1
I use logical connectors in my writing.	5 4 3 2 1

In a successful experiment to introduce self-assessment in his advanced intermediate pre-university ESL class, Phillips (2000) created a questionnaire (Figure 10.2) through which his students evaluated themselves on their class participation. The items were simply formatted with just three options to check for each category, which made the process easy for students to perform. They completed the questionnaire at midterm, which was followed up immediately with a teacher–student conference during which students identified weaknesses and set goals for the remainder of the term.

Of course, indirect self- and peer-assessment is not confined to scored rating sheets and questionnaires. An ideal genre for self-assessment is through journals, where students engage in more open-ended assessment and/or make their own further comments on the results of completed checklists.

3. Metacognitive assessment [for setting goals]. Some kinds of evaluation are more strategic in nature, with the purpose not just of viewing past performance or competence but of setting goals and maintaining an eye on the process of their pursuit. Personal goal-setting has the advantage of fostering intrinsic motivation and of providing learners with that extra-special impetus from having set and accomplished one's own goals. Strategic planning and self-monitoring can take the form of journal entries, choices from a list of possibilities, questionnaires, or cooperative (oral) pair or group planning.

A simple illustration of goal-setting self-assessment was offered by Smolen, Newman, Wathen, and Lee (1995). In response to the assignment of making "goal cards," a middle-school student wrote:

1. *My goal for this week is to stop during reading and predict what is going to happen next in the story.*

2. *My goal for this week is to finish writing my Superman story.*

CLASS PARTICIPATION

Please fill out this questionnaire by checking the appropriate box:

Yes, Definitely	**Sometimes**	**Not Yet**
☐	☐	☐

A. I attend class.   Y S N

I come to class.   ☐ ☐ ☐

I come to class on time.   ☐ ☐ ☐

Comments: _____

B. I usually ask questions in class.

I ask the teacher questions.   ☐ ☐ ☐

I ask my classmates questions.   ☐ ☐ ☐

Comments: _____

C. I usually answer questions in class.

I answer questions that the teacher asks.   ☐ ☐ ☐

I answer questions that my classmates ask.   ☐ ☐ ☐

Comments: _____

D. I participate in group-work.

I take equal turns in all three roles (C, W and R).   ☐ ☐ ☐

I offer my opinion.   ☐ ☐ ☐

I cooperate with my group members.   ☐ ☐ ☐

I use appropriate classroom language.   ☐ ☐ ☐

Comments: _____

E. I participate in pair-work.   Y S N

I offer my opinion.   ☐ ☐ ☐

I cooperate with my partner.   ☐ ☐ ☐

I use appropriate classroom language.   ☐ ☐ ☐

Comments: _____

F. I participate in whole-class discussions.

I make comments.   ☐ ☐ ☐

I ask questions.   ☐ ☐ ☐

I answer questions.   ☐ ☐ ☐

I respond to things someone else says.   ☐ ☐ ☐

I clarify things someone else says.   ☐ ☐ ☐

I use the new vocabulary.   ☐ ☐ ☐

Comments: _____

G. I listen actively in class.

I listen actively to the teacher.   ☐ ☐ ☐

I listen actively to my classmates.   ☐ ☐ ☐

Comments: _____

H. I complete the peer-reviews.

I complete all of the peer-reviews.   ☐ ☐ ☐

I respond to every question.   ☐ ☐ ☐

I give specific examples.   ☐ ☐ ☐

I offer suggestions.   ☐ ☐ ☐

I use appropriate classroom language.   ☐ ☐ ☐

Comments: _____

Figure 10.2. Self-assessment of class participation (Phillips, 2000)

On the back of this same card, which was filled out at the end of the week, was the student's self-assessment:

> *The first goal help me understand a lot when I'm reading.*
>
> *I met my goal for this week.*

Brown's (1999) *New Vistas* series offers end-of-chapter self-evaluation checklists that give students the opportunity to think about the extent to which they have reached a desirable competency level in the specific objectives of the unit. Figure 10.3 shows a sample of this "checkpoint" feature. Through this technique, students are reminded of the communication skills they have been focusing on and are given a chance to identify those that are essentially accomplished, those that are not yet fulfilled, and those that need more work. The teacher follow-up is to spend more time on items on which a number of students checked "sometimes" or "not yet," or possibly to individualize assistance to students working on their own points of challenge.

I can	Yes!	Sometimes	Not Yet
say the time in different ways.	☐	☐	☐
describe an ongoing action.	☐	☐	☐
ask about and describe what people are wearing.	☐	☐	☐
offer help.	☐	☐	☐
accept or decline an offer of help.	☐	☐	☐
ask about and describe the weather and seasons.	☐	☐	☐
write a letter.	☐	☐	☐

Figure 10.3. Self-assessment of lesson objectives (Brown, 1999, p. 59)

4. *Socioaffective assessment.* Yet another type of self- and peer-assessment comes in the form of methods of examining affective factors in learning. Such assessment is quite different from looking at and planning linguistic aspects of acquisition. It requires looking at oneself through a psychological lens and may not differ greatly from self-assessment across a number of subject-matter areas or for any set of personal skills. When learners resolve to assess and improve motivation, to gauge and lower their own anxiety, to find mental or emotional obstacles to learning and then plan to overcome those barriers, an all-important socioaffective domain is invoked. A checklist form of such items may look like many of the questionnaire items in Brown (2002), in which test-takers must indicate preference for one statement over the one on the opposite side:

Self-assessment of styles (Brown, 2002, pp. 2, 13)

I don't mind if people laugh at me when I speak.	A B C D	I get embarrassed if people laugh at me when I speak.
I like rules and exact information.	A B C D	I like general guidelines and uncertain information.

In the same book, multiple intelligences are self-assessed on a scale of definite agreement (4) to definite disagreement (1):

Self-assessment of multiple intelligences (Brown, 2002, p. 37)

4 3 2 1	I like memorizing words.
4 3 2 1	I like the teacher to explain grammar to me.
4 3 2 1	I like making charts and diagrams.
4 3 2 1	I like drama and role plays.
4 3 2 1	I like singing songs in English.
4 3 2 1	I like group and pair interaction.
4 3 2 1	I like self-reflection and journal writing.

The *New Vistas* series (Brown, 1999) also presents an end-of-unit section on "Learning Preferences" that calls for self-assessment of an individual's learning preferences (Figure 10.4). This information is of value to both teacher and student in identifying preferred styles, especially through subsequent determination to capitalize on preferences and to compensate for styles that are less than preferred.

Learning Preferences

Think about the work you did in this unit. Put a check next to the items that helped you learn the lessons. Put two checks next to the ones that helped a lot.

☐ ☐ Listening to the teacher
☐ ☐ Working by myself
☐ ☐ Working with a partner
☐ ☐ Working with a group
☐ ☐ Asking the teacher questions

☐ ☐ Listening to the tapes and doing exercises
☐ ☐ Reading
☐ ☐ Writing paragraphs
☐ ☐ Using the Internet

Figure 10.4. Self-assessment of learning preferences (Brown, 1999, p. 59)

5. *Student-generated tests.* A final type of assessment that is not usually classified strictly as self- or peer-assessment is the technique of engaging students in the process of constructing tests themselves. The traditional view of what a test is would never allow students to engage in test construction, but student-generated tests can be productive, intrinsically motivating, autonomy-building processes.

Gorsuch (1998) found that student-generated quiz items transformed routine weekly quizzes into a collaborative and fulfilling experience. Students in small groups were directed to create content questions on their reading passages and to collectively choose six vocabulary items for inclusion on the quiz. The process of creating questions and choosing lexical items served as a more powerful reinforcement of the reading than any teacher-designed quiz could ever be. To add further interest, Gorsuch directed students to keep records of their own scores to plot their progress through the term.

Murphey (1995), another champion of self- and peer-generated tests, successfully employed the technique of directing students to generate their own lists of words, grammatical concepts, and content that they think are important over the course of a unit. The list is synthesized by Murphey into a list for review, and all items on the test come from the list. Students thereby have a voice in determining the content of tests. On other occasions, Murphey has used what he calls "interactive pair tests" in which students assess each other using a set of quiz items. One student's response aptly summarized the impact of this technique:

> We had a test today. But it was not a test, because we could study for it beforehand. I gave some questions to my partner and my partner gave me some questions. And we students decided what grade we should get. I hate tests, but I like this kind of test. So please don't give us a surprise test. I think, that kind of test that we did today is more useful for me than a surprise test because I study for it.

Many educators agree that one of the primary purposes in administering tests is to stimulate review and integration, which is exactly what student-generated testing does, but almost without awareness on the students' part that they are reviewing the material. I have seen a number of instances of teachers successfully facilitating students in the self-construction of tests. The process engenders intrinsic involvement in reviewing objectives and selecting and designing items for the final form of the test. The teacher of course needs to set certain parameters for such a project and be willing to assist learners in designing items.

Guidelines for Self- and Peer-Assessment

Self- and peer-assessment are among the best possible *formative* types of assessment and possibly the most rewarding, but they must be carefully designed and administered for them to reach their potential. Four guidelines will help teachers bring this intrinsically motivating task into the classroom successfully.

1. *Tell students the purpose of the assessment.* Self-assessment is a process that many students—especially those in traditional educational systems—will initially find quite uncomfortable. They need to be sold on the concept. It is therefore essential that you carefully analyze the needs that will be met in offering both self- and peer-assessment opportunities, and then convey this information to students.

2. *Define the task(s) clearly.* Make sure the students know exactly what they are supposed to do. If you are offering a rating sheet or questionnaire, the task is not complex, but an open-ended journal entry could leave students perplexed about what to write. Guidelines and models will be of great help in clarifying the procedures.

3. *Encourage impartial evaluation of performance or ability.* One of the greatest drawbacks to self-assessment is the threat of subjectivity. By showing students the advantage of honest, objective opinions, you can maximize the beneficial washback of self-assessments. Peer-assessments, too, are vulnerable to unreliability as students apply varying standards to their peers. Clear assessment criteria can go a long way toward encouraging objectivity.

4. *Ensure beneficial washback through follow-up tasks.* It is not enough to simply toss a self-checklist at students and then walk away. Systematic follow-up can be accomplished through further self-analysis, journal reflection, written feedback from the teacher, conferencing with the teacher, purposeful goal-setting by the student, or any combination of the above.

A Taxonomy of Self- and Peer-Assessment Tasks

To sum up the possibilities for self- and peer-assessment, it is helpful to consider a variety of tasks within each of the four skills.

Self- and peer-assessment tasks

Listening Tasks

listening to TV or radio broadcasts and checking comprehension with a partner
listening to bilingual versions of a broadcast and checking comprehension
asking when you don't understand something in pair or group work
listening to an academic lecture and checking yourself on a "quiz" of the content
setting goals for creating/increasing opportunities for listening

Speaking Tasks

filling out student self-checklists and questionnaires
using peer checklists and questionnaires
rating someone's oral presentation (holistically)
detecting pronunciation or grammar errors on a self-recording
asking others for confirmation checks in conversational settings
setting goals for creating/increasing opportunities for speaking

Reading Tasks

reading passages with self-check comprehension questions following
reading and checking comprehension with a partner
taking vocabulary quizzes
taking grammar and vocabulary quizzes on the Internet
conducting self-assessment of reading habits
setting goals for creating/increasing opportunities for reading

Writing Tasks

revising written work on your own
revising written work with a peer (peer editing)
proofreading
using journal writing for reflection, assessment, and goal-setting
setting goals for creating/increasing opportunities for writing

An evaluation of self- and peer-assessment according to our classic principles of assessment yields a pattern that is quite consistent with other alternatives to assessment that have been analyzed in this chapter. Practicality can achieve a moderate level with such procedures as checklists and questionnaires, while reliability risks remaining at a low level, given the variation within and across learners. Once students accept the notion that they can legitimately assess themselves, then face validity can be raised from what might otherwise be a low level. Adherence to course objectives will maintain a high degree of content validity. Authenticity and washback both have very high potential because students are centering on their own linguistic needs and are receiving useful feedback.

Table 10.1 is a summary of all six of the alternatives in assessment with regard to their fulfillment of the major assessment principles. The caveat that must accom-

Table 10.1. Principled evaluation of alternatives to assessment

Principle	Portfolio	Journal	Conference	Interview	Observation	Self/Peer
Practicality	low	low	low	mod	mod	mod
Reliability	mod	mod	low	mod	mod	low
Face validity	high	mod	high	high	high	mod
Content validity	high	high	high	high	high	high
Washback	high	high	high	mod	mod	high
Authenticity	high	high	high	mod	high	high

pany such a chart is that none of the evaluative "marks" should be considered permanent or unchangeable. In fact, the challenge that was presented at the beginning of the chapter is reiterated here: take the "low" factors in the chart and create assessment procedures that raise those marks.

§   §   §   §   §

Perhaps it is now clear why "alternatives in assessment" is a more appropriate phrase than "alternative assessment." To set traditional testing and alternatives against each other is counterproductive. All kinds of assessment, from formal conventional procedures to informal and possibly unconventional tasks, are needed to assemble information on students. The alternatives covered in this chapter may not be markedly different from some of the tasks described in the preceding four chapters (assessing listening, speaking, reading, and writing). When we put all of this together, we have at our disposal an amazing array of possible assessment tasks for second language learners of English. The alternatives presented in this chapter simply expand that continuum of possibilities.

EXERCISES

[Note: (**I**) Individual work; (**G**) Group or pair work; (**C**) Whole-class discussion.]

1. (**C**) Using Brown and Hudson's (1998) 12 characteristics of alternatives in assessment (quoted at the beginning of the chapter), discuss the differences between traditional and "alternative" assessment. Some performance assessments are relatively traditional (oral interview, essay writing, demonstrations), yet they fit most of the criteria for alternatives in assessment. In this light, identify a continuum of assessments, ranging from highly traditional to alternative.
2. (**G**) In a small group, refer to Figure 10.1, which depicts the relationship between practicality/reliability and authenticity/washback. With each group assigned to a separate skill area (L, S, R, W), select perhaps 10 or 12 techniques that were described earlier in this book and place them into this same graph. Show your graph to the rest of the class and explain.
3. (**G**) In pairs or groups assigned to procure a sample of a portfolio from a teacher you know, or from a school you have some connection with, evaluate the portfolio on as many of the seven guidelines (pages 257–259) as possible. Present the portfolio and your evaluation to the rest of the class.
4. (**G**) In pairs or groups, follow the same procedure as #3 above for a journal.
5. (**I/C**) If possible, observe a teacher–student conference or a student–student peer-assessment. The most common type of conference might be over a draft of an essay. Report back to the class on what you observed and offer an evaluation of its effectiveness.

6. **(I/C)** Plan to observe an ES/FL class. Select specific students to observe, and define the form of linguistic performance you will focus on. Such an observation could include attention to students' processing of the teacher's error treatment. Report your findings to the class.
7. **(C)** Look at the self-assessments in Figures 10.2, 10.3, and 10.4. Evaluate their effectiveness in terms of the guidelines offered in this chapter.
8. **(G)** At the end of the chapter, Table 10.1 offers a broad estimate of the extent to which the alternatives to assessment in this chapter measure up to basic principles of assessment. In pairs or small groups, each assigned to one of the six alternatives, decide whether you agree with these evaluations. Defend your decisions and report them to the rest of the class.

FOR YOUR FURTHER READING

Brown, J.D. (Ed.) (1998). *New ways of classroom assessment.* Alexandria, VA: Teachers of English to Speakers of Other Languages.

This volume in TESOL's "New Ways" series offers an array of nontraditional assessment procedures. Each procedure indicates its appropriate level, objective, class time required, and suggested preparation time. Included are examples of portfolios, journals, logs, conferences, and self- and peer-assessment. Alternatives to traditional assessment of listening, speaking, reading, and writing are also given. All techniques were contributed by teachers in varying contexts around the world.

O'Malley, J. Michael, and Valdez Pierce, Lorraine. (1996.) *Authentic assessment for English language learners: Practical approaches for teachers.* White Plains, NY: Addison-Wesley.

This practical guide for teachers targets English Language Learners (ELLs) from K–12, but has applications beyond this context. It is a valuable collection of techniques and procedures for carrying out performance assessments that are authentic and that offer beneficial washback to learners. It contains reproducible checklists, rating scales, and charts that can be adapted to one's own context. It offers a comprehensive treatment of portfolios, journals, observations, and self- and peer-assessments.

TESOL Journal 5 (Autumn, 1995). Special Issue on Alternative Assessment.

This entire issue is devoted to alternatives in assessment. Included are articles from practicing teachers on portfolios, self-assessment, collaborative teacher assessment, test review activities, and general reflections on the benefits of assessment that promotes collaboration and reflection.

CHAPTER 11

GRADING AND STUDENT
EVALUATION

Grades must be the most-talked-about topic in anyone's school years.

> "How'd you do, Jennifer?"
> "Oh, pretty good. Got an A minus."
> "Wow, that's cool. I did so-so. Got a B."

> "Ready for the test tomorrow?"
> "No, gotta pull an all-nighter, I think."
> "Oh, yeah, how've you been doing in the course?"
> "Barely squeaking by with a C. You?"
> "Not bad. Somewhere in the B range."

> "Did you hear about Christina? Professor Kind gave her an A!"
> "You're kidding. Christina? She was never in class."
> "Yeah, maybe that winning smile helped some."

> "Mr. Smart, I see that your overall GPA is a 4.3 out of 4."
> "Well, uh, yes sir, I took quite a few advanced placement courses."
> "Splendid work, Mr. Smart. Outstanding."
> "Oh, thank you, Dr. Dean, thank you."
> "Yes, we certainly would welcome you into the College of Hard Knocks!"

Isn't it ironic that untold hours of reading, listening to lectures, note-taking, writing papers, doing assignments, and going to classes are invariably reduced to one of five letters of the alphabet? And after all that grueling labor, the only thing that seems to really matter is that the letter goes onto a transcript? Even more mysterious is that those tiny little letters actually mean something: a person's whole sense of academic self-esteem is summed up and contained in one alphabetic symbol. An A: I'm really, really okay! A C−: Ouch, not so good, something wrong with me. An F (God forbid): Woe is me, wretched soul that I am.

If our lives are too often controlled by tests, as mentioned in the opening lines of this book, then our educational lives are certainly governed by the grades that are greatly determined by those tests. Educational systems define honors students, marginal students, college-bound students, exceptional students (on either end of the scale), failing students, and average students not so much by the quality of their performance(s) and not necessarily by demonstrated skills that have been observed, but rather by grades.

Perhaps even more ironic is that the standards for assigning grades are extraordinarily variable across teachers, subject matter, courses, programs, institutions, school systems, and even cultures. Every institution from high school on up has its "easy" teachers and "tough" teachers who differ in their grading standards. Sometimes mathematics and science courses gain the reputation for being strict in assigning grades because one incorrect part of a complicated problem means a failing grade. Certain institutions are "known" by transcript evaluators to be stingy with high grades, and therefore a B in those places is equivalent to an A in others. American grading systems are demonstrably different from some systems in Europe and Asia; a course grade of 85 percent may be considered noteworthy in some countries, while in the United States the same percentage score is a B or possibly a B−.

Books and manuals on language assessment generally omit the topic of grading and student evaluation, and possibly for good reason. Focusing on the evaluation of a plethora of different separate assessment procedures may be sufficient for a course in language testing and assessment, without the complexity of tackling the summing up of all those assessments. On the other hand, every new teacher that I know has questions about grading, and every experienced teacher has opinions, and therefore a book about language assessment would not be complete without discussing a few principles and practices of grading.

This chapter addresses topics like these: What should grades reflect? How should different objectives, tasks, and components of a course figure into a formula for calculating grades? How do cultural and institutional philosophies dictate standards for grading? How can a teacher achieve reliability in grading students? What are some alternatives to letter grades? From this discussion, we will be able to derive some generalizations about the nature of grading, some principles of grading, and some specific guidelines to follow in assigning grades.

PHILOSOPHY OF GRADING: WHAT SHOULD GRADES REFLECT?

You are teaching a course in English in a context of your choice (choose a country, institutional situation, course content, and proficiency level). You have been given a questionnaire to fill out (see page 283). Complete the questionnaire now, before reading on.

Grading questionnaire

Directions: Look at the items below and circle the letters for all items that should be considered (however greatly or minimally) in a set of criteria for determining a final grade in a course.

_____ a. language performance of the student as formally demonstrated on tests, quizzes, and other explicitly scored procedures

_____ b. your intuitive, informal observation of the student's language performance

_____ c. oral participation in class

_____ d. improvement (over the entire course period)

_____ e. behavior in class ("deportment")—being cooperative, polite, disruptive, etc.

_____ f. effort

_____ g. motivation

_____ h. punctuality and attendance

  ☺ i. how many times the student brings you chocolate chip cookies

Now look back at the items you circled, and in the blank next to those items only, write in a percentage that represents the weight that you would assign to each circled item. Make sure your total percentages add up to 100. If they don't, adjust them until they do.

By completing this exercise, you have made a quick, intuitive allocation of factors that you think should be included in deciding the final grade for a course. In the second part of the exercise, you have also established a weighting system for each factor. You have essentially begun to articulate a philosophy of grading—at least for this (possibly hypothetical) course.

In a recent administration of this questionnaire to teachers at the American Language Institute at San Francisco State University, the item on which the teachers had most agreement was item (a), which received percentage allocations from 50 percent to 75 percent. It is safe to assert that formal tests, quizzes, exercises, homework, essays, reports, presentations—all of which are usually marked in some way (with a grade, a "check" system [such as $\sqrt{+}$, $\sqrt{}$, or $\sqrt{-}$], a score, or a credit/no credit notation)—are universally accepted as primary criteria for determining grades. These tasks and assignments represent observable performance and can be conveniently recorded in a teacher's record book.

Items (b) and (c) also drew relatively strong support, but a word of caution is in order here. If intuitive, informal observations by the teacher figure into the final grade, it is very important to inform the students in advance how those observations and impressions will be recorded throughout the semester. Likewise, if oral participation is listed as one of the objectives of a course and is listed as a factor in a final grade, the challenge to all teachers is to quantify that participation as clearly and directly as possible. Leaving either of these factors to a potentially whimsical or impressionistic evaluation at the end of the course not only risks unnecessary unreliability but leaves the student at the mercy of the teacher. Failure to decide *how* informal assessments and observations will be summed up risks confusing a student's "nice" cooperative behavior with actual performance.

On items (d) through (h) there was some disagreement and considerable discussion after the exercise, but all those items received at least a few votes for inclusion. How can those factors be systematically incorporated into a final grade? Some educational assessment experts state definitively that none of these items should ever be a factor in grading. Gronlund (1998), a widely respected educational assessment specialist, gave the following advice:

> Base grades on student achievement, and achievement only. Grades should
> represent the extent to which the intended learning outcomes were achieved by
> students. They should *not* be contaminated by student effort, tardiness, misbehavior,
> and other extraneous factors. . . . If they are permitted to become part of the grade,
> the meaning of the grade as an indicator of achievement is lost. (pp. 174–175)

Earlier in the same chapter, Gronlund specifically discouraged the inclusion of improvement in final grades, as it "distorts" the meaning of grades as indicators of achievement.

Gronlund's point is well worth considering as a strongly empirical philosophy of grading. Before you rush to agree with him, consider some other points of view. Not everyone agrees with Gronlund. For example, Grove (1998), Power (1998), and Progosh (1998) all recommended considering other factors in assessing and grading. And how many teachers do you know who are consistently impeccable in their objectivity as graders in the classroom?

To look at this issue in a broader perspective, think about some of the characteristics of assessment that have been discussed in this book. The importance of *triangulation*, for one, tells us that all abilities of a student may not be apparent on achievement tests and measured performances. One of the arguments for considering alternatives in assessment is that we may not be able to capture the totality of students' competence through formal tests; other observations are also significant indicators of ability. Nor should we discount most teachers' intuition, which enables them to form impressions of students that cannot easily be verified empirically. These arguments tell us that improvement, behavior, effort, motivation, and attendance might justifiably belong to a set of components that add up to a final grade.

Guidelines for Selecting Grading Criteria

If you are willing to include some nonachievement factors in your grading scheme, how do you incorporate them, along with the other more measurable factors? Consider the following guidelines.

1. It is essential for all components of grading to be consistent with an *institutional philosophy* and/or regulations (see below for a further discussion of this topic). Some institutions, for example, mandate deductions for unexcused absences. Others require that only the final exam determines a course grade. Still other institutions may implicitly dictate a relatively high number of As and Bs for each class of students. Embedded in institutional philosophies are the implicit *expectations* that students place on a school or program, and your attention to those impressions is warranted.

2. All of the components of a final grade need to be *explicitly stated in writing* to students at the beginning of a term of study, with a designation of percentages or weighting figures for each component.

3. If your grading system includes items (d) through (g) in the questionnaire above (improvement, behavior, effort, motivation), it is important for you to recognize their subjectivity. But this should not give you an excuse to avoid converting such factors into observable and measurable results. *Challenge yourself to create checklists, charts, and note-taking systems that allow you to convey to the student the basis for your conclusions.* It is further advisable to guard against final-week impressionistic, summative decisions by giving ongoing periodic feedback to students on such matters through written comments or conferences. By nipping potential problems in the bud, you may help students to change their attitudes and strategies early in the term.

4. Finally, consider allocating *relatively small weights* to items (c) through (h) so that a grade primarily reflects achievement. A designation of 5 percent to 10 percent of a grade to such factors will not mask strong achievement in a course. On the other hand, a small percentage allocated to these "fuzzy" areas can make a significant difference in a student's final course grade. For example, suppose you have a well-behaved, seemingly motivated and effort-giving student whose quantifiable scores put him or her at the top of the range of B grades. By allocating a small percentage of a grade to behavior, motivation, or effort (and by measuring those factors as empirically as possible), you can justifiably give this student a final grade of A−. Likewise, a reversal of this scenario may lead to a somewhat lower final grade.

Calculating Grades: Absolute and Relative Grading

I will never forget a university course I took in Educational Psychology for a teaching credential. There were regular biweekly multiple-choice quizzes, all of which were included in the final grade for the course. I studied hard for each test and consistently received percentage scores in the 90–95 range. I couldn't understand in the first few weeks of the course (a) why my scores warranted grades in the C range (I thought that scores in the low to mid-90s should have rated at least a B+, if not an A−) and (b) why students who were, in my opinion, not especially gifted were getting better grades!

In another course, Introduction to Sociology, there was no test, paper, nor graded exercise until a midterm essay-style examination. The professor told the class nothing about the grading or scoring system, and we simply did the best we could. When the exams came back, I noted with horror that my score was a 47 out of 100! No grade accompanied this result, and I was convinced I had failed. After the professor had handed back the tests, amid the audible gasps of others like me, he announced "good news": no one received an F! He then wrote on the blackboard his grading system for this 100-point test:

A	51 and above
B	42–50
C	30–41
D	29 and below

The anguished groans of students became sighs of relief.

These true stories illustrate a common philosophy in the calculation of grades. In both cases, the professors adjusted grades to fit the distribution of students across a continuum, and both, ironically, were using the same method of calculation:

A	Quartile 1 (the top 25 percent of scores)
B	Quartile 2 (the next 25 percent)
C	Quartile 3 (the next 25 percent)
D	Quartile 4 (the lowest 25 percent)

In the Educational Psychology course, many students got exceptionally high scores, and in the Sociology course, almost everyone performed poorly according to an absolute scale. I later discovered, much to my chagrin, that in the Ed Psych course, more than half the class had had access to quizzes from previous semesters and that the professor had simply administered the same series of quizzes! The Sociology professor had a reputation for being "tough" and apparently demonstrated toughness by giving test questions that offered little chance of a student answering more than 50 percent correctly.

Among other lessons in the two stories is the importance of specifying your approach to grading. If you pre-specify standards of performance on a numerical point system, you are using an **absolute** system of grading. For example, having established points for a midterm test, points for a final exam, and points accumulated for the semester, you might adhere to the specifications in Table 11.1.

There is no magic about specifying letter grades in differentials of 10 percentage points (such as some of those shown in Table 11.1). Many absolute grading systems follow such a model, but variations occur that range from establishing an A as 95 percent and above, all the way down to 85 percent and above. The decision is usually an institutional one.

The key to making an absolute grading system work is to be painstakingly clear on competencies and objectives, and on tests, tasks, and other assessment techniques

Table 11.1. Absolute grading scale

	Midterm (50 points)	Final Exam (100 points)	Other Performance (50 points)	Total # of Points (200)
A	45–50	90–100	45–50	180–200
B	40–44	80–89	40–44	160–179
C	35–39	70–79	35–39	140–159
D	30–34	60–69	30–34	120–139
F	below 30	below 60	below 30	below 120

that will figure into the formula for assigning a grade. If you are unclear and hap-hazard in your definition of criteria for grading, the grades that are ultimately assigned are relatively meaningless.

Relative grading is more commonly used than absolute grading. It has the advantage of allowing your own interpretation and of adjusting for unpredicted ease or difficulty of a test. Relative grading is usually accomplished by ranking students in order of performance (percentile ranks) and assigning cut-off points for grades. An older, relatively uncommon method of relative grading is what has been called grading "on the curve," a term that comes from the normal bell curve of normative data plotted on a graph. Theoretically, in such a case one would simulate a normal distribution to assign grades such as the following: A = the top 10 percent; B = the next 20 percent; C = the middle 40 percent; D = the next 20 percent; F = the lowest 10 percent. In reality, virtually no one adheres to such an interpretation because it is too restrictive and usually does not appropriately interpret achievement test results in classrooms.

Table 11.2. Hypothetical rank-order grade distributions

	Percentage of Students		
	Institution X	Institution Y	Institution Z
A	~15%	~30%	~60%
B	~30%	~40%	~30%
C	~40%	~20%	~10%
D	~10%	~ 9%	
F	~ 5%	~ 1%	

An alternative to conforming to a normal curve is to pre-select percentiles according to an institutional expectation, as in the hypothetical distributions in Table 11.2. In Institution X, the expectation is a curve that is slightly skewed to the right (higher frequencies in the upper levels), compared to a normal bell curve. The expectation in Institution Y is for virtually no one to fail a course and for a large majority of students to achieve As and Bs; here the skewness is more marked. The third institution may represent the expectations of a university postgraduate program where a C is considered a failing grade, a B is acceptable but indicates adequate work only, and an A is the expected target for most students.

Pre-selecting grade distributions, even in the case of relative grading, is still arbitrary and may not reflect what grades are supposed to "mean" in their appraisal of performance. A much more common method of calculating grades is what might be called *a posteriori* relative grading, in which a teacher exercises the latitude to determine grade distributions after the performances have been observed. Suppose you have devised a midterm test for your English class and you have adhered to objectives, created a variety of tasks, and specified criteria for evaluating responses. But when your students turn in their work, you find that they performed well below your expectations, with scores (on a 100-point basis) ranging from a high of 85 all the way down to a low of 44. Would you do what my Sociology professor did and establish four quartiles and simply assign grades accordingly? That would be one solution to adjusting for difficulty, but another solution would be to adjust those percentile divisions to account for one or more of the following:

a. your own philosophical objection to awarding an A to a grade that is perhaps as low as 85 out of 100
b. your well-supported intuition that students really did not take seriously their mandate to prepare well for the test
c. your wish to include, after the fact, some evidence of great effort on the part of some students in the lower rank orders
d. your suspicion that you created a test that was too difficult for your students

One possible solution would be to assign grades to your 25 students as follows:

A	80–85	(3 students)
B	70–79	(7 students)
C	60–69	(10 students)
D	50–59	(4 students)
F	below 50	(1 student)

Such a distribution might confirm your appraisal that the test was too difficult, and also that a number of students could have prepared themselves more adequately, therefore justifying the Cs, Ds, and F for the lower 15 students. The distribution is also faithful to the observed performance of the students, and does not add unsubstantiated "hunches" into the equation.

Is there room in a grading system for a teacher's intuition, for your "hunch" that the student should get a higher or lower grade than is indicated by performance? Should teachers "massage" grades to conform to their appraisal of students beyond the measured performance assessments that have been stipulated as grading criteria? The answer is no, even though you may be tempted to embrace your intuition, and even though many of us succumb to such practice. We should strive in all of our grading practices to be explicit in our criteria and not yield to the temptation to "bend" grades one way or another. With so many alternatives to traditional assessments now available to us, we are capable of designating numerous observed performances as criteria for grades. In so doing we can strive to ensure that a final grade fully captures a summative evaluation of a student.

Teachers' Perceptions of Appropriate Grade Distributions

Most teachers bring to a test or a course evaluation an interpretation of estimated appropriate distributions, follow that interpretation, and make minor adjustments to compensate for such matters as unexpected difficulty. This prevailing attitude toward a relative grading system is well accepted and uncontroversial. What is surprising, however, is that teachers' preconceived notions of their own standards for grading often do not match their actual practice. Let me illustrate.

In a workshop with English teachers at the American Language Institute at San Francisco State University, I asked them to define a "great bunch" of students—a class that was exceptionally good—and to define another class of "deadbeats" who performed very poorly. Here was the way the task was assigned.

Grading distribution questionnaire

You have 20 students in your ALI class. You've done what you consider to be a competent job of teaching, and your class is what you would academically call a "great bunch of students." What would be an estimated number of students in each final grade category to reflect this overall impression of your Ss? Indicate such a distribution in the column on the left. Then do the same for what you would describe as a "bunch of deadbeats" in a class in which you've done equally competent teaching. Indicate your distribution of the "deadbeats" in the column on the right.

	"Great bunch"	"Deadbeats"
Number of	As _____	As _____
	Bs _____	Bs _____
	Cs _____	Cs _____
	Ds _____	Ds _____
	Fs _____ (total # = 20)	Fs _____ (total # = 20)

When the responses were tabulated, the distribution for the two groups was as indicated in Figure 11.1. The workshop participants were not surprised to see the distribution of the "great bunch," but were quite astonished to discover that the "deadbeats" actually conformed to a normal bell curve! Their conception of a poorly performing group of students certainly did not *look* that bad on a graph. But their

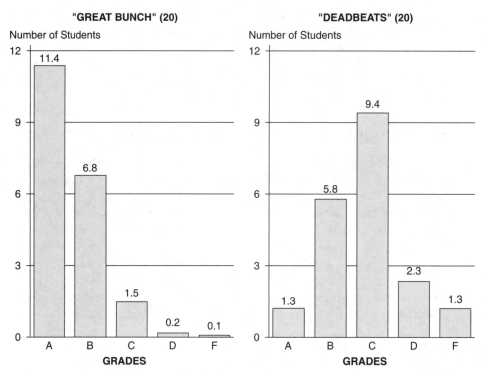

Figure 11.1. Projected distribution of grades for a "great bunch" and "deadbeats"

raised eyebrows turned to further surprise when the next graph was displayed, a distribution of the previous term's grades across the 420 grades assigned to students in all the courses of the ALI (see Fig. 11.2). The distribution was a virtual carbon copy of what they had just defined as a sterling group of students. They all agreed that the previous semester's students had not shown unusual excellence in their performance; in fact, a calculation of several prior semesters yielded similar distributions.

Two conclusions were drawn from this insight. First, teachers may hypothetically subscribe to a pre-selected set of expectations, but in practice may not conform to those expectations. Second, teachers all agreed they were guilty of **grade inflation** at the ALI; their good nature and empathy for students predisposed them toward assigning grades that were higher than ALI standards and expectations. Over the course of a number of semesters, the implicit expected distribution of grades had soared to 62 percent of students receiving As and 27 percent Bs. It was then agreed that ALI students, who would be attending universities in the United States, were done a disservice by having their expectations of American grading systems raised unduly. The result of that workshop was a closer examination of grade assignment with the goal of conforming grade distributions more closely to that of the undergraduate courses in the university at large.

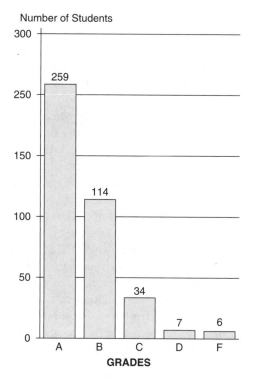

Figure 11.2. Actual distribution of grades, ALI, fall 1999

INSTITUTIONAL EXPECTATIONS AND CONSTRAINTS

A consideration of philosophies of grading and of procedures for calculating grades is not complete without a focus on the role of the institution in determining grades. The insights gained by the ALI teachers described above, for example, were spurred to some extent by an examination of institutional expectations. In this case, an external factor was at play: all the teachers were students in, or had recently graduated from, the Master of Arts in TESOL program at San Francisco State University. Typical of many graduate programs in American universities, this program manifests a distribution of grades in which As (from A+ to A−) are awarded to an estimated 60 percent to 70 percent of students, with Bs (from B+ to B−) going to almost all of the remainder. In the ALI context, it had become commonplace for the graduate grading expectations to "rub off" onto ALI courses in ESL. The statistics bore that out.

Transcript evaluators at colleges and universities are faced with variation across institutions on what is deemed to be the threshold level for entry from a high school or another university. For many institutions around the world, the concept of letter grades is foreign. Point systems (usually 100 points or percentages) are more common globally than the letter grades used almost universally in the United States. Either way, we are bound by an established, accepted system. We have become accustomed in the United States to calculating grade point averages (GPAs) for defining admissibility: $A = 4, B = 3, C = 2, D = 1$. (Note: Some institutions use a 5-point system, and others use a 9-point system!) A student will be accepted or denied admission on the basis of an established criterion, often ranging from 2.5 to 3.5, which usually translates into the philosophy that a B student is admitted to a college or university.

Some institutions refuse to employ either a letter grade or a numerical system of evaluation and instead offer **narrative evaluations** of students (see the discussion on this topic below). This preference for more individualized evaluations is often a reaction to the overgeneralization of letter and numerical grading.

Being cognizant of an institutional philosophy of grading is an important step toward a consistent and fair evaluation of your students. If you are a new teacher in your institution, try to determine what its grading philosophy is. Sometimes it is not explicit; the assumption is simply made that teachers will grade students using a system that conforms to an unwritten philosophy. This has potentially harmful washback for students. A teacher in an organization who applies a markedly "tougher" grading policy than other teachers is likely to be viewed by students as being out of touch with the rest of the faculty. The result could be avoidance of the class and even mistrust on the part of students. Conversely, an "easy" teacher may become a favorite or popular teacher not because of what students learn, but because students know they will get a good grade.

Cross-Cultural Factors and the Question of Difficulty

Of further interest, especially to those in the profession of English language teaching, is the question of *cultural expectations* in grading. Every learner of English comes from a native culture that may have implicit philosophies of grading at wide variance with those of an English-speaking culture. Granted, most English learners worldwide are learning English within their own culture (say, learning English in Korea), but even in these cases it is important for teachers to understand the context in which they are teaching. A number of variables bear on the issue. In many cultures,

- it is unheard of to ask a student to self-assess performance.
- the teacher assigns a grade, and nobody questions the teacher's criteria.
- the measure of a good teacher is one who can design a test that is so difficult that no student could achieve a perfect score. The fact that students fall short of such marks of perfection is a demonstration of the teacher's superior knowledge.
- as a corollary, grades of A are reserved for a highly select few, and students are delighted with Bs.
- one single final examination is the accepted determinant of a student's entire course grade.
- the notion of a teacher's preparing students to do their best on a test is an educational contradiction.

As you bear in mind these and other cross-cultural constraints on philosophies of grading and evaluation, it is important to construct your own philosophy. This is an extra-sensitive issue for teachers from English-speaking countries (and educational systems) who take teaching positions in other countries. In such a case, you are a guest in that country, and it behooves you to tread lightly in your zeal for overturning centuries of educational tradition. Yes, you can be an agent for change, but do so tactfully and sensitively or you may find yourself on the first flight home!

Philosophies of grading, along with attendant cross-cultural variation, also must speak to the issue of gauging *difficulty* in tests and other graded measures. As noted above, in some cultures a "hard" test is a good test, but in others, a good test results in a distribution like the one in the bar graph for a "great bunch" (Fig. 11.1): a large proportion of As and Bs, a few Cs, and maybe a D or an F for the "deadbeats" in the class. How do you gauge such difficulty as you design a classroom test that has not had the luxury of piloting and pre-testing? The answer is complex. It is usually a combination of a number of possible factors:

- experience as a teacher (with appropriate intuition)
- adeptness at designing feasible tasks
- special care in framing items that are clear and relevant
- mirroring in-class tasks that students have mastered
- variation of tasks on the test itself
- reference to prior tests in the same course
- a thorough review and preparation for the test
- knowledge of your students' collective abilities
- a little bit of luck

After mustering a number of the above contributors to a test that conforms to a predicted difficulty level, it is your task to determine, within your context, an expected distribution of scores or grades and to pitch the test toward that expectation. You will probably succeed most of the time, but every teacher knows the experience of evaluating a group of tests that turn out to be either too easy (everyone achieves high scores) or too hard. From those anomalies in your pedagogical life, you will learn something: the next time you will change the test, prepare your students better, or predict your students' performance better.

What Do Letter Grades "Mean"?

An institutional philosophy of grading, whether it is explicitly stated or implicit, presupposes expectations for grade distribution and for a *meaning* or description of each grade. We have already looked at several variations on the mathematics of grade distribution. What has yet to be discussed is the meaning of letter grades.

Typically, institutional manuals for teachers and students will list the following descriptors of letter grades:

A	excellent
B	good
C	adequate
D	inadequate/unsatisfactory
F	failing/unacceptable

Notice that the C grade is described as "adequate" rather than "average." The former term has in recent years been considered to be more descriptive, especially if a C is not mathematically calculated to be centered around the mean score.

Do these adjectives contain enough meaning to evaluate a student appropriately? What the letter grades ostensibly connote is a **holistic** score that sums up a multitude of performances throughout a course (or on a test, possibly consisting of multiple methods and traits). But do they? In the case of holistic scoring of writing or of oral production, each score category specifies as many as six different qualities or competencies that are being met. Can a letter grade provide such information? Does it tell a student about areas of strength and weakness, or about relative performance across a number of objectives and tasks? Or does a B just mean "better than most, but not quite as good as a few"? Or even more complex, what does a GPA across four years of high school or college tell you about a person's abilities, skills, talents, and potential?

The overgeneralization implicit in letter grading underscores the meaninglessness of the adjectives typically cited as descriptors of those letters. And yet, those letters have come to mean almost everything in their gate-keeping role in admissions decisions and employment acceptance. Is there a solution to this semantic conundrum? The answer is a cautious yes, with a twofold potential answer. First, every teacher who uses letter grades or a percentage score to provide an evaluation, whether a summative, end-of-course assessment or on a formal assessment procedure, should

a. use a carefully constructed system of grading,
b. assign grades on the basis of explicitly stated criteria, and
c. base the criteria on objectives of a course or assessment procedure(s).

Second, educators everywhere must work to persuade the gatekeepers of the world that letter/numerical evaluations are simply one side of a complex representation of a student's ability. Alternatives to letter grading are essential considerations.

ALTERNATIVES TO LETTER GRADING

I can remember on occasion receiving from a teacher a term paper or a final examination with nothing on it but a letter grade or a number. My reaction was that I had put in hours and in some cases weeks of toil to create a product that had been reduced to a single symbol. It was a feeling of being demeaned, discounted, and unfulfilled. In terms of washback alone, a number or a grade provides absolutely no information to a student beyond a vague sense that he or she has pleased or displeased the teacher, or the assumption that some other students have done better or worse.

The argument for alternatives to letter grading can be stated with the same line of reasoning used to support the importance of alternatives in assessment in the previous chapter. Letter grades—and along with them numerical scores—are only one form of student evaluation. The principle of triangulation cautions us to provide as many forms of evaluation as are feasible.

For assessment of a test, paper, report, extra-class exercise, or other formal, scored task, the primary objective of which is to offer *formative* feedback, the possibilities beyond a simple number or letter include

- a teacher's marginal and/or end comments,
- a teacher's written reaction to a student's self-assessment of performance,
- a teacher's review of the test in the next class period,
- peer-assessment of performance,
- self-assessment of performance, and
- a teacher's conference with the student.

For *summative* assessment of a student at the end of a course, those same additional assessments can be made, perhaps in modified forms:

- a teacher's marginal and/or end of exam/paper/project comments
- a teacher's summative written evaluative remarks on a journal, portfolio, or other tangible product
- a teacher's written reaction to a student's self-assessment of performance in a course
- a completed summative checklist of competencies, with comments
- narrative evaluations of general performance on key objectives
- a teacher's conference with the student

Most of the alternatives to grading for formative tests and other sets of tasks have been discussed in previous chapters. A more detailed look is now appropriate for a few of the summative alternatives to grading, particularly self-assessment, narrative evaluations, checklists, and conferences.

1. Self-assessment. A good deal was said in Chapter 10 about self-assessment. Here, the focus is specifically on the feasibility of students' commenting on their own achievement in a whole course of study. Self-assessment of end-of-course attainment of objectives is recommended through the use of the following:

- checklists
- a guided journal entry that directs the student to reflect on the content and linguistic objectives

- an essay that self-assesses
- a teacher–student conference

In all of the above, the assessment should not simply end with the summation of abilities over the past term of study. The most important implication of reflective self-assessment is the potential for setting goals for future learning and development. The intrinsic motivation engendered through the autonomous process of reflection and goal-setting will serve as a powerful drive for future action.

2. Narrative evaluations. In protest against the widespread use of letter grades as exclusive indicators of achievement, a number of institutions have at one time or another required narrative evaluations of students. In some instances those narratives replaced grades, and in others they supplemented them. What do such narratives look like? Here are three narratives, all written for the same student by her three teachers in a pre-university intensive English program in the United States. Notice the use of third-person singular, with the expectation that the narratives would be read by admissions personnel in the student's next program of study. Notice, too, that letter grades are also assigned.

Narrative evaluation

FINAL EVALUATION

COURSE: OCS/Listening   **Instructor:**   **Grade:** B+

Mayumi was a very good student. She demonstrated very good listening and speaking skills, and she participated well during class discussions. Her attendance was good. On tests of conversations skills, she demonstrated very good use of some phrases and excellent use of strategies she learned in class. She is skilled at getting her conversation partner to speak. On tape journal assignments, Mayumi was able to respond appropriately to a lecture in class, and she generally provided good reasons to support her opinions. She also demonstrated her ability to respond to classmates' opinions. When the topic is interesting to her, Mayumi is particularly effective in communicating her ideas. On the final exam, Mayumi was able to determine the main ideas of a taped lecture and to identify many details. In her final exam conversation, she was able to maintain a conversation with me and offer excellent advice on language learning and living in a new culture. Her pronunciation test shows that her stress, intonation, and fluency have improved since the beginning of the semester. Mayumi is a happy student who always is able to see the humor in a situation. I could always count on her smile in class.

COURSE: Reading/Writing   **Instructor:**   **Grade:** A−

Mayumi is a very serious and focused student. It was a pleasure having her in my class. She completed all of her homework assignments and wrote in her journal every day. Mayumi progressed a lot throughout the semester in developing her writing skills. Through several drafts and revision, she created some excellent writing products which had a main idea, examples, supporting details, and clear organization. Her second essay lacked the organization and details necessary for a good academic essay. Yet her third essay was a major improvement, being one of the best in the class. Mayumi took the opportunity to read a novel outside of class and wrote an extra-credit journal assignment about it. Mayumi has a good understanding of previewing, predicting, skimming, scanning, guessing vocabulary in context, reference words, and prefixes and suffixes. Her O. Henry reading presentation was very creative and showed a lot of effort; however, it was missing some parts. Mayumi was an attentive listener in class and an active participant who asked for clarification and volunteered answers.

COURSE: Grammar   **Instructor:**   **Grade:** A

Mayumi was an outstanding student in her grammar class this semester. Her attendance was perfect, and her homework was always turned in on time and thoroughly completed. She always participated actively in class, never hesitating to volunteer to answer questions. Her scores on the quizzes throughout the semester were consistently outstanding. Her test scores were excellent, as exemplified by the A+ she received on the final exam. Mayumi showed particular strengths in consistently challenging herself to learn difficult grammar; she sometimes struggled with assignments, yet never gave up until she had mastered them. Mayumi was truly an excellent student, and I'm sure she will be successful in all her future endeavors.

The arguments in favor of this form of evaluation are apparent: individualization, evaluation of multiple objectives of a course, face validity, and washback potential. But the disadvantages have worked in many cases to override such benefits: narratives cannot be quantified easily by admissions and transcript evaluation offices; they take a great deal of time for teachers to complete; students have been found to pay little attention to them (especially if a letter grade is attached); and teachers have succumbed, especially in the age of computer-processed writing, to formulaic narratives that simply follow a template with interchangeable phrases and modifiers.

3. Checklist evaluations. To compensate for the time-consuming impracticality of narrative evaluation, some programs opt for a compromise: a checklist with brief comments from the teacher, ideally followed by a conference and/or a response from the student. Here is a form that is used for midterm evaluation in one of the high-intermediate listening-speaking courses at the American Language Institute.

Midterm evaluation checklist

Midterm Evaluation Form

Course _____ Tardies _____ Absences _____ Grade _____
Instructor _____ [signature] _____

	Excellent progress	Satisfactory progress	Needs improvement	Unsatisfactory progress
Listening skills	☐	☐	☐	☐
Note-taking skills	☐	☐	☐	☐
Public speaking skills	☐	☐	☐	☐
Pronunciation skills	☐	☐	☐	☐
Class participation	☐	☐	☐	☐
Effort	☐	☐	☐	☐

Comments: _____

_____

_____

_____

Goals for the rest of the semester:

The advantages of such a form are increased practicality and reliability while maintaining washback. Teacher time is minimized; uniform measures are applied across all students; some open-ended comments from the teacher are available; and the student responds with his or her own goals (in light of the results of the checklist and teacher comments). When the checklist format is accompanied, as in this case, by letter grades as well, virtually none of the disadvantages of narrative evaluations remain, with only a small chance that some individualization may be slightly reduced. In the end-of-term chaos, students are also more likely to process checked boxes than to labor through several paragraphs of prose.

4. Conferences. Perhaps enough has been said about the virtues of conferencing. You already know that the impracticality of scheduling sessions with students is offset by its washback benefits. The end of a term is an especially difficult time to add more entries to your calendar, but with judicious use of classroom time (take students aside one by one while others are completing assigned work) and a possible office hour here and there, and with clear, concise objectives (to minimize time consumption and maximize feedback potential), conferences can accomplish much more than can a simple letter grade.

SOME PRINCIPLES AND GUIDELINES FOR GRADING AND EVALUATION

To sum up, I hope you have become a little better informed about the widely accepted practice of grading students, whether on a separate test or on a summative evaluation of performance in a course. You should now understand that

- grading is not necessarily based on a universally accepted scale,
- grading is sometimes subjective and context-dependent,
- grading of tests is often done on the "curve,"
- grades reflect a teacher's philosophy of grading,
- grades reflect an institutional philosophy of grading,
- cross-cultural variation in grading philosophies needs to be understood,
- grades often conform, by design, to a teacher's expected distribution of students across a continuum,
- tests do not always yield an expected level of difficulty,
- letter grades may not "mean" the same thing to all people, and
- alternatives to letter grades or numerical scores are highly desirable as additional indicators of achievement.

With those characteristics of grading and evaluation in mind, the following principled guidelines should help you be an effective grader and evaluator of student performance:

Summary of guidelines for grading and evaluation

1. Develop an informed, comprehensive personal philosophy of grading that is consistent with your philosophy of teaching and evaluation.
2. Ascertain an institution's philosophy of grading and, unless otherwise negotiated, conform to that philosophy (so that you are not out of step with others).

3. Design tests that conform to appropriate institutional and cultural expectations of the difficulty that students should experience.
4. Select appropriate criteria for grading and their relative weighting in calculating grades.
5. Communicate criteria for grading to students at the beginning of the course and at subsequent grading periods (mid-term, final).
6. Triangulate letter grade evaluations with alternatives that are more formative and that give more washback.

§   §   §   §   §

This discussion of grading and evaluation brings us full circle to the themes presented in the first chapter of this book. There the interconnection of assessment and teaching was first highlighted; in contemplating grading and evaluating our students, that co-dependency is underscored. When you assign a letter grade to a student, that letter should be symbolic of your approach to teaching. If you believe that a grade should recognize only objectively scored performance on a final exam, it may indicate that your approach to teaching rewards end products only, not process. If you base some portion of a final grade on improvement, behavior, effort, motivation, and/or punctuality, it may say that your philosophy of teaching values those affective elements. You might be one of those teachers who feel that grades are a necessary nuisance and that substantive evaluation takes place through the daily work of optimizing washback in your classroom. If you habitually give mostly As, a few Bs, and virtually no Cs or below, it could mean, among other things, that your standards (and expectations) for your students are low. It could also mean that your standards are very high and that you put monumental effort into seeing to it that students are consistently coached throughout the term so that they are brought to their fullest possible potential!

As you develop your own philosophy of grading, make some attempt to conform that philosophy to your approach to teaching. In a communicative language classroom, that approach usually implies meaningful learning, authenticity, building of student autonomy, student–teacher collaboration, a community of learners, and the perception that your role is that of a facilitator or coach rather than a director or dictator. Let your grading philosophy be consonant with your teaching philosophy.

EXERCISES

[Note: **(I)** Individual work; **(G)** Group or pair work; **(C)** Whole-class discussion.]

1. **(G)** In pairs, check with each other on how you initially responded to the questionnaire on page 283. Now that you have read the rest of the chapter,

how might you change your response, if at all? Defend your decisions and share the results with the rest of the class.

2. **(C)** Look again at the quote from Gronlund on page 284. To what extent do you agree that grades should be based on student achievement and achievement only?

3. **(G)** In pairs or groups, each assigned to interview a different teacher in a number of different institutions, determine what that institution's philosophy of grading is. Start with questions about the customary distribution of grades; what teachers and student perceive to be "good," "adequate," and "poor" performance in terms of grades; absolute and relative grading; and what should be included in a final course grade. Report your findings to the class and compare different institutions.

4. **(C)** The cross-cultural interpretations of grades provide interesting contrasts in teacher and student expectations. In a culture that you are familiar with, answer and discuss the following questions in reference to a midterm examination that counts for about 40 percent of a total grade in a course:

   a. Is it appropriate for students to assign a grade to themselves?

   b. Is it appropriate to ask the teacher to raise a grade?

   c. Consider these circumstances. You have a class of reasonably well motivated students who have put forth an acceptable amount of effort and whose scores (out of 100 total points) are distributed as follows:

5 Ss:	90–94 (highest grade is 94)
10 Ss:	between 85 and 89
15 Ss:	between 80 and 84
5 Ss:	below 80.

      Is it appropriate for you, the teacher, to assign these grades?

A	95 and above (0 Ss)
B	90–94 (5 Ss)
C	85–89 (10 Ss)
D	80–84 (15 Ss)
F	below 80 (5 Ss)

   d. How appropriate or feasible are the alternatives to letter grading that were listed on page 295?

5. **(G)** In groups, each assigned to one of the four alternatives to letter grading (self-assessment, narrative evaluations, checklist evaluations, and conferences), evaluate the feasibility of your alternative in terms of a specific, defined context. Present your evaluation to the rest of the class.

6. **(C)** Look at the summary of guidelines for grading and evaluation at the end of the chapter and determine the adequacy of each and whether other guidelines should be added to this list.

FOR YOUR FURTHER READING

Gronlund, Norman E. (1998). *Assessment of student achievement.* Sixth Edition. Boston: Allyn & Bacon.

In Chapter 9 of his classic book on assessment of various subject matter content, Gronlund offers a substantive treatment of issues surrounding grading. The chapter deals with absolute and relative grading, mathematical considerations in grading, and six major guidelines for effective and fair grading.

O'Malley, J. Michael, and Valdez Pierce, Lorraine. (1996). *Authentic assessment for English language learners: Practical approaches for teachers.* White Plains, NY: Addison-Wesley.

Turn to page 29 for a succinct three-page overview of issues in grading. Included are comments about criteria for assigning grades, methods of grading, group grading, grading in the context of authentic assessment, and a list of practical suggestions for maximizing the washback effect of grading.

BIBLIOGRAPHY

Acton, William. (1979). *Second language learning and the perception of difference in attitude.* Unpublished doctoral dissertation, University of Michigan.

Alderson, J. Charles. (2000). *Assessing reading.* Cambridge: Cambridge University Press.

Alderson, J. Charles. (2001). Language testing and assessment (Part 1). *Language Teaching, 34,* 213-236.

Alderson, J. Charles. (2002). Language testing and assessment (Part 2). *Language Teaching, 35,* 79-113.

Alderson, J. Charles, Clapham, C., & Wall, D. (1995). *Language test construction and evaluation.* Cambridge: Cambridge University Press.

Armstrong, Thomas. (1994). *Multiple intelligences in the classroom.* Philadelphia: Association for Curriculum Development.

Bachman, Lyle F. (1988). Problems in examining the validity of the ACTFL oral proficiency interview. *Studies in Second Language Acquisition, 10,* 149-164.

Bachman, Lyle F. (1990). *Fundamental considerations in language testing.* New York: Oxford University Press.

Bachman, Lyle F. & Palmer, Adrian S. (1996). *Language testing in practice.* New York: Oxford University Press.

Bailey, Kathleen M. (1998). *Learning about language assessment: Dilemmas, decisions, and directions.* Cambridge, MA: Heinle & Heinle.

Banerjee, Jayanti. (2003). Test review: The TOEFL CBT. *Language Testing, 20,* 111-123.

Bernstein, Jared, DeJong, J., Pisoni, D., & Townshend, Brent. (2000, August). Two experiments on automatic scoring of spoken language proficiency. *Integrating Speech Technology in Learning,* pp. 57-61.

Brindley, Geoff. (2001). Assessment. In Ronald Carter & David Nunan (Eds.), *The Cambridge guide to teaching English to speakers of other languages* (pp. 137-143). Cambridge: Cambridge University Press.

Brown, H. Douglas. (1999). *New vistas: An interactive course in English.* White Plains, NY: Pearson Education.

Brown, H. Douglas. (2000). *Principles of language learning and teaching.* Fourth Edition. White Plains, NY: Pearson Education.

Brown, H. Douglas. (2001). *Teaching by principles: An interactive approach to language pedagogy.* Second Edition. White Plains, NY: Pearson Education.

Brown, H. Douglas. (2002). *Strategies for success: A practical guide to learning English.* White Plains, NY: Pearson Education.

Brown, H. Douglas & Sahni, Sabina. (1994). *Vistas: An interactive course in English, student test package.* Englewood Cliffs, NJ: Prentice Hall Regents.

Brown, James Dean. (1991). Do English faculties rate writing samples differently? *TESOL Quarterly, 25,* 587–603.

Brown, James Dean. (1996). *Testing in language programs.* Upper Saddle River, NJ: Prentice Hall Regents.

Brown, James Dean. (1998). *New ways of classroom assessment.* Alexandria, VA: Teachers of English to Speakers of Other Languages.

Brown, James Dean & Bailey, Kathleen M. (1984). A categorical instrument for scoring second language writing skills. *Language Learning, 34,* 21–42.

Brown, James Dean & Hudson, Thom. (1998). The alternatives in language assessment. *TESOL Quarterly, 32,* 653–675.

Buck, Gary. (2001). *Assessing listening.* Cambridge: Cambridge University Press.

Canale, Michael. (1984). Considerations in the testing of reading and listening proficiency. *Foreign Language Annals, 17,* 349–357.

Canale, Michael & Swain, Merrill. (1980). Theoretical bases of communicative approaches to second language teaching and testing. *Applied Linguistics, 1,* 1–47.

Carroll, John B. (1981). Twenty-five years of research on foreign language aptitude. In Karl C. Diller (Ed.), *Individual differences and universals in language learning aptitude* (pp. 83–118). Rowley, MA: Newbury House.

Carroll, John B. (1990). Cognitive abilities in foreign language aptitude: Then and now. In Thomas S. Parry & Charles W. Stansfield (Eds.), *Language aptitude reconsidered.* Englewood Cliffs, NJ: Prentice Hall Regents.

Carroll, John B. & Sapon, Stanley M. (1958). *Modern Language Aptitude Test.* New York: The Psychological Corporation.

Cascallar, Eduardo & Bernstein, Jared. (2000, March). *The assessment of second language learning as a function of native language difficulty measured by an automated spoken English test.* Paper presented at the American Association of Applied Linguistics Conference, Vancouver, BC, Canada.

Celce-Murcia, Marianne, Brinton, Donna, & Goodwin, Janet. (1996). *Teaching pronunciation: A reference for teachers of English to speakers of other languages.* Cambridge: Cambridge University Press.

Chinen, Nagomi. (2000, March). *Has CLT reached Japan?* Paper presented at the American Association of Applied Linguistics Conference, Vancouver, BC, Canada.

Clark, John L. D. (1983). Language testing: Past and current status—directions for the future. *Modern Language Journal, 67,* 431–443.

Cloud, Nancy. (2001, Fall). TESOL standards standing committee created. *Friends in TESOL,* p. 3.

Cohen, Andrew D. (1994). *Assessing language ability in the classroom.* Second Edition. Boston: Heinle & Heinle.

Cooper, J. D. (1997). *Literacy: Helping children construct meaning.* Third Edition. Boston: Houghton Mifflin.

Cziko, Gary A. (1982). Improving the psychometric, criterion-referenced, and practical qualities of integrative language tests. *TESOL Quarterly, 16,* 367–379.

Davidson, Fred, Hudson, Thom, & Lynch, Brian. (1985). Language testing: Operationalization in classroom measurement and L2 research. In Marianne Celce-Murcia (Ed.), *Beyond basics: Issues and research in TESOL.* Rowley, MA: Newbury House.

Davies, Alan. (1975). Two tests of speeded reading. In R. L. Jones & B. Spolsky (Eds.), *Testing language proficiency.* Washington, DC: Center for Applied Linguistics.

Dörnyei, Zoltan & Katona, L. (1992). Validation of the C-test amongst Hungarian EFL learners. *Language Testing, 9,* 187–206.

Douglas, Dan & Smith, Jan. (1997). *Theoretical underpinnings of the Test of Spoken English revision project.* TOEFL Monograph Series RM-97-2, May 1997. Princeton, NJ: Educational Testing Service.

Dunkel, Patricia. (1991). Listening in the native and second/foreign language: Toward an integration of research and practice. *TESOL Quarterly, 25,* 431–457.

Duran, Richard P., Canale, Michael, Penfield, Joyce, Stansfield, Charles W., & Liskin-Gasparro, Judith E. (1985). *TOEFL from a communicative viewpoint on language proficiency: A working paper.* TOEFL Research Report #17. Princeton, NJ: Educational Testing Service.

Edgeworth, F. Y. (1888). The statistics of examinations. *Journal of the Royal Statistical Society, 51,* 599–635.

Elder, Catherine. (2001). *Experimenting with uncertainty: Essays in honour of Alan Davies.* (Studies in Language Testing #11). Cambridge: Cambridge University Press.

Fair Test. (2002). Florida: Politically referenced tests? *16,* 5–8.

Farhady, Hossein. (1982). Measures of language proficiency from the learner's perspective. *TESOL Quarterly, 16,* 43–59.

Farr, R. & Tone, B. (1994). *Portfolio and performance assessment: Helping students evaluate their progress as readers and writers.* Orlando, FL: Harcourt Brace.

Fields, Sara. (2000). ELD test in the pipeline for 2000–2001 school year. *CATESOL News, 32,* 3.

Frase, R., Faletti, J., Ginther, A., & Grant, L.A. (1999). *Computer analysis of the TOEFL Test of Written English*. TOEFL Research Report #64. Princeton, NJ: Educational Testing Service.

Gardner, David. (1996). Self-assessment for self-access learners. *TESOL Journal, 6,* 18–23.

Gardner, Howard. (1983). *Frames of mind: The theory of multiple intelligences*. New York: Basic Books.

Gardner, Howard. (1999). *Intelligence reframed: Multiple intelligences for the 21st century*. New York: Basic Books.

Gardner, Howard. (2000). *The disciplined mind: Beyond facts and standardized tests—the K–12 education that every child deserves*. New York: Penguin Putnam.

Genesee, Fred (Ed.). (1994). *Educating second language children: The whole child, the whole curriculum, the whole community*. New York: Cambridge University Press.

Genesee, Fred & Upshur, John A. (1996). *Classroom-based evaluation in second language education*. Cambridge: Cambridge University Press.

Ginther, April. (2001). *Effects of the presence and absence of visuals on performance on TOEFL CBT listening-comprehensive stimuli*. TOEFL Research Report #66. Princeton, NJ: Educational Testing Service.

Goleman, Daniel. (1995). *Emotional intelligence*. New York: Bantam Books.

Golub-Smith, Marna, Reese, N., & Steinhaus, G. (1993). *Topic and topic type comparability on the Test of Written English*. TOEFL Research Report #42. Princeton, NJ: Educational Testing Service.

Goodman, Kenneth. (1970). Reading: A psycholinguistic guessing game. In H. Singer & R. B. Ruddell (Eds.), *Theoretical models and processes of reading*. Newark, DE: International Reading Association.

Gorsuch, Greta J. (1998). Let them make quizzes: Student-created reading quizzes. In James Dean Brown (Ed.), *New ways of classroom assessment* (pp. 215–218). Alexandria, VA: Teachers of English to Speakers of Other Languages.

Gottlieb, Margo. (1995). Nurturing student learning through portfolios. *TESOL Journal, 5,* 12–14.

Gronlund, Norman E. (1998). *Assessment of student achievement*. Sixth Edition. Boston: Allyn and Bacon.

Grove, Ron. (1998). Getting the point(s): An adaptable evaluation system. In J. D. Brown (Ed.), *New ways of classroom assessment* (pp. 236–239). Alexandria, VA: Teachers of English to Speakers of Other Languages.

Hale, Gordon. (1992). *Effects of amount of time allowed on the Test of Written English*. TOEFL Research Report #39. Princeton, NJ: Educational Testing Service.

Hale, Gordon, Taylor, C., Bridgeman, B., Carson, J., Kroll, B., & Kantor, R. (1996). *A study of writing tasks assigned in academic degree programs*. TOEFL Research Report #54. Princeton, NJ: Educational Testing Service.

Hamp-Lyons, Liz. (2001). Ethics, fairness(es), and developments in language testing. In Catherine Elder (Ed.), *Experimenting with uncertainty: Essays in honour of Alan Davies* (pp. 222–227). (Studies in Language Testing #11). Cambridge: Cambridge University Press.

Hamp-Lyons, L. & Condon, W. (2000). *Assessing the portfolio: Principles for practice theory and research.* Cresskill, NJ: Hampton Press.

Harp, B. (1991). Principles of assessment in whole language classrooms. In B. Harp (Ed.), *Assessment and evaluation in whole language programs* (pp. 35–50). Norwood, MA: Christopher-Gordon.

Henning, Grant & Cascallar, Eduardo. (1992). *A preliminary study of the nature of communicative competence.* TOEFL Research Report #36. Princeton, NJ: Educational Testing Service.

Hosoya, Michiko. (2001). *Is SFSU's Graduate Essay Test fair or unfair for international students?* Unpublished paper, Department of English, San Francisco State University.

Huerta-Macías, Ana. (1995). Alternative assessment: Responses to commonly asked questions. *TESOL Journal, 5,* 8–11.

Hughes, Arthur. (1989). *Testing for language teachers.* Cambridge: Cambridge University Press.

Hughes, Arthur. (2003). *Testing for language teachers.* Second Edition. Cambridge: Cambridge University Press.

Imao, Yasuhiro. (2001). *Validating a new ESL placement test at SFSU.* Unpublished master's thesis, Department of English, San Francisco State University.

Imao, Yasuhiro, Castello, Alessandra, Kotani, Aika, Scarabelli, Andrea, & Suk, Namhee. (2000). *Toward a revision of the ESLPT at SFSU.* Unpublished paper, Department of English, San Francisco State University.

Jacobs, H., Zinkgraf, S., Wormuth, D., Hartfiel, V., & Hughey, J. (1981). *Testing ESL composition: A practical approach.* Rowley, MA: Newbury House.

Jamieson, Joan. (1992). The cognitive styles of reflection/impulsivity and field independence and ESL success. *Modern Language Journal, 76,* 491–501.

Kahn, Roshan. (2002). *Revision of an ALI level 46 midterm exam.* Unpublished paper, Department of English, San Francisco State University.

Klein-Braley, C. (1985). A cloze-up on the C-test: A study in the construct validation of authentic tests. *Language Testing, 2,* 76–104.

Klein-Braley, C. & Raatz, U. (1984). A survey of research on the C-test. *Language Testing, 2,* 134–146.

Kohn, Alfie. (2000). *The case against standardized testing.* Westport, CT: Heinemann.

Kuba, Akiko. (2002). *Strategies-based instruction in Japanese high schools.* Unpublished master's thesis, Department of English, San Francisco State University.

Kuhlman, Natalie. (2001, April). *Standards for teachers, standards for children.* Paper presented at the California Teachers of English to Speakers of Other Languages Conference, Ontario, CA.

Language Testing. (1997). Ethics in Language Testing. Special Issue (14:3).

Lazaraton, Anne & Wagner, Stacie. (1996). *The Revised Test of Spoken English (TSE): Discourse analysis of native speaker and nonnative speaker data.* TOEFL Monograph Series RM-96-10. Princeton, NJ: Educational Testing Service.

Leacock, Claudia & Chodorow, Martin. (2001). *Automatic assessment of vocabulary usage without negative evidence.* TOEFL Research Report #67. Princeton, NJ: Educational Testing Service.

Lloyd-Jones, R. (1977). Primary trait scoring. In C. R. Cooper & L. Odell (Eds.), *Evaluating writing* (pp. 33–69). New York: National Council of Teachers of English.

Longford, Nicholas T. (1996). *Adjustment for reader rating behavior in the Test of Written English.* TOEFL Research Report #55. Princeton, NJ: Educational Testing Service.

Lowe, Pardee Jr. (1988). The unassimilated history. In Pardee Lowe & Charles W. Stansfield (Eds.), *Second language proficiency assessment: Current issues* (pp. 11–51). Englewood Cliffs, NJ: Prentice-Hall.

Lowe, Pardee & Stansfield, Charles W. (Eds.) (1988). *Second language proficiency assessment: Current issues.* Englewood Cliffs, NJ: Prentice Hall Regents.

Lynch, Brian K. (2001). The ethical potential of alternative language assessment. In Catherine Elder (Ed.), *Experimenting with uncertainty: Essays in honour of Alan Davies* (pp. 228–239). (Studies in Language Testing #11). Cambridge: Cambridge University Press.

Madsen, Harold. (1983). *Techniques in testing.* New York: Oxford University Press.

McNamara, Martha. (1998). Self-assessment: Keeping a language learning log. In James Dean Brown (Ed.), *New ways of classroom assessment* (pp. 38–41). Alexandria, VA: Teachers of English to Speakers of Other Languages.

McNamara, Tim. (2000). *Language testing.* Oxford: Oxford University Press.

Medina, Noe & Neill, D. Monty. (1990). *Fallout from the testing explosion.* Cambridge, MA: National Center for Fair and Open Testing.

Mendelsohn, David J. (1998). Teaching listening. *Annual Review of Applied Linguistics, 18,* 81–101.

Messick, S. (1989). Validity. In R. Linn (Ed.), *Educational measurement* (pp. 13–103). New York: Macmillan.

Moskowitz, Gertrude. (1971). The classroom interaction of outstanding foreign language teachers. *Foreign Language Annals, 9,* 125–157.

Mousavi, Seyyed Abbas. (1999). *Dictionary of language testing.* Second Edition. Tehran: Rahnama Publications.

Mousavi, Seyyed Abbas. (2002). *An encyclopedic dictionary of language testing.* Third Edition. Taiwan: Tung Hua Book Company.

Murphey, Tim. (1995). Tests: Learning through negotiated interaction. *TESOL Journal, 4,* 12–16.

Myford, Carol M. & Wolfe, Edward W. (2000). *Monitoring sources of variability within the Test of Spoken English assessment system.* TOEFL Research Report #65. Princeton, NJ: Educational Testing Service.

Myford, Carol M., Marr, D. B., & Linacre, J. M. (1996). *Reader calibration and its potential role in equating for the Test of Written English.* TOEFL Research Report #52. Princeton, NJ: Educational Testing Service.

Norris, J. M., Brown, J. D., Hudson, T., & Yoshioka, J. (1998). *Designing second language performance assessments.* Honolulu: University of Hawaii Press.

Nuttall, Christine. (1996). *Teaching reading skills in a foreign language.* Second Edition. Oxford: Heinemann.

Oller, John W. (1971). Dictation as a device for testing foreign language proficiency. *English Language Teaching, 25,* 254–259.

Oller, John W. (1973). Cloze tests of second language proficiency and what they measure. *Language Learning, 23,* 105–119.

Oller, John W. (1976). A program for language testing research. *Language Learning,* Special Issue #4, 141–165.

Oller, John W. (1979). *Language tests at school: A pragmatic approach.* London: Longman.

Oller, John W. (1983). *Issues in language testing research.* Rowley, MA: Newbury House.

O'Malley, J. Michael & Valdez Pierce, Lorraine. (1996.) *Authentic assessment for English language learners: Practical approaches for teachers.* White Plains, NY: Addison-Wesley.

Peyton, J. K. & Reed, L. (1990). *Dialogue journal writing with nonnative English speakers: A handbook for teachers.* Alexandria, VA: Teachers of English to Speakers of Other Languages.

Phillips, Deborah. (2001). *Longman Introductory Course for the TOEFL Test.* White Plains, NY: Pearson Education.

Phillips, Eric. (2000). *Self-assessment of class participation.* Unpublished paper, Department of English, San Francisco State University.

Pimsleur, Paul. (1966). *Pimsleur Language Aptitude Battery.* New York: Harcourt, Brace & World.

Power, Michael A. (1998). Developing a student-centered scoring rubric. In J. D. Brown (Ed.), *New ways of classroom assessment* (pp. 219–222). Alexandria, VA: Teachers of English to Speakers of Other Languages.

Powers, Donald E., Albertson, W., Florek, T., Johnson, K., Malak, J., Nemceff, B., Porzuc, M., Silvester, D., Wang, M., Weston, R., Winner, E., & Zelazny, A. (2002). *Influence of irrelevant speech on standardized test performance.* TOEFL Research Report #68. Princeton, NJ: Educational Testing Service.

Prator, Clifford H. (1972). *Manual of American English pronunciation.* New York: Holt, Rinehart & Winston.

Progosh, David. (1998). A continuous assessment framework. In J. D. Brown (Ed.), *New ways of classroom assessment* (pp. 223–227). Alexandria, VA: Teachers of English to Speakers of Other Languages.

Raimes, Ann. (1991). Out of the woods: Emerging traditions in the teaching of writing. *TESOL Quarterly, 25,* 407–430.

Raimes, Ann. (1998). Teaching writing. *Annual Review of Applied Linguistics, 18,* 142–167.

Read, John. (2000). *Assessing vocabulary.* Cambridge: Cambridge University Press.

Reed, Daniel J. & Cohen, Andrew D. (2001). Revisiting raters and ratings in oral language assessment. In Catherine Elder (Ed.), *Experimenting with uncertainty: Essays in honour of Alan Davies* (pp. 82–96). (Studies in Language Testing #11). Cambridge: Cambridge University Press.

Reid, Joy. (1993). *Teaching ESL writing.* Englewood Cliffs, NJ: Prentice Hall Regents.

Richards, Jack C. (1983). Listening comprehension: Approach, design, procedure. *TESOL Quarterly, 17,* 219–239.

Sakamoto, Yumiko. (2002). *Japanese high school English teachers' attitudes toward communicative and traditional methodologies.* Unpublished master's thesis, Department of English, San Francisco State University.

Savignon, Sandra J. (1982). Dictation as a measure of communicative competence in French as a second language. *Language Learning, 32,* 33–51.

Seow, Anthony. (2002). The writing process and process writing. In Jack C. Richards & Willy A. Renandya (Eds.), *Methodology in language teaching: An anthology of current practice* (pp. 315–320). Cambridge: Cambridge University Press.

Shepard, L. & Bliem, C. (1993). *Parent opinions about standardized tests, teacher's information, and performance assessments.* Los Angeles: Center for Research on Evaluation, Standards, and Student Testing.

Shohamy, Elana. (1995). Performance assessment in language testing. *Annual Review of Applied Linguistics, 15,* 188–211.

Shohamy, Elana. (1997, March). *Critical language testing and beyond.* Paper presented at the American Association of Applied Linguistics Conference, Orlando, FL.

Skehan, Peter. (1988). State of the art: Language testing (Part I). *Language Teaching, 21,* 211–221.

Skehan, Peter. (1989). State of the art: Language testing (Part II). *Language Teaching, 22,* 1–13.

Smolen, Lynn, Newman, Carole, Wathen, Tracey, & Lee, Dennis. (1995). Developing student self-assessment strategies. *TESOL Journal, 5,* 22–27.

Spada, Nina & Frölich, Maria. (1995). *Communicative orientation of language teaching observation scheme.* Sydney: National Centre for English Language Teaching and Research, Macquarie University.

Spolsky, Bernard. (1997). The ethics of gatekeeping tests: What have we learned in a hundred years? *Language Testing, 14,* 242–247.

Stack, Lydia, Stack, Jim, & Fern, Veronica. (2002, April). *A standards-based ELD curriculum and assessment.* Paper presented at the Teachers of English to Speakers of Other Languages Convention, Salt Lake City, UT.

Staton, J., Shuy, R. W., Peyton, J. K., & Reed, L. (1987). *Dialogue journal communication: Classroom, linguistic, social and cognitive views.* Norwood, NJ: Ablex.

Sternberg, Robert J. (1988). *The triarchic mind: A new theory of human intelligence.* New York: Viking Press.

Sternberg, Robert J. (1997). *Thinking styles.* Cambridge: Cambridge University Press.

Stevenson, D. K. (1985). Authenticity, validity, and tea party. *Language Testing, 2,* 41–47.

Swain, Merrill. (1984). Large scale communicative language testing. In Sandra Savignon & Margie Berns (Eds.), *Initiatives in communicative language teaching: A book of readings.* Reading, MA: Addison-Wesley.

Swain, Merrill. (1990). The language of French immersion students: Implications for theory and practice. In James E. Alatis (Ed.), *Georgetown University round table on languages and linguistics.* Washington: Georgetown University Press.

TESOL Journal. (1995). Alternative Assessment. Special Issue (5:1).

Test of Spoken English: Examinee handbook. (1987). Princeton, NJ: Educational Testing Service.

TOEFL score user guide. (2001). Princeton, NJ: Educational Testing Service.

TOEFL test and score manual. (2001). Princeton, NJ: Educational Testing Service.

Townshend, Brent, Bernstein, Jared, Todic, O., & Warren, E. (1998, May). Estimation of spoken language proficiency. *Proceedings of the ESCA Workshop on Speech Technology and Language Learning,* pp. 179–182.

Underhill, Nic. (1987). *Testing spoken language: A handbook of oral testing techniques.* Cambridge: Cambridge University Press.

Ur, Penny. (1984). *Teaching listening comprehension.* Cambridge: Cambridge University Press.

Valdez Pierce, L. & O'Malley, J. M. (1992). *Performance and portfolio assessments for language minority students.* Washington: National Clearinghouse for Bilingual Education.

Valdman, Albert. (1988). The assessment of foreign language oral proficiency. *Studies in Second Language Acquisition, 10,* Special Issue.

Weigle, Sara Cushing. (2002). *Assessing writing.* Cambridge: Cambridge University Press.

Weir, Cyril J. (1990). *Communicative language testing.* London: Prentice Hall International.

Weir, Cyril J. (2001). The formative and summative uses of language test data: Present concerns and future directions. In Catherine Elder (Ed.), *Experimenting with uncertainty: Essays in honour of Alan Davies* (pp. 117–123). (Studies in Language Testing #11). Cambridge: Cambridge University Press.

White, John. (1998). *Do Howard Gardner's multiple intelligences add up?* London: University of London Institute of Education.

Wolcott, W. (1998). *An overview of writing assessment: Theory, research and practice.* Urbana, IL: National Council of Teachers of English.

Yoshida, Kensaku. (2001, March). *From the fishbowl to the open seas: Taking a step towards the real world of communication.* Paper presented at the Teachers of English to Speakers of Other Languages Convention, St. Louis, MO.

Young, Richard & He, Agnes Weiyun. (1998, March). *Talking and testing: Discourse approaches to the assessment of oral proficiency.* Colloquium presented at the American Association of Applied Linguistics Conference, Seattle, WA.

NAME INDEX

SUBJECT INDEX